Pressure Politics in Contemporary Britain

Pressure Politics in Contemporary Britain

Graham Wootton
Tufts University

Lexington Books
D.C. Heath and Company
Lexington, Massachusetts
Toronto

Library of Congress Cataloging in Publication Data

Wootton, Graham.
  Pressure politics in contemporary Britain.

  Includes index.
  1. Pressure groups—Great Britain. I. Title.
JN329.P7W67   322.4'3'0941   77-26372
ISBN 0-669-02167-9

Published simultaneously in Canada.

Printed in the United States of America.

International Standard Book Number: 0-669-02167-9

Library of Congress Catalog Card Number: 77-26372

Louisetta
con amore

Contents

42441

Preface

Americans of all ages, all walks of life, and all dispositions are forever joining together. Not only do they have commercial and industrial companies in which all take part, but also societies of a thousand other kinds: religious, moral, serious, trifling, very broad and very specific, vast and minute.
—Alexis de Tocqueville

Having cast an eye over England following his more celebrated journey to America, Alexis de Tocqueville could have characterized the British in much the same terms. It is not even certain that Britain had by then been any the less prolific than the United States. Whatever the truth of that, "England . . . has certainly been a paradise of groups," as political theorist Sir Ernest Barker would say a century or so later. His remarks serve as an extended epigraph to this book.

Like him and the great legal historian, Maitland whom he cites, I am (I may as well confess) fascinated by such social riches—people-in-motion, forming and reforming, striving, achieving, falling by the wayside. But of course I have not attempted the stupendous task of surveying, even for a limited period of time in one country, the whole field of what de Tocqueville called, in that context, the associations of civil life. Rather I have focused on one subclass—pressure, or interest, groups—of what he had earlier identified as political associations, which (in his second volume) he acknowledged to be but a single feature on a great canvas. If so, why does this inquiry open with a sketch of civil associations (in contemporary Britain)? Because, as de Tocqueville hypothesized, there is a natural and perhaps a necessary connection between these two kinds of associations. What he meant in part was that civil associations facilitate political associations.

Insofar as his concept of political association included pressure groups as well as political parties—he was for once not entirely clear—his hypothesis receives ample support from the evidence assembled and analysed in Part II of this book. Yet the truth about the relationship is not exhausted by what he then perceived. Civil associations *facilitate* political association *in this particular form* because they constitute the fundamental continuing source of it. Some pressure groups are indeed so specialized that they have little else to do but blaze a single trail, or, as it sometimes seems, carry a cross of their own making to some secular Calvary. But the basic pressure groups are essentially *the* civil associations out to achieve some of their objectives by political means. That is why in these pages, against the common practice, individual companies and local unions are counted as pressure groups in addition to those usually put on parade by academic persons.

This flexibility of function resting, over a wide range, on identity of structure, or at most slight differentiation, creates some technical difficulties in the classification of pressure groups that the reader is prudently left to savour in the text. But it also suggests some conclusions of general political significance. One is the absurdity of populist proposals to break up, demolish, or otherwise deal with the pressure groups. Being to such a considerable extent none other than the civil associations going about their business in a certain way, pressure groups could be dealt with only by tearing a very large hole in the fabric of British (and by extension, American and Canadian) society.

Does this imply that citizens and governments have to put up with whatever the pressure groups do? By no means. But what, exactly, *do* they do? What do they want and how do they go about getting it? In Part II a preliminary attempt is made to answer such questions in contemporary British terms (the decade or more from the mid-sixties to the late seventies). In that I was assisted by a series of free-ranging interviews (1973-1976) with Cabinet Ministers, other Parliamentarians, senior civil servants, and officials of pressure groups and of the two main political parties. This section of the work could be read without any reference to de Tocqueville simply for the light that I believe it does cast on the working of the British political system.

Not that these mini-cases are offered as complete accounts of all the sources of influence upon the particular issues and policies. As someone who, in the course of studying (wartime) policy making from a base in the Cabinet Office, was once able to turn from the Cabinet Memoranda and Conclusions and Churchill's private files to some of the flesh-and-blood participants in Whitehall and beyond, I learned to doubt whether such complete accounts could ever be provided. My more recent interviews confirmed that more youthful impression. Here, in any case, the focus is upon the groups—immediately on what they do to achieve what ends.

Nor are these mini-cases historical narratives as such: hence they have different cut-off points within the period studied. On the other hand, they were not chosen by random sample, so the conclusions are not, in the strict sense, scientific either. But then, in the study of concrete politics, many are the questions that do not lend themselves to such scientific treatment but yet require an answer, or judgment, however tentative and provisional. The issues raised here are, I believe, of that kind. So what I have done is to select on the basis of apparent political significance, in my eyes and in the eyes of others. The effect of adopting this procedure is as follows. If the assessment yielded little or nothing to be perturbed about, that would be inconclusive: Perturbing cases might have been overlooked. But in fact I conclude that there is something to be perturbed about, or at least to be thought about. This points to a minimum cause for concern about the impact of pressure groups on the British polity—a prima facie case for further investigation and debate.

"Perturbed" is perhaps not the most common term in the political scientist's lexicon. But then I hold that a basic purpose of political science is to refine political judgment. So in Part III, I proceed to discuss impact. Here I hope to help sustain the momentum that has already carried recent political science towards the study of outputs (or policies) as distinct from inputs (or process) alone. Much remains to be investigated about impact. The concept also needs to be broadened from the impact (or outcome) of policy—important as that still neglected subject is—to impact on the polity *as a whole* of *both* policy and process. Since that is a rather large subject, I focus upon three dimensions of it: the methods adopted, some of which do seem to erode some of the virtues of a democratic polity; the observed or feared tendencies towards pluralist stagnation on the one hand and the Corporate State on the other. In discussing corporatism, we shall find ourselves reverting to the significance of identity, over a wide range, of group structure despite differentiation of function. If the pressure groups are to a considerable degree none other than the civil associations, presumably the substance of group politics resembles the substance of civil association-*al* politics in general. This might mean that pressure politics and class politics are (as Kipling wrote in *The Ladies*) like "the Colonel's Lady an' Judy O'Grady—sisters under their skins." Pressure politics might then be properly represented as the continuation of class politics in another form. Using evidence garnered in Part II, I touch upon that issue in the final chapter, but do not pursue it far.

I wish to acknowledge with thanks the help of the following who found time to be interviewed: two Ministers who had not only written with insight about the role of pressure groups in the contemporary period but had had some experience of them in running their Departments, the Rt. Hon. Ian Gilmour and the Rt. Hon. Anthony Wedgwood Benn; Mr. Frank Barlow, secretary of the Parliamentary Party; John Mackintosh, M.P.; Miss Margaret Jackson, since elevated from Labour Party Research to the House of Commons; Sir Michael (later Lord) Fraser of the Conservative Central Office and Mr. James Douglas, then head of the Conservative Research Department; Mr. Len Murray, General Secretary of the TUC; Sir John Partridge, former President of the CBI, and its then Director of Information, Mr. Michael King; another significant business leader, Sir Reay Geddes, as well as one who, then in the City of London (or Wall Street), had straddled Whitehall and Washington, D.C., the late Sir Richard (Otto) Clarke; Mr. T.C. Fraser, the trade association executive who had been drawn into national economic development planning; Mr. J.A. Raven (ABCC); Mr. Michael Strauss and Mr. Donald Willcox (NFU); Mr. Anthony Thistlethwaite (BMA); Mr. Fred Jarvis (NUT); Mr. Martin Wright (Howard League for Penal Reform); Mr. M.V. Beaumont (National Trust); Dr. John Davoll and Mr. Edward Dawson (Conservation Society); Mr. Tom Burke and Mr. Mick Hamer (Friends of the Earth); and Mr. A.J. Woolford (Save our Seafront, Dover). As usual, civil servants promptly declined to be identified, but I was able to persuade Sir Antony Part, then permanent Secretary of the Department of Industry, to lend me his name.

I wish also to thank Lord Douglas of Barloch; Mr. Robert Cant, M.P.; Mr.

Philip Goodhart, M.P. (Secretary of the 1922 Committee); the Rt. Hon. Sir John Vaughan-Morgan, Bt., and Mrs. E. Heyman; Mr. Graham Perkins (ABCC); Mr. R.J.V. Dixon (CBI); Mr. J.W. Stevenson (National Chamber of Trade); Mr. H.F. Tucker (Engineering Employers' Federation); Mrs. H.A. Rosser (NUT); Mrs. Diane Munday (Abortion Law Reform Association); Mr. Richard Wiggs (Anti-Concorde Project); Mr. Tony Dawe (*Sunday Times*); and Mr. Peter Kenya, a student from Kenya who for some time laboured with me—but cheerfully—in this vineyard.

Part I:
Foundations

1

A Paradise of Groups

The text for this discussion is taken from an address given to the Institute of Sociology in London in 1937 by the classical scholar and political theorist, Ernest Barker. Considering "Maitland as a sociologist," he said:

Now whatever else we may say about England, it has certainly been a paradise of groups. They begin in old Anglo-Saxon frith-gilds (mutual insurance societies, as I should call them, for the safer commission and the surer compensation of cattle-raids), if they are not even earlier than the frith-gilds: they continue through mediaeval religious gilds, mediaeval societies of lawyers called Inns of Court, seventeenth-century Free Churches, seventeenth-century East India and other companies, down to modern groups such as Lloyd's, the Stock Exchange, the Trade Union, the London Club (such as the Athenaeum), and, as I am in private duty bound to mention, this Institute of Sociology which I am now addressing. These riches fascinated Maitland. They may well fascinate any Englishman. How shall we count them, and in what denominations and under what categories shall we classify them?[1]

Whether he really meant England or whether he had been carried away by his Lancashire pride into mistaking the part for the whole is not entirely clear. In any case, it is the United Kingdom of Great Britain and Ireland (to use the pre-1921 title) that has been a paradise of groups. In fact some of the important groups since 1760, when the first Catholic Association was formed, have been Irish.

Britain is still a paradise of groups. To facilitate one's entry into a not altogether delighted world there are the Association for the Improvement of Maternity Services and the National Childbirth Trust, one section of which is out to encourage a particular mode of receiving early nourishment (the Breastfeeding Promotion Group). To ensure that one *is* born and not aborted is the purpose of the Society for the Protection of Unborn Children. Children admitted to a hospital have the Mother Care for Children in Hospital Association (Battersea, 1962)—rechristened the Welfare of Children in Hospital—to insist that parents be allowed to visit whenever they can and that mothers of children under five should even be put up at the hospital, a recommendation of the Platt Committee (1959) honoured mainly in the breach. For children who suffer in one way or another there are, in addition to the National Society for the Prevention of Cruelty to Children (NSPCC, but "Royal" in its Scottish form), several benevolent societies, general (Dr. Barnado's Homes, the Church of England

3

Children's Society—the former Waifs and Strays—and the Catholic Child Welfare Council) and specific (offspring of theatrical players or of ex-servicemen or ex-servicewomen). The Child Poverty Action Group set out (in 1967) to "relieve poverty among families with children." The society helping the "thalidomide children" constitutes a special case, as does, in its different way, the National Association for Gifted Children.

Exit from this world is facilitated by at least eight societies in burial and cremation, including the Funeral Directors and the Funeral Furnishing Manufacturers, both of whom (indeed all of whom) are obviously on to a good thing. For the service of embalming (that *spécialité de la maison* of the Funeral Home), there is the British Institute of Embalmers to maintain dignity and proper standards of craftsmanship.

In between the polar extremes of entry and exit, almost everything one has ever heard of has been made the object of organization. A Campaign for Nuclear Disarmament, a Union of Democratic Control (of foreign policy); a society for "the extension of patriotism" (Royal Society of St. George, that Palestinian who so improbably became the patron saint of the English); the Monarchist League, "to uphold rightful Monarchy against disintegrating tendencies of whatever nature"; a Richard III Society, to defend his reputation against both Henry VII, his victor, and Shakespeare, who followed the Tudor party line; a Marlowe Society, whose claim for Marlowe to the authorship of Shakespeare's plays would, if successful, at least absolve Shakespeare from having traduced Richard III; societies for the advancement of state education, reimbursing parents whose dearest wish is to retreat from the state system bearing vouchers equal to the relevant imputed cost, educational standards in schools, against Secret Records on Schoolchildren; for legalizing paedophilia (adult sexual relations with children); helping parents of drug addicts; counselling and befriending homosexuals, women and men (Friend); for the redemption of the 3.5 percent War Loan (whose value has been largely eroded since it was issued, but prudently undated, in 1917). There is a Reindeer Council of the U.K. (based on Cambridge, where reindeers do not often appear); a Royal National Homing Union, devoted to pigeons, and a related "Royal" for the Protection of Birds, as well as, of course, the Royal Society for the Prevention of Cruelty to Animals (RSPCA), whose work is supplemented by the Council of Justice to Animals and Humane Slaughter Association. For those whose remarks on trains would, given the opportunity, rise above mere oaths and exclamations, a Conversant Travellers Association was founded (Letchworth, 1950). Whether its one thousand members lived to tell the tale is not known. Certainly the Society for the Suppression of Yunno Yunno Yunno in the Diction of Broadcasters (1969) has not been an unalloyed success. The Rolls-Royce Enthusiasts Club of Great Britain has been, unavoidably, a rather exclusive group, but it made up in ardour what it lacked in numbers. In 1971, when the famous company seemed on its last legs, the secretary said that if it were sold off to the highest bidder, "I for one would like to leave this country." If he had thought of the ultimate rather than the penultimate sacrifice, he might have been deterred from *hara-kiri* by the Samaritans. There are societies to prevent the other forms of self-destruction, through drugs and also alcohol. Fifteen or sixteen societies, if church-related bodies are counted, advocate temperance. The United Kingdom Alliance for the Total Suppression of Liquor Traffic, which is mid-Victorian, stands for the root-and-branch policy, as in a sense does Alchoholics Anonymous, composed of those who have made their recovery and maintain it by complete abstention.

Unconnected except for the echo of the name (apparently) is Sewers Synonymous. With members drawn from the Public Health Engineering Department, London Region, it is rather limited in scope, whether based on occupation or recreation. In 1969 the Leader of the Greater London Council, Desmond Plummer, was pictured climbing into a sewer that extended beneath the forecourt of Buckingham Palace, where he was made an honorary member of Sewers Synonymous. That may have been carrying loyalty to all things royal rather to excess.

Sewers Synonymous is not the only group composed of people who walk alone. The Flat Earth Society has survived those space-shots appearing to demonstrate that the earth is indeed round. The Society of Individualists hopes to protect the "rights and liberties of the freeborn Briton." But, in the implied circumstances, freeborn Britons would be well advised to rely rather more upon the National Council for Civil Liberties (NCCL), with its penchant for helping the uninformed and underprivileged, "the hopeless and the helpless" (as the general secretary, Tony Smythe, puts it); or Justice, lawyers particularly concerned with upholding the rule of law in those lands where the British writ still runs, more or less; or, in some situations, the Howard League for Penal Reform. Amnesty keeps track of political prisoners, wherever incarcerated, and works for their release. Those who have done time in the commoner sense may be assisted on release by the National Association for the Care and Resettlement of Offenders. Persistent offenders have their own group—Recidivists Anonymous.

Justice in another sense has been pursued by the Campaign Against Racial Discrimination, Equal Rights, and similar bodies, also by the National Council for the Single Woman and her Dependants. The cause of the homeless has been served by the Squatters Protection Society (in the North after World War II) and the London Squatters Campaign (from 1968), by HELL (Help Expose Lousy Landlords) in Paddington (1970), and on a broader front by Shelter (the National Campaign for the Homeless) and the Family Squatting Advisory Service.

Environmentalists and preservationists are thicker on the ground even than squatters. Four generations (not equal in length) may be distinguished. To the first (say 1860-1914) belong the Commons Registration Society (now Commons, Open Spaces and Footpaths), the Society for the Protection of Ancient

Buildings, the National Trust, and the Town and Country Planning Association. The period 1914 to 1939 saw the launching of the Town Planning Institute, the Council for the Protection of Rural England (under another name), the National Society for Clean Air (also under another name), the Georgian Group, and the Central Council of Civic Societies. The post-World War II period produced the Victorian Society and the Civic Trust. In the sixties and seventies a qualitative change may be detected: the worldwide concern for the environment as such, especially in the sense of ecological balance, precipitated many new organizations. In Britain the Conservation Society (1966) exemplifies the new species. Friends of the Earth U.K. (1970) is another of the kind. Some of the new societies have a narrower focus: the Transport and Environment Group (1972) and Transport 2000 (1973). Transport by air has also been attacked on environmentalist grounds, as by the Anti-Concorde Project (1967), active in the United States as well as England, and on amenity grounds (if that rough distinction is acceptable), as by the British Association for the Control of Aircraft Noise and by the Noise Abatement Society, although its range is obviously wider. Many other names could appear even under this one subheading, and some have a certain charm. The Men of the Trees, for example, are redolent of Sherwood Forest but have the very practical goal of saving the country's trees from the developer's axe. In 1964 it criticized Lord Cadogan's proposal to cut down the trees of Cadogan Square and plant new ones over an underground car park. Replanting could not be done in six feet of earth, the chairman, Sir John Austin, argued. And if permission were granted all London's trees would thereafter be at risk. Evidently London's trees are not friendless (and happily so), but there tend to be friendless churches, the ones made redundant by, for example, the movement of population. So, of course, a group exists, under the paradoxical title of Friends of Friendless Churches. In the early 1970s it fought to save a church in Warwickshire, apparently friendless since the fourteenth century when the villagers moved away from the Black Death. It had a medieval screen and benches that the Friends wished to preserve *in situ.* (How Ernest Barker would have applauded.)

Meanwhile some of the older societies, not as such environmentalist in their objectives, have been responding to the new imperative: the Soil Association, for example; also the Royal Institute of British Architects, which has even spent its own money on a PR campaign on the theme of environmental protection, admittedly stressing "the *built* environment."

Some groups rest on a leisure-time activity, sport or common enterprise: cricket umpires, riflemen, practitioners of judo, pursuers of the inedible fox, conchologists, and spediologists. To encourage staring at the sky, there are two astronomical bodies and, for those who like to add a *soupçon* of divination, a federation of astrologers. For falling out of the sky, there are parachutes and the British Parachute Association. Impatient telephone users (or would-be users) band together as the Telephone Users' Association. The Patients Association

(1963) presumably serves those who are not patient with aspects of the National Health Service. For those determined to walk, there is the Ramblers' Association; to walk and survive, the Pedestrians' Association for Road Safety. Even anarchists have eaten of the forbidden fruit in this paradise of groups—hence, the Federation of British Anarchists.

These are national bodies: If we trawled the localities, we could make a very large catch. The Civic Trust, which has replaced the Central Council of Civic Societies as the co-ordinating body, is in touch (1975) with perhaps twelve hundred local civic and amenity societies. Scores of other such bodies have responded to particular local crises; for example, in Bedfordshire, the Blunham Village Society, formed in 1972 to save a Victorian rectory from demolition. There are (or have been) the Kennett Valley Preservation Society, opposing with others particular routes for the Berkshire section of the M4; the various Motorway Action Groups (Hampstead/London, Midlands, Roding Valley, Aire Valley, and so forth), out to forestall, not promote; various other such London groups ranging from the Golbourne Social Rights Committee, demonstrably against the extension of their bit of Westway (White City to Paddington), which they could have done without, to the Campaign Against the Lorry Menace (1975), a coalition of some seventy bodies whose response to the Greater London Council's proposal to designate 425 miles of the area's existing main roads as lorry (truck) routes made the acronym of the title rather incongruous. Nor have other forms of transport been left unscathed. SKAR (Surrey and Kent Against the Rail Link) was launched in 1974 to prevent high-speed trains racing to the Channel through the Marden Valley. At Dover in 1976, SOS (Save Our Seafront Action Committee) argued against the particular proposals made by the Harbour Board for a new Hoverport at the Western Docks.

***

Most of the groups so far mentioned, which of course represent only a sampling of the field, are *for* something or other: the practice or pursuit of some intrinsically interesting or pleasurable activity; the treatment, protection or support of certain categories of persons or animals; the accomplishment of certain public-policy objectives. Beyond that the group members need have nothing in common. By contrast, a great many groups are *of* rather than, or as well as, *for*. Some of these are based on a sex distinction: Mothers' Union; Guild of Lady Drivers; Women's Institutes and Townswomen's Guilds; the National Council of Women of Great Britain; women, electrical, engineering, executive, medical, and advertising; Women's Liberation Workshop, Women's Liberation Front, and women sufficiently liberated to acknowledge their lesbianism (*Kenric*). Other groups embody an age distinction. Secondary-school children organized the Schools Action Union in the Greater London area. Its slogan was the one that had already haunted some colleges in Britain and the United States: "Don't demand—occupy." When older, they might have encountered the

Anti-Violence and Anti-Aggression Students Movement, launched in London after the Grosvenor Square "demo" in June 1968. Survivors of those lively times might eventually be served by the National Federation of Old Age Pensions Associations. For an earlier, and unluckier, generation there was (early 1960s) an Old Age Non-Pensioners Association based on Worthing.

That ethnicity or race may be the matrix from which pressure groups rise is also clear, most obviously, and harrowingly, from the terrible story of English-Irish relations: as well as the United Irishmen, Irish Tenant Right League, United Irish League, and the rest, one should count, if not the paramilitary groups, the several Catholic Associations and Catholic Committees from 1760 to Emancipation in 1829, all essentially Irish. But since the 1960s, with the arrival of large numbers of immigrants from areas of the old British Empire, ethnicity has become even more productive of associations: Indian, Pakistani, Bangladeshi; West Indian, Caribbean and so on.

Whether churches should be counted as organizations of is more debatable, but there is perhaps a sense in which church membership or affiliation is—for the millions—almost as given, or inherited, as ethnicity or sex. One notes, in any case, the many mansions of the Christian church, including Christian Aid for some practical applications of the faith, including, over a certain range, political influence. British Jewry is represented by the Board of Deputies of British Jews, which appeared on stage with George III (and the first Catholic Association) in 1760. Sephardic Jews, often regarded as a kind of aristocracy, were already organized, however, as the Community of Spanish and Portuguese Jews (1657). The British Council of Churches is the central body. Outside but fervently looking in, so to speak, are the National Secular Society, which is late Victorian, and the British Humanist Association, which is recent.

The greatest single source of organizations of is clearly the occupational structure. Some occupational roles and the resulting associations are so unfamiliar that they send one scurrying to the dictionary: tarpavoirs, rheologists, and labologists. But most are readily identifiable, ranging from bartenders and income tax inspectors to toastmasters and the Taxpayers' Union, not forgetting licensed kosher butchers or master steeplejacks (who have gone up in the world, being nowadays dignified with the additional title, "and lightning conductors engineers").

The professions produce a rich harvest. The law provides the bedrock for about fourteen associations, including the Institute of Legal Executives, described as the "professional body" for those employed by solicitors, and the British Legal Association, the "independent professional" society for solicitors in Scotland as well as England and Wales (independent, in a sense, of the Law Society and the Law Society of Scotland). If we scoured the interconnecting worlds of medicine and surgery, dentistry, hospital administration, nursing, and public health, we could collect the names of about 110 organizations. Medical societies alone number about fifty, a dozen or so with roots in the British

Medical Association (BMA) itself. The Central Committee for Hospital Medical Services (CCHMS), reproduced in Scotland, Wales, and Northern Ireland, is a little known but important example. It is an autonomous BMA Committee dealing with issues affecting doctors in hospital practice. Its own subcommittee of eighteen negotiates with the Department of Health and Social Security over terms and conditions of service within the hospital field. The educational service is the matrix for about 125 organizations. The National Union of Teachers (NUT) is one of the household names; the National Association of School-masters, originally a breakaway from the NUT, is a familiar one, although not with the new addition to the title, "Union of Women Teachers." Increasingly familiar is the Association of Teachers in Technical Institutions.

All three have found their way into the Trades Union Congress (TUC), which harbours 114 unions in all (1975) with a membership approaching eleven million, about two thirds of it from the ten largest. The T.& G. (Transport and General Workers' Union) leads the field with 1,850,000 members.

The Trade Union did find a place in Ernest Barker's list, which, however, contained no examples drawn from the "other side" of industrial capitalism. Even merchant capitalism was represented only by such early manifestations as the East India Company, yet it had peaked, even before he was born, as the Associated (now Association of) British Chambers of Commerce (1860). During Barker's own lifetime industrial capitalism had produced such complex structures as the British Employers' Confederation (BEC) and the Federation of British Industries (FBI).[2] The FBI was a trade association (or TA) designed to further a collective trade interest, as distinct from an employers' organization (EO), built for bargaining over wages and conditions of work. In 1972 an authoritative commission found an ostensible 2,500 "representative associations" (in this general area, counting EOs as well as TAs). Of that total nearly 150 were "almost certainly dead"; 830 failed to respond to a circular, but that may merely have been the mark of sturdy independence. The Commission did discover "860 associations which are certainly alive and with 800 more associations affiliated to them."[3] That makes a firm total, then, of about 1,600 "representative associations" in that particular sector. The current peak is the Confederation of British Industry, which absorbed the BEC and FBI (and another) in 1965.

From those few numbers we gain a rudimentary idea of the scale of the representative institutions of industrial capitalism, although, as we shall see at the proper time, a place has to be found for the individual companies themselves if we are to obtain a more complete view than the literature now offers of group-government interaction and its consequences for the political system as a whole (which is the subject we are gradually approaching). Finance capitalism (to persist with the old-fashioned but still serviceable terminology) naturally provides its own quota. At its centre is the Committee of London Clearing Banks, which has its origin in a body formed in 1821.[4] It speaks for the deposit bankers of England and Wales (some 12,000 branches) to the Bank of England, the Treasury, and the Government. Its EO is the Federation of London Clearing Bank Employers, which keeps in touch and perhaps in line with the corresponding Scottish and Irish organizations. The British Bankers' Association is the most ecumenical if also the most innocuous. It has in membership the six London Clearing Banks and some minor English ones, British banks abroad, the Irish "big four," the Scottish "big three," and Commonwealth banks in London. The city's still more specialized institutions provide the basis for the Accepting Houses Committee (1914), with seventeen such houses in membership, overlapping to that extent with the Issuing Houses Association (1945), a TA made up of sixty issuing houses. The 280 companies that between them transact most of the city's worldwide insurance business are banded together in the British Insurance Association (BIA), which does not, however, have insurance brokers or Lloyd's, the underwriters of marine insurance mentioned in Ernest Barker's list. Nine societies harness the specializations; for example, the Life Offices' Association and the Associated Scottish Life Offices. Each of the nine interlocks with the BIA through representation on its Council, apart from some overlapping membership. To facilitate commerce in other senses some new bodies have been founded: the British Shippers' Council (1955), to help importers and exporters move their goods expeditiously; the British Importers Confederation (1972), which clearly looks only one way.

Agriculture provides fertile soil for groups, which, excluding horticulture but including dairying and poultry-keeping and some related activities such as the sale of corn and cattle foods, totalled about ninety in the early 1970s. The National Farmers' Union of England and Wales is a name for all seasons. A hybrid (EO and TA), the NFU suffered a breakaway in 1955, when some Welsh farmers, dissatisfied with the treatment of Welsh affairs within the organization, set up the Farmers' Union of Wales. Welsh affairs, about which the NFU staff at Agriculture House in Knightsbridge remain unusually sensitive and perhaps even a little apprehensive, are now covered by the Welsh Council of the NFU, a consultative body.[5] As usual, the Scots already had their own National Farmers' Union of Scotland, which, however, with the Ulster Farmers' Union has always worked closely with the NFU of England and Wales. The English/Scottish distinction is also apparent among two of the "Royals" (Agricultural Society of England; Highland and Agricultural Society). Among the remainder in this category are the English Butter Conference and a number of British-ers (Poultry Association, Ploughing Association, and Society of Animal Production). Horticulture, allowing for double-counting with agriculture, accommodates about thirty associations, not only TAs but also the organized arboriculturists, tree surgeons and arborists, tree transplanters, and flower growers generally and in particular of roses, orchids, and dahlias.

So Britain is indeed "a paradise of groups" and perhaps more richly endowed than even Ernest Barker quite realized. In any case, transposing one word (though discounting the hyperbole), he might well have echoed Alexis de Tocqueville's remarks about the United States in the 1830s:

Americans of all ages, all conditions, and all dispositions, constantly form associations. They have not only commercial and manufacturing companies, in which all take part, but associations of a thousand other kinds—religious, moral, serious, futile, extensive or restricted, enormous or diminutive.[6]

2 Pressure Groups

The focus of this book, however, is not on all such civil associations (technically, secondary groups), only on some: pressure groups, defined as those (not counting political parties) that influence or attempt to influence the public authorities, mainly the central government. Why, then, have we been approaching the narrower topic through the wider concept? The answer should become apparent as we proceed. Here it is enough to observe that some groups have obviously been built with virtually nothing in mind but the exercise of political influence. Examples from the mid- and late seventies include the incongruously named, or acronymed, CALM (Campaign Against the Lorry Menace), the Conservation for Survival Campaign, and the organizations that underpinned them (such as the Islington-based *Intersoc* and the Conservation Society); Friends of the Earth (FoE), and Population Stabilization (to keep Britain's total numbers in the year 2010 to 65 million by taking various steps now, such as withdrawing maternity benefits); Life (anti-abortion), and Doctors for women's choice in abortion; Confederation for the Advancement of State Education (CASE), Campaign for Comprehensive Education and the associated PRISE (Programme for Reform in Secondary Education), a specific counter to the sombre "Black Papers" on education, which, however, had the backing of the National Council for Educational Standards, the Parents' Action Group for Educational Standards (descending on M.P.s en masse), FEVER (Friends of the Education Voucher Experiment in Representative Regions), made up of those parents wanting "their money back"; PIE (Paedophile Information Exchange), which, seeking to legalize adult sexual relations with children, was hardly as wholesome as the acronym might suggest; the Sexual Law Reform Society (immediate successor to the earlier Homosexual Law Reform Society), and the Campaign for Homosexual Equality. Even a group to facilitate some forms of pressure-group activity has been known: the Community Action Union (1968), designed to coordinate experience and information so that people could form their own street associations to campaign for better living and housing conditions.

By contrast a high proportion of the private entities that engage in pressure politics do so, as it were, only part-time. For example: the president of the Royal College of Veterinary Surgeons denounces the cropping of dogs' tails and proposes legislation to stop such "cosmetic surgery" (1973); the Law Society writes to the Chancellor about the value-added tax (VAT), expressing anxiety that the search powers to be authorised by the 1972 legislation would make

13

confidential letters (solicitors-barristers-clients) open to inspection by the tax authorities, and recommending a limited application to solicitors' offices. Even the TUC and CBI have other-than-pressure-group functions to discharge for members or constituents, although the functional mix will naturally be of quite a different order. What all this means is that, except for the pure specialization (CALM, LIFE, PRISE, FEVER, and the rest), a pressure group (as stipulatively defined above) is not a species of the genus, secondary group: it is a secondary group whose work includes "pressing."

It follows that Ernest Barker's characterization of Britain ("England") as "a paradise of groups" can be rephrased as "the land is alive with pressure groups," which appeared in the *Sunday Telegraph* in 1962.[1] But once that is done, we are moved to inquire: Are there no serpents in this paradise? Are not some of the methods incompatible with a democratic system? Is not PR, in particular, a black art? But, then, what do all these group strivings really amount to? Is it all sound and simulated fury, or does it make a difference? If it does, is the power of groups excessive? An affirmative answer may be inferred from such character- izations of contemporary society as The New Feudalism. Used by the *Economist* in 1938, this concept apparently came in the post-war period to embrace not only the TUC and FBI but some of the giant unions and companies, perceived as the new estates or baronies, if not as haughty or arrogant as their medieval prototypes, overmighty and overbearing nonetheless. Since the late sixties, however, it has tended to be superseded, in the minds of some well placed observers, by the New Corporatism. This belongs to the same family of ideas (and fears), but whereas the New Feudalism often implied "medieval concep- tions of separate autonomies" (as J.M. Keynes put it in 1926), the New Corporatism points to a fusion of politico-economic authority—Government, Capital and Labour—in which the traditional, territorially based institutions, such as Parliament, tend to be by-passed and, in the extreme case, to wither and die. The old corporatism from which the new immediately derives is that body of ideas, essentially counter-Marxist, which developed in Continental Europe after 1890; the institutional model may be Mussolini's (meant-to-have-been) Corporate State from the late twenties until its expiration in the early forties. If the analogy seems far-fetched, the telltale signs (these British Cassandras say) are or include the NEDC and the little "Neddies"; the statutory control of incomes but also the social contract, with its *quid pro quo*-s for the unions; the planning agreements with individual companies; the Manpower Services Commission, the Health and Safety Commission, and the like.

No doubt, if for by no means that reason alone, Parliament has declined in *relative* importance to the other central institutions of government (though not, of course, to the social order as a whole). The general point emerges again from Michael Shanks' revival of Bagehot's distinction between "efficient" government (headed by the Prime Minister) and "dignified" government (graced by the Queen).[2] Remarking that the content of the categories had "changed a lot since

Bagehot's day," Mr. Shanks added: "Among the 'efficient' institutions, in the sense of wielding power, which have emerged in recent years one must include bodies like the TUC, the Confederation of British Industry and now also the Commission of the EEC in Brussels. The Crown remains a 'dignified' institution, a repository of influence but not of power. And I'm inclined to think that Parliament itself should now be included in that category too, because it seems to me that the occasions on which Parliament as an institution can decisively influence events are rather few. On the other hand, the party machines are powerful and thus came in the 'efficient' category. About the Cabinet I'm not sure. It depends on the style of the prime minister."[3]

The broader issues are complicated and controversial. Some, like Ian Gilmour, backbencher, Minister and political analyst, have come round to the view that the influence of Parliament is greater than outsiders commonly assume. But he would not wish to deny that the "estates" have gained some ground at the expense of Parliament, as in the consultation of interests and the work of the NEDC, which provides no place for Parliamentarians as such.

Although not necessarily unperturbed by the activities and power of at least some of the "estates," other political analysts express concern about some of the propagational groups. The Abortion Law Reform Association (ALRA) is one offender named, and "power without responsibility" the charge developed. The Abortion Act of 1967 (wrote Ronald Butt) "was pushed through Parliament as a private member's bill under the steam of a minority pressure group, while Ministers stood safely on the sidelines, but gave it a helping hand with parliamentary time."[4] Yet (Mr. Butt argued) the government had no mandate from the electors for it, nor for the Divorce Reform Bill of 1969, which "is being pushed through Parliament mainly by the same people. It is not right that it should be hustled through a thinly attended Parliament, without proper amendment, by the will of a pressure group, without the Government taking any responsibility for what is being done."

In that passage both language and thought evoke historical memories, suggesting that the issues posed are of enduring, not passing, concern. "The steam of a minority pressure group" recalls the remark made by Joseph Parkes, organizer of the Reform Association, about getting the Municipal Reform Bill of 1835 on the statute book: "Steam alone could do the business." Is that generally true of reforms, and if so does our view of pressure groups depend on our evaluation of what the steam is generated for? We are also reminded of Sir Frederick Pollock's comment on the Trades Dispute Act of 1906, that triumph for the TUC:

... it remains to be seen whether the Act represents any general movement of legislative ideas, or anything else than the pressure of very powerful interests astutely applied at a critical moment.[5]

Against the grain of the implied arguments, Anthony Wedgwood Benn has commended the "new centres of democratic initiative outside the party system [which] were developing as pressure groups or action groups dealing with specific issues. . . ."[6] His concept of a pressure group or action group was wide, embracing the CBI and trade associations as well as the TUC and those nationalist parties that were virtually single-issue groups as "a very powerful factor in our system of government," but not to be condemned. The number of political issues "was increasing enormously" but the public's confidence in the capacity of political parties to cope with them was in decline. Besides, the public would no longer put up with imposed solutions, even ones favoured in principle; they wished to participate in the solving. Thus Mr. Benn's concept of the role of pressure groups is congruent with his concern for workers' participation in industry.

On another view, not every "centre of democratic initiative" is to be commended. That other Anthony, Mr. Crosland, also a Cabinet Minister, castigated the Wing Airport Resistance Association (WARA) for its efforts to save Cublington from what it regarded as a fate akin to death—becoming London's third airport: "WARA is in danger of giving the impression that it does not care tuppence for anybody else's noise and environment." More broadly, it is bad enough that the "conservationist lobby" wholly neglects "the economic case" (i.e., sets its face against economic growth); in so doing, it also exhibits "class bias," ranking its own "middle and upper class" values higher than the "lower housing densities and better schools and hospitals" that economic growth would tend to bring the working class. Five months later Mr. Crosland managed to get both groups with one barrel. Why, he asked, did the Government choose Foulness for the third London airport in the teeth of overwhelming objections? Partly because "they were scared off the inland sites [such as Cublington] by the rich and powerfully organized pressure-groups, by the environmental lobby. . . ."[7]

This case of Anthony v. Anthony is obviously contrived, but the juxtaposition is useful in disclosing variations in attitudes towards pressure groups even on the part of those who stood together, more or less, on many other issues as (in this example) concurrent members of Labour Cabinets. Whatever else it may have been, WARA has to count as a centre of democratic initiative. And it worked well, helping to deflect the proposed third airport from its own territory. But that had already been deflected from Stansted, partly by the North-West Essex and East Herts Preservation Society. These victories entailed still further delay in meeting an authoritatively defined national need. Ought we to praise such pressure groups for their democratic virility or denounce them for passing the buck?

That case alone raises serious questions about the methods used by groups. Are groups guilty of stooping to conquer, of exceeding the democratic proprieties in their determination to get their own way? Are groups now too much imbued with the spirit of the famous American football coach: Winning isn't everything—it's the only thing. Beyond the issue of acceptable methods lie perturbing questions about the cumulative effect of the several activities, however innocent. The general point was made two centuries ago (apparently under the inspiration of the seventeenth-century French Cardinal de Retz) by the Scottish philosopher, Adam Ferguson, writing about political establishments (*An Essay on the History of Civil Society*, Boston, 1809):

Mankind, in following the present sense of their minds, in striving to remove inconveniences, or to gain apparent and contiguous advantages, arrive at ends which even their imagination could not anticipate. . . . Every step and every movement of the multitude, even in what are termed enlightened ages, are made with equal blindness to the future; and nations stumble upon establishments, which are indeed the result of human action, but not the execution of any human design.

Transposed from that context to this, the notion emerges as "pluralist stagnation" (Robert McKenzie) or "pluralistic stagnation" (Samuel Beer). As applied to groups (rather than parties), it seems to have arisen in or with reference to Sweden, whose society is well known to be *genomorganiserad*, or saturated with organizations. The danger, which Professor McKenzie (in 1958 at least) was inclined to discount, is that the existence of so many group (or plural) centres of power prevents the carrying out of policies essential to the nation. Thinking mainly of the great producer groups, and their perceived role as a counterbalance to centralized government, Professor Beer remarked: "We may breathe a sigh of relief for the liberties of the subject . . . ," but was the danger for Britain not "oppressive efficiency" (from centralized government) but rather "pluralistic stagnation"? Noel (now Lord) Annan agreed: "The interests are so faithfully represented and bring such pressure to bear indicating how far each is prepared to move—which is usually little distance at all—that the degree of movement is negligible."[8]

The problem has already received some attention, notably in the context of trade unions and incomes policy,[9] but going by Mr. Crosland's comments on WARA, it may not be limited to the producer groups. This, and the related issues, we shall be better qualified to judge after we have completed this inquiry, which covers the contemporary period, broadly interpreted as the mid-sixties to the mid-seventies. Cases will be chosen not by random sample but for their apparent political significance, so the method is exploratory—rather like making holes in the ice at a number of points and fishing—and the judgments correspondingly tentative. Even so these will either augment or diminish current concerns and apprehensions (unless the verdict is "not proven"), and throw light on some of the other issues.

A Typology of Pressure Groups

This universe of pressure groups now requires more systematic subdivision. The problem at once encountered is that the traditional ways of doing it hardly seem adequate. The oldest classification in the technical literature is the one introduced in 1935 by Harwood Childs of Princeton University, who distinguished between those groups "whose community of interests is based on such fundamental differentials as age, sex, occupation, and race, from those existing merely to further special ideas or groups of ideas. . . . For want of better labels, these two types of pressure groups may be referred to as 'interest' and 'idea' groups respectively."[10]

In Britain the most influential classification was introduced by another American scholar but one long resident there, Allen Potter. As a pioneer in the field, he played out several hands between 1956 and 1961, but essentially split the pack into two: sectional groups (whom one stands for), and programmatic or promotional groups (what one stands for).[11] This reasonable distinction is congruent not only with Childs' a generation earlier but with the one drawn by groups themselves between organizations *of* and organizations *for*.[12] All the same it runs into difficulties in practical application partly because what is presented as a promotional group may have a distinctly sectional character. When it was called the National Smoke Abatement Society, the National Society for Clean Air was partly financed by the makers of smokeless fuels and the Solid Smokeless Fuels Federation.[13] Some prewar groups promoting birth control were, in effect, subsidized by the manufacturers of birth-control devices.[14] In the mid-sixties both the London Foundation for Marriage Education and its virtual successor the Genetic Study Unit, advocates of mechanical (including rubber) as opposed to oral contraceptives, were found to be unacknowledged offspring of London Rubber Industries, the largest manufacturers in Britain of rubber contraceptives.[15]

Ostensible promotional groups really grounded in sectional ones have elsewhere been christened 'anchored'.[16] This phenomenon of anchorage may be more significant than has so far been recognized. Historically one might hypothesize that, of the ostensible promotional (or cause) groups, the markedly successful ones tended to be anchored—that is, had some sectional character. If that were true, the classification sectional/promotional would have obstructed rather than advanced one's understanding of, at least, the methods adopted by ostensible promotional groups and the conditions of their success. By the same token it would have failed to bring to light some of the methods adopted by sectional groups and have led to an underestimate of their real strength.

What compounds one's doubts about the received classification is that it compels the sectional box to accommodate not simply a vast number of groups but such a variety in terms of political significance. It puts the Tomato and Cucumber Growers' Association cheek by jowl with the NFU, the Wholesale

Poultry Merchants in the same coop as the ABCC. So, too, with promotional groups. Such varying degrees of political involvement (i.e., of pressure group-*ness*) surely ought to be brought out in the subdivision.

A Constructed Typology

For these reasons alone we need to make room in our sorting for at least one other attribute or property—call it, *degree of political specialization.* We have already inherited the distinction between interest/idea: of/for: sectional/promotional, the implied basis of which, however, seems to be well caught in the attribute properly if tiresomely expressed as *degree of openness of membership,* (or perhaps of *recruitment*). So we acquire two attributes to work with, and advance beyond a logical classification into a constructed typology. For this we resort to the familiar social-science device of "property space,"[1][7] by which properties, or attributes, are arrayed in conceptual space and divided as finely as their nature allows and the research design or discussion requires. In this instance the two properties will themselves be divided into two (i.e., dichotomized): low or high political specialization; closed or open membership. This will create a matrix of four cells (or a two-by-two). Each cell will harbour a type (in the straightforward English sense of "a class of things, etc., with common character-istics"). Figure 2-1 portrays the typology diagramatically, with examples.

Types 1 and 2, then, are groups that rest at any particular moment upon a given or closed membership: occupation or function, age, sex, ethnicity, and, arguably, both church affiliation and locality. But they differ in practice in the extent of their political involvement. This of course is a matter of gradation, sometimes fine, whereas all that can be managed here is a gross distinction between low and high involvement. Thus the Law Society is placed in cell 1; the British Legal Association, representing the militant 10 percent of practising solicitors, in cell 2. The Indian Social Club (Birmingham) and the National Federation of Pakistani Associations go in cell 1; the Indian Workers' Associ-ation, Great Britain, and the League of Overseas Pakistanis (Tower Hamlets) in cell 2. Obviously, these and many of the other placings represent rough and challengeable judgments, but that is mainly because we lack sufficient knowl-edge of the functional mix (politics/other-than-politics) in each instance, which is in principle discoverable.

Cell 4 contains the pure pressure groups, high in political involvement but also open-ended. It does not, however, harbour all the groups that other authors have called "programmatic," "promotional," or "cause." Those pursuing a cause from a given base (i.e., anchored groups), not being really open-ended, are put in with their parent group; for example, the Genetic Study Unit goes in with London Rubber Industries; Transport 2000 (arguably) with the National Union of Railwaymen and the other railway workers' unions on the assumption that

POLITICAL SPECIALIZATION

	LOW	HIGH
	1	**2**
CLOSED	T & G, NUR	TUC
	British Aircraft, Burmah Oil, London Rubber Industries, House of Fraser, Hill Samuel	CBI, ABCC, NFU, British Road Federation
	Law Society	British Legal Association
	Townwomen's Guilds, Women's Institutes	National Joint Action Campaign for Women's Equal Rights
	National Federation of Pakistani Associations	League of Overseas Pakistanis (Tower Hamlets)
	Urdd Gobaith Cymru (Welsh League of Youth)	Welsh Language Society
	Saffron Walden Countryside Association	Saffron Walden Anti-Airport Committee, Stansted Working Party (etc.), WARA
	(Operational)	(Representative)
	3	**4**
OPEN	National Trust, Georgian Society, Ulster Architectural Heritage Society, Association for the Protection of Rural Scotland	Conservation Society, FoE, Population Stabilization
	Friend	Campaign for Homosexual Equality
	Society of Individualists	Justice, Amnesty, NCCL
	National Allotments and Garden Society	Child Poverty Action Group, Shelter
	Workers' Educational Association	CASE, FEVER, PRISE
	(Expressive)	(Propagational)

(Left axis label, top to bottom: M E M B E R S H I P)

Figure 2-1. A Typology of Pressure Groups

those who pay the piper call the tune. Another divergence from the traditional classification is that such a body as the Wing Airport Resistance Association (WARA) does not appear in cell 4 as a cause group but rather in cell 2. The rationale is that politically specialized groups with distinctive local roots, especially when defending their territory, will prove to be more like *of* groups than *for* groups.

Types 1, 2, and 4 contain elements that had shown themselves before the eighteenth century was over (in terms of government relationships, British Aircraft, for example, reflecting the East India Company; ABCC, the Manchester Commercial Committee; the CBI, the General Chamber of Manufacturers; the Campaign for Homosexual Equality, the Committee for effecting the Abolition of the Slave Trade, and so on). But type 3, including the Society for the Protection of Ancient Buildings, the Georgian Society and the Scottish Georgian Society, the Ulster Architectural Heritage Society, and the like, seems a newer development. This might be interpreted in part to mean that Britain has been ceasing to stand aside from the Continental-European (or Graeco-Roman) life of "common enjoyment," as historian J.L. Hammond would come to call it, thinking of leisure-time recreation in towns, for the many rather than the few. In any case, much of the activity in this cell (or sector) is valued for itself (e.g., admiring the balance and proportions of a Georgian building). In the language of Professor Salisbury's exchange theory of interest (or pressure) groups, the benefits of group membership are solidary,[18]—that is, intrinsic to the members rather than instrumental. However, many such groups are increasingly drawn into politics. A few are indeed so political that they almost seem to belong with the pure pressure groups. The Town and Country Planning Association is an example.[19] Founded in the late 1890s, it "started life [wrote the *Guardian*] as a garden cities propaganda outfit but has gradually changed character down the years. Now it operates by a mixture of pamphleteering and old boy jollying in committee that is the real mark of influence."[20]

This assessment, made in 1967, would not have been endorsed by everyone in as good or better position to judge as that journalist. Only a few years earlier, Dame Evelyn Sharp, who had come "from the planning side of things" to the permanent secretaryship of the Ministry of Housing and Local Government, characterized the Town and Country Planning Association as "a mere cypher."[21] By the early 1970s, in any case, the Association was no longer relying entirely on what the *Guardian* diarist called "corridor work" but openly conferring with other organizations (e.g., at Manchester) to discuss the Welfare State, community power and action techniques, and the mobilization of the resources of the inner city. Still, bodies such as these do not in general give themselves up wholly to activities of the kind; they exist autonomously and stand apart, which marks them off from the pure pressure groups of cell 4.

Names for the four types are still lacking. A distinction will first be drawn between the top row in the diagram and the bottom one. Taking our cue from the eighteenth century, we shall call groups in the bottom row by the illuminating term "self-created," as opposed to the top row of, say, "given" groups (based, directly or at one or more removes, on occupational role; such attributes as age, sex or ethnicity; or, more tentatively, neighbourhood and church membership). We also need a name for groups in each cell of each row. Those in cell 1 will be called *operational*; in cell 2, *representative*;[22] in cell 3, *expressive* (partly echoing sociologist Peter Blau); in cell 4, *propagational* (as in "propagation of the Gospel"). Obviously this choice of terms is arbitrary; the meaning is not in the name, however, but in the combination of attributes, or properties, specified. And that has empirical (or historical) support.

Having embarked upon the subject of terminology, one may as well acknowledge that the attribution of "pressure group" does tend to raise hackles. When in 1973, for example, a leading official of the TUC heard it incautiously referred to as a pressure group, he exclaimed: "Blow that" (or words to that effect). In fact the TUC itself frequently uses the language of pressure; for example, in 1975: ". . . we have been putting strong pressure on the Government to reflate the economy selectively and to introduce selective temporary controls on imports," and many other instances could be cited.[23] In all this the TUC is in perfectly good company, the language of pressure having been resorted to, approvingly and on occasion even with pride, for at least a century by such varied and respectable bodies as the ancestor of the ABCC, the London Chamber of Commerce, organized ex-servicemen, and the Central (now Country) Land-owners' Association.[24] Today's examples include even the National Trust: "In the Lake District continued pressure by the Trust induced the Cumberland County Council to drop its plans for a southern bypass round Keswick . . . "; and the Commons Society's "It is a striking tribute to the pressure exerted by the Society and other amenity organizations on this matter in recent years that *all three* of the 1968 Acts . . . contained substantial provisions regarding traffic limitation control."[25] The use of the language of pressure surely implies the possession of an attitudinal structure to match, but in any case the characteriza-tion "pressure group" seems a reasonable extrapolation from what the groups themselves say.

Admittedly, when that characterization is put forward *about* groups, the reference is quite often derogatory. Even so the groups need not be on the defensive unless their behaviour has been indefensible. Although it has (so far) escaped the net of the Oxford English Dictionary, "pressure" in just this political sense has been in use since the 1840s at least. That is really one index of the rising tide of democracy. Originally, those who gave "pressure" a bad name were the entrenched elites challenged by new social forces, in much the same way as it was opponents and critics who adapted or invented "Whig" and "Tory," "Quaker" and "Methodist," and other such terms in the vocabulary of derision and abuse. No doubt pressure groups may from time to time deserve criticism, but that will be in virtue of what they do, not what they are called.

**Part II:
Representations:
Substance and Style**

3

Expressive Groups: The Amenities of Life

Sector 3

Making a hole in the ice and dropping a fishing line yields a very varied catch, as Figure 2-1 in Part I suggests. Most of these groups may be conveniently left to their own happy devices. We shall concentrate here upon a single subclass, the amenity groups, which are more political (in the pressure-group sense) than most expressive groups, yet not so much so as to require their being placed within sector 4. Even with that limitation only a taste can be provided of what goes on—substance as well as method—in sector 3.

What one finds here may be displayed (impressionistically) as variations in the degree to which amenity groups are politicized or otherwise put in the nature of the apparent functional mix within the total role. Towards the lower end of the scale, one finds the National Allotments and Garden Society. Any notion that its members are invariably content to lean on their shovels, compare notes about their cabbages and onion sets, and "let the world slide," should be promptly dispelled. At its 1967 Conference, for example, four resolutions called for amendments to the 1925 Allotments Act. One wanted "all allotment land nationalized," the movers (Glamorgan) being "at pains to explain that by nationalization they really meant that allotments should be made the ward of the government in a manner similar to that adopted in the case of 'national' parks." The Society also took on the Prime Minister and other Cabinet Ministers over the anticipated increases in the price of vegetables if Britain joined the Common Market. It was in reply officially advised that "the 47.5 percent increase for vegetables which you envisage would be most unlikely to occur at all widely." The Prime Minister's private secretary added this comment on the Society's statistics: "The more fundamental criticism is that the average British housewife buys much greater quantities of potatoes and of tomatoes than of spring cabbage, cauliflowers and lettuce. The suggested increase in her grocery bill could, therefore, be calculated only a weighted basis."[1]

Evidently, within the breast of the humble allotment-holder, there may be a lobbyist struggling to get out. In the same general vicinity as the Allotments Society stands the Society for the Protection of Ancient Buildings (SPAB). It began with a bang in 1877 after poet and artist William Morris had taken up arms against the restoration (which seemed often to mean desecration) of old buildings in general and Tewkesbury Abbey in particular. Joined by John Ruskin, Burne Jones, Holman Hunt and others, the "Anti-Scrape" naturally won some battles if not the war. Since then, it has gradually become less belligerent and correspondingly more technical, consultative, and advisory. But it makes forays from time to time. It came on the scene too late to save Woburn Square (1969), but its intervention precipitated the important decision by the Ministry of Housing to add some two hundred Bloomsbury buildings to the list of those not to be demolished or even altered without planning permission.

In its own self-perception, that other late Victorian creation, the National Trust also belongs at the lower end of the scale (of politicization). "First and foremost a preservation society" is how it has described itself. Consistently with that and quite self-consciously, the Trust has tried to keep its distance from the other amenity societies on "important conservation issues," which did not "directly affect Trust property," leaving it to "those organizations that have been primarily set up as expressions of the public concern or to act as pressure groups," meaning the CPRE, CPRW, Georgian Group, and others, including the SPAB.[2] In 1971, for example, as Brookes and Richardson have remarked, the Trust declined to take part in the National Parks Campaign.[3] However, remaining a member of the Standing Committee on National Parks (formed in the 1930s to press for their establishment), the Trust did become "actively involved in making representations to the Government over the future of the National Parks,"[4] arguing, with the force of the third largest landowner in Britain and indeed with land in all the National Parks, that these should be independently administered—that is, no longer left as a patchwork quilt in which the colours of the County Councils predominated, which was the goal of the Campaign. Only the previous year (as noted towards the end of Chapter 2) the Trust claimed that its own "continued pressure" had made the Cumberland County Council do what the Trust wanted it to do. At the higher level of the Budget, the 1972 Finance Act contained valuable concessions for the Trust in Scotland as well as the rest of the country: Bequests, "however large," were made "wholly exempt from estate duty and aggregation" and all gifts relieved from capital gains tax.[5] These fiscal gifts did not come unsolicited. On the right sort of issue the Trust will even stake out a position openly (in *The Times*, in Parliament, and so forth), as in its opposition to the siting of the Third London Airport at Cublington.[6]

What is true then is that the character of the National Trust does put constraints upon its political style. "Character" refers not only to its being a statutory body[7] but a charity, which always tends to put a damper on the methods that a pressure group can use. But quiet persuasion of the public authorities remains an available method, and the National Trust through its social network is well placed to take advantage of it and does, for interaction with government in *some* form is crucial to the discharge of its duties.

The Civic Trust, not Victorian but Elizabethan (1957), also occupies a fairly central position along this political dimension. Financed by grants from industry and commerce, it is charged with fostering high standards of architecture and civic planning in British towns and with improving their appearance. Holding the threads of a dense network of some 1200 local civic and amenity societies, it is, to a considerable degree, inevitably political (in the pressure-group sense). It even goes into business on its own account as, for example, "the major pressure group behind"[8] the Civic Amenities Act of 1967. Originating in a Private Members' Bill introduced by former Minister Duncan Sandys as the Trust's president, the Act empowered local authorities to designate conservation areas, preserve trees and dispose of abandoned cars, partly reflecting the "beautification" Acts of 1965-66 in the United States.

More political still, probably, are the CPRE and its Welsh counterpart, the CPRW (both singled out in that sense by the National Trust in the comment quoted above). The CPRE is indeed politically active. In 1967, it pressed the Ministry of Housing and Local Government to make local councils provide permanent camping sites for Britain's estimated 25,000 gipsies, the immediate problem being caused by the peripatetic Irish tinkers whose invasion of Kent, for example, was said by Sir George Langley Taylor, then CPRE chairman, to have done much harm to the countryside.[9] Early in 1969 three of its county branches (Buckinghamshire, Northamptonshire, and Oxfordshire) "formed a joint standing committee to organize the opposition" to siting the third London airport at Silverstone, or indeed *"anywhere else inland,"*[10] which was national CPRE policy. When, in December 1970, the choice fell on Cublington, headquarters called on branches to write in protest to both Prime Minister and the Secretary of State for the Environment, Peter Walker. In the Lords debate the following February, the chairman himself (by now, Lord Molson) kept up the running fire. Some two months later Cublington was indeed reprieved, although at the cost (which Cublington and district bore with equanimity) of making Foulness the new victim.

The Juggernauts

With others, the CPRE played a notable part in the continuous struggle to keep Britain safe from the heavy lorry (or truck), the kind that, before the *autoroutes* were built in France, so often intimidated British car drivers *en route*, they hoped, for the South. As the sixties advanced, the shadow of Europe grew longer too, and with it the demand for longer vehicles. The Economic Development Committee on the Movement of Exports in its report (*Through Transport to Europe*) recommended increases in the permitted length of certain types of vehicles that were implemented after the Ministry's consultation with the interests in 1967. But as one of those consulted, the ABCC (representing transport users), was quick to tell the Ministry: "The changes would be of limited practical value so long as existing limitations of gross permitted weights and axle loadings remained in force."[11] (Gross weight = weight of vehicle + load carried. The limitations were the Ministry regulations that controlled gross weight according to the number of axles and the distance between them, or wheelbase.) The logic of the comment was accepted by or in the Ministry, which had in fact authorised some such dialectical increase in size and weight from the mid-fifties onwards. In due course, the upper limit became 32 tons and the maximum length, except for combinations (= lorries + trailers), a little over 49 feet. By 1969 the manufacturers were openly seeking authority for much greater increases, to 44 tons (and perhaps, for combinations, 56 tons), with a slight increase in length to carry a 40-foot shipping container without overhanging the back of the lorry.

The Ministry's response in part was to sound out the other interests, including the users, spoken for by the ABCC. The idea behind the Ministry's approach "was that the present vehicle dimensions can accommodate a standard 40-foot container but it cannot be carried anything like fully laden."[12] Since through traffic to Europe would increase and Britain could not afford to lag behind the European standards, the ABCC gave its support to the particular proposals. That seemed a good augury for change. The Ministry itself did not need to be persuaded, and its new political master, Richard Marsh (if not his predecessor, Barbara Castle) was sympathetic.

The signs, however, proved deceptive. Even the return of a Conservative Government in 1970, which on past experience should have favoured the industry's claims, failed to produce the expected result. Just in time for Christmas John Peyton, the Minister of Transport, announced that he had "decided not to allow the maximum weight of goods vehicles to be raised above 32 tons. I am primarily concerned that greater efforts should be made to reduce the noise, congestion and pollution which lorries cause, and to improve their ability to operate within the physical limitations of our road system."[13]

Thus, his reasons were essentially environmental—aptly enough for the holder of an office that had been absorbed within the recently created Department of the Environment. But the hands that had turned fortune's wheel, defeating the industry's earlier expectations, belonged to the press, the amenity societies and the local authorities' associations. The *Sunday Times* struck first through reporter Tony Dawe, whose opening article in September 1969 was intended to be a shot over the Minister's bows. Two weeks later he wrote another piece stressing the danger of damaging historic buildings, and early in the new year he extended the point to include the cost to the country in a broader sense.[14] Whether or not as cause and effect, the amenity societies were by then up and running, with (of course) letters to *The Times*, questions in the House, a debate in both Houses, a public meeting not far from the precincts, and private meetings with officials at the Ministry and at the Scottish Development Office.

Except for Mr. Dawe's writings (he published in all five or six shorter pieces after his January article), the public debate subsided in the spring. A General

Election in the summer produced a new government. In the autumn the campaign picked up again to take advantage of the new Parliamentary session. The CPRE and the Pedestrians' Association for Road Safety were again prominent as they had been a year earlier and since. But another early opponent, the Civic Trust, may have made an important contribution through its "detailed 200-page report . . . which condemned existing heavy lorries on the grounds of noise, vibration and danger and listed examples from throughout Britain of the damage they have caused."[15] Asked for its views in January 1970, the Trust had written to all its 700 registered amenity societies on the broad environmental impact of lorries, not merely the specific proposal on which it was being consulted. On the basis of 300 responses, it quickly provided an interim answer opposing the proposed change. The final report, written by Arthur Percival of the Trust's staff, reached the Minister in October. No doubt the analysis supported by a massive catalogue of concrete examples did open "many people's eyes to the seriousness and widespread nature of the problem," as the environment reporter of *The Times*, Tony Aldous, remarked.[16] Whether it was really decisive is much more difficult to judge. The crucial achievement may have been to hold the line in the period October 1969 to January 1970 before the round of consultations began that produced the report. If so, then the press (not the *Sunday Times* alone) and a number of groups, including the Civic Trust itself but also some not mentioned above, such as the Royal Institute of British Architects (RIBA), deserve credit. It has also to be recalled that local government, especially the County Councils' Association and for the boroughs, the Association of Municipal Corporations, had taken up arms against the *juggernauts*.[17] Possibly the real significance of the report is that it filled a gap, since the "detailed study into every aspect of the problem by the Road Research Laboratory—commissioned earlier this year to help the Government reach a decision—has not yet been completed."[18] The report may even have provided the Minister with evidence to support a decision already reached on environmental grounds. For as John Peyton's "boss," Peter Walker, Secretary of State for the Environment, would soon say in a public lecture at Cambridge, had it not been for his Department, the decision would probably have gone the other way.[19] The only certainty is that the Civic Trust, CPRE, Pedestrians' Association, RIBA, and others, including the Scottish societies, routed the Society of Motor Manufacturers and Traders, the Road Haulage Association and perhaps even a section within the Ministry itself. As a *Sunday Times* subeditor put it, victory "in the lorry war" went to "the giant killers."

After that famous victory of December 1970, the forces that had secured it did not rest upon their laurels. The Pedestrians' Association went on to argue for a *reduction* in the current 32-ton limit. Attempting to meet the threat at one of its sources on the Continent, both CPRE and RIBA tried to influence their counterparts there. The CPRE even carried the argument to Brussels as the administrative headquarters of the EEC, claiming that most British people opposed further weight increases and proposing a thorough reconsideration of EEC transport policy. At home the Civic Trust floated a compromise plan to specify routes that existing heavy lorries would be compelled to take, and even defrayed some of the expenses of a private members' bill designed to achieve that end. Introduced in February 1973 by a Conservative member, Hugh Dykes, it would have placed the burden of regulating the movement of heavy lorries upon an Advisory Council acting after consultation with the local councils and such other interested parties as the road hauliers.

However realistic in one sense, that was an idea whose time would never have come in that form because it entailed the exercise of detailed zoning power by an unrepresentative body. The obvious way out was to bring the local authorities—the county councils—fully in, and for once it was followed. Advised by a benevolent (Conservative) Government, Mr. Dykes made the appropriate amendments as to zoning power and enforcement, thus enabling the county councils to come into their own. The final policy output went under the unlovely name of the Heavy Commercial Vehicles (Controls and Regulations) Act, 25 July 1973.

Of course, whether local government would really do the job—the obverse of the realistic coin—was quite another question. In June 1974, Peter Harland of the *Sunday Times* would write: "Local authorities should use their powers under the Heavy Commercial Vehicles Act 1973 to regulate the routes of heavy lorries."[20] Yet important ground had been gained: Not only had the nation stumbled into the idea of designated routes for heavy lorries, but this had in the end been accepted, however grudgingly, by the road haulage interests.

What had come over them? In that other area, the post-World War II period, the Road Haulage Association (RHA) won a not undeserved reputation for aggressiveness or, from another vantage point, for splendid vigour in self-defence (when trying to ward off nationalization). And for some years after 1969, when the Freight Transport Association (FTA) arose out of the ashes of three such bodies, the RHA enjoyed, de facto, an accession of strength, since the FTA, ostensibly speaking for the industrial users of any form of transport—rail and water as well as road—then showed itself tender to the road haulage interests.[21] Drawing upon the work of Richard Rose (and Samuel Beer), Richard Kimber and his colleagues explained this apparent (but probably not very Christian) resignation over the 1973 Bill as an instance of group acceptance of a marked change in the cultural (or normative) constraints upon its freedom of action.[22]

That such a change had occurred is clear. It is signalled again in the consultation document (two volumes of well over 200 pages)[23] issued by the (Labour) Government for public discussion in April, 1976; for example, "Commercial vehicles, especially heavy lorries, should meet environmental as well as resource costs." But Kimber et al. added a gloss of their own to the effect that the road hauliers might in due course turn the change to their own advantage, accepting designated routes "as a factor likely to increase the chances of higher weights being eventually accepted by both the Government and the amenity interests."

This comment, published early in 1974, proved to be very perceptive: Within a few years *that* was exactly what the road haulage interests and the lorry manufacturers went after, except that they were pressing not only for an increase in maximum weight from 32 to 40 tons but in length (an extra half meter, to 50 ft. 10 in). Exerting themselves in part on and through the EEC—evidently destined to be an important new channel for pressure-group influence of certain kinds—they seemed to exude confidence in the ultimate result. For in 1976, 12,000 or so *more* lorries of over 28 tons were registered (about one in five of all new lorries). Of these, some 7,000 were designed to carry more than the 32-ton limit. As John Wardroper of the *Sunday Times* (which still kept a sharp eye on the subject) remarked: "The lorry men have a big investment in a rise in the legal limit."[24]

Once again an amenity group picked up the gauntlet. Early in 1977, the Civic Trust set out to mobilize its nationwide network of local societies, asking these to let the Transport Minister (William Rodgers) have the benefit of their views. Meanwhile industry pressure of another kind continued to mount. During 1975 the number of lorries over 28 tons increased by 11,000, making a total of some 66,000, which meant that something like one out of eight lorries was then a juggernaut. By 1977 the total had reached about 73,000. Connoisseurs of the policy studies distinction between *output* and *outcome* should also note that the Heavy Commercial Vehicles . . . Act of 1973 seemed to have been little used. By mid-year, when yet another in the long line of transport White Papers was published, it even appeared that some kinds of local bans, such as Cirencester's "access only" restriction on vehicles over three tons, had little appeal to the Government, because, as Mr. Wardroper noted, "these often mean that people on busy roads are hit even harder."[25] The problem of how to "civilize" the heavy lorry (the Minister's word) remained.

It is also a problem, some might think, of how to civilize the heavy-lorry interests. One is in any case reminded of some far from pious remarks about *The Motor God* made by Anthony Wedgwood Benn in 1964 some months after he (and William Rodgers) had made spirited criticisms of the Conservative Government in the debate on the celebrated Buchanan Report dealing with the long-term development of roads and traffic in urban areas and their influence on the urban environment.[26] Discussing road safety specifically, Mr. Benn wrote, "Any Minister of Transport who really decided to take [it] seriously would have to brace himself for the most bitter hostility from the unthinking worshippers of the Motor God," predicting that "the pressure groups that surround the motor industry would lobby ferociously against him. . . ."[27] The proposition could be extended to other road vehicles than the motor car and to more than road safety: one way or another, as we advance towards the eighties, a great deal of civilizing remains to be accomplished all round.

***

The CPRE is not wholly given up to the exercise of political influence. One thinks of a 20-mile walk sponsored by the CPRE (Oxfordshire Branch), the Soil Association, and the Naturalists—the three societies "having mutual interest in furthering the study and enjoyment of our countryside." The organizers did not miss the opportunity of marking out a route that followed (and thus confirmed) fieldpaths that were public rights of way, but the route was also "exciting" in its own terms, "on the dividing ridge" between the valleys of Thames and Severn, passing "Jurassic Way (the oldest road in Britain, known here as Ditchedge Lane)," by Gallow Hill and Traitor's Ford to the headwaters of the Stour. To make the most of the occasion, good advice was offered in advance: "Rub feet with methylated spirit each day for a week. . . . No fizzy drinks. Chocolate and apple are suggested."[28] All this, in the end, marks off the CPRE (and its sister bodies in Wales and Scotland) from the pure pressure group. It is indeed dedicated to what Lord Esher once termed "the preservation of the greatest work of art this country has ever produced, its landscape."[29] That entails political action. But the principal goal is the enjoyment, direct and not vicarious, of the work of art itself—that makes the CPRE "expressive."

4

Propagational Groups: Conservation, Human Rights, Morals

Sector 4

Cultivated continually since the 1780s, this corner of the land is characterized by luxuriant growth. Many are of course ephemeral, such as the thirty or so groups lined up in relation to British entry into the EEC (assuming here, which would not be true of all, that they were autonomous and not anchored). Some of the thirty were revived in 1974 in order to counter the Get Britain Out Campaign, the movement to make a perhaps not very graceful exit from the EEC by way of the unprecedented referendum. But with Britain's membership confirmed, such groups will naturally fade away.[1]

Faced with such lush growth, one picks out a few features and then concentrates upon a particular patch in the hope of gaining some political insights, thus refining one's political judgment. One's roving eye alights upon the conservation lobby, upon groups protecting or advancing human rights and upon those dealing with what are called "moral issues": abortion, homosexual relations, and divorce (as if ecology or human rights did not constitute or entail moral questions, or for that matter, food adulteration or dangerous working conditions in factory or mine).

The Conservation Lobby

We often talk about the environmental groups, or the environmental lobby. The usage is not inconvenient but could perhaps be improved upon by resolving the concept into two parts: amenity lobby and conservation lobby. The former would be held to embrace such bodies as the SPAB, Civic Trust and CPRE; the latter, the Conservation Society, FoE and other specimens of the pure pressure group. The distinction, however, goes beyond the degree of specialization as such. The Noise Abatement Society is politically specialized. In our period it worked, for example, to amend the law so as to authorize the public health authorities or the police to take immediate action without having to wait for a formal complaint, with secretary John Connell saying: "If someone's hitting you over the head with noise . . . you've got to put up with it for at least a fortnight [whereas] if somebody's hitting you over the head with a crowbar, you can get him arrested immediately." The point is rather that in this domain a qualitative shift occurred during the late sixties and early seventies. Environmental politics then passed beyond preservation, protection, and the territorial imperative towards an understanding of and concern for conservation, ecology, and ecosystems. According to a standard formulation (by Ernst Haeckel of the University of Jena in the late 1860s), ecology focuses upon the total relations of an animal to both its organic and its inorganic environment, which was not exactly what the founders of the late-Victorian amenity societies had in mind even assuming they had heard of the German biologist. Similarly, the founders of the Georgian Group in 1936 would not have been thinking of ecosystems (those "resulting from the integration of all living and nonliving factors of the environment"), which A.G. Tansley had formulated the year before. Conservation may have been nearer to what the pioneers of the amenity societies had had in mind. This is a vaguer concept, owing something perhaps to ideas of conservancy advanced by the foresters of British India. In the relevant sense the term *conservation* itself, however, may be American, coined in about 1907 by Overton Price, one of a dedicated band of public servants that included Gifford Pinchot, a forester by training, who defined it as "the use of natural resources for the greatest good of the greatest number for the longest time."

Combined with the interrelated Malthusian notion then enjoying one of its periodic revivals, a concern for ecology, ecosystems, and conservation gained ground during the 1960s, not only in Britain. There the catalyst was a letter to the *Observer* in 1966 by a Scottish physical chemist, Dr. Douglas MacEwan, which produced the Conservation Society, to conserve all kinds of resources (food and water, land and raw materials, wild life). Expressing the key ecological idea of balance between the various forms of life, Lady Eve Balfour (Field Director of the Soil Association) argued at the inauguration for a limit to the "uncontrolled expansion of mankind." But as a corollary of its central concern, the Society also moved to stop the contamination of the environment by smoke, effluents, and toxic pesticides. By 1974 the local branches were displaying the same catholicity. For example, the Thames Valley branch, based on Hampton Hill, was trying to get traffic noise reduced in the town centres in and around Richmond and Twickenham. The Reading and District branch (whose secretary had been a theoretical physicist) published a leaflet *How to Protect Yourself Against Pollution*, which was sold to local authorities throughout the country. Its researches into the danger arising from the lead content in petrol (gas, to Americans) became the basis of the Conservation Society's national policy.[2]

Nationally the Society was on the move in more senses than one—from an Honourable Secretary in Potter's Bar to a full-time Director (the Cambridge-educated research chemist, Dr. John Davoll) in Walton-on-Thames and then Chertsey, where an operations officer was taken on board. Policy, too, was developing from an emphasis on population control to what Dr. Davoll, in a paper discussing political action, identified as the "far more serious problems [that] arise from attempts to control that component of environmental destruction and depletion that arises from industrial operations."[3] This merged easily into the theme of *a sustainable economy* addressed by members in several booklets, including one by Colin Hutchinson, derived from a membership survey, that was used as fuel to fire the Conservation for Survival Campaign started in November 1975. The theme was bleak: *"industrialized society has acquired a way of life that cannot be sustained . . .* material equilibrium is not an option but a necessity, although its character and timing are debatable."[4]

Such more or less ecological self-consciousness marks off the Conservation Society from the older amenity groups as such (not necessarily their individual members). It differs also in self-perception, seeing itself quite straightforwardly as a pressure group,[5] and so tending to act differently from the typical amenity groups—that is, less conventionally and more vigorously (which once cost it a vice president who straddled several of these realms, Lord Esher.[6] He had objected to "the Society's policy and tactics" at motorway inquiries). So too with Friends of the Earth (FoE), the 1970 British incarnation (hence *Ltd.*) of the American *Inc.* launched by activist David Brower in San Francisco the previous year[7] and thus the local component of Friends of the Earth International, a more or less federal body: In its written evidence to the Wolfenden Committee on Voluntary Organizations, FoE, too, described itself quite straightforwardly as a pressure group.[8] It, too, is vigorous, as Whitehall is aware. Thus, on the issue of the control of endangered species, over which it had been consulted at an early stage, it did not get the resulting press release possibly because (director Tom Burke speculated) its criticism had been feared.[9] Certainly it is unconventional. Its office puts one in mind of a newsroom close to the deadline after war has just been unexpectedly declared or some king has inconsiderately allowed himself to be assassinated. Refused a press card for a Department of the Environment news conference, it got one out of the *New Scientist*, which then surprisingly sported two representatives. This enterprising move did not endear FoE to the Department.

On the other hand, FoE, if no less ardent than the Conservation Society in its commitment to "the conservation, restoration and rational use of the Ecosphere" (on the masthead of its Supporters' Bulletin), does express its concern in a different form. Where the Society argues (making an appeal to reason and the imagination), FoE acts: against the nonreturnable bottle, making Schweppes a present initially of 1,500 bottles (1971), followed by Bottle Day (1974); for endangered species (Adopt-a-Species 1972), followed two years later by promotion of an Endangered Species Bill; against the import of baleen whale products (1973), followed by Whale Week in 1975; Bike Day at County Hall, London, part of a campaign against the road programme. This last item serves as a reminder that the contrast presented above between the two organizations is of course too sharp: FoE does argue, and at length, as in Mick Hamer's analysis of the road lobby (1974). But to a substantial degree the argument is *in* the action: One is reminded of the old anarchist slogan, "the propaganda of the deed." This is all the more apt if one thinks of methods in a narrower sense—that is, presenting Prime Minister Heath with a bike for circumnavigating traffic jams (1972), a demonstration at the Motor Show (1973), sending the Minister of State responsible for policy on whales a giant Christmas card bearing a condemnation by some thirty M.P.s of sperm-oil imports (1975). All the while, of course, cultivating the Press, often successfully.

Whether these two bodies, so much concerned with survival, can themselves survive long enough to do the job they defined was not entirely clear as the decade advanced. Much depends no doubt on the fate of the conservation movement in Britain and elsewhere: There are some disquieting signs that the first fine careless rapture is already over. Amalgamation is not unthinkable and has in fact been thought about by the professional staffs. They know what it is to work together, as on energy policy. In June 1976, Secretary of State for Energy, Anthony Wedgwood Benn, in line with his views (quoted early in Chapter 2) about using "new centres of democratic initiative outside the party system," convened a National Energy Conference in order to help crystallize a national energy strategy. The two societies presented a joint paper.[10]

Still, each may well continue individually to defy the odds. The conservation movement ought to be big enough to accommodate both.

Human Rights

On the broad definition (recalling "freedom from want"), the Child Poverty Action Group (CPAG) would appear here. Off the mark in the summer of 1967,[11] it was quickly into its stride and by the end of the following year was described by the *Guardian* as a major lobby. It is but one of a subclass of groups that emerged in the late sixties to grapple with the interrelated problems of poverty and bad housing and even homelessness (at a time when about 675,000 houses stood empty in England and Wales alone and perhaps as many as 100,000 in the London Area). After the plight of the homeless in the great cities had been dramatized on TV (*Cathy Come Home*, 1966), Shelter was launched. As the National Campaign for the Homeless, it developed, under the leadership of Des Wilson, a national network. Its Family Squatting Advisory Service also makes it practical as well as propagational. With the London Squatters Campaign, however, the boot is on the other foot. It is practical first (getting people into empty flats or houses) and propagational mainly in consequence. It, too, was born of *Cathy Come Home,* but of the third showing in November 1968, which convinced Ron Bailey, a political activist, that the homeless or hopelessly housed simply had to be installed in empty accommodation without further ado. In December the Squatters infiltrated a block of flats, one third unoccupied, on the east side of London and climbed on to the roof. With banners unfurled ("Luxury Flats Stand Empty as Homeless Rot"), they made the front pages (as of *The Times*).

It is characteristic of this issue area that the groups tend to burst their bonds. Thus in May 1974, the CPAG, with the Catholic Housing Aid Society and the Campaign for the Homeless and Rootless, formed a new group, the Ten Million, with the title reflecting the number of persons said to lack decent homes. In the same month, on the initiative of the CPAG and of the War on Want, six of the groups in the poverty lobby were represented on a deputation to the Prime Minister, (Sir) Harold Wilson, who was supported by three other Ministers, including Mrs. Judith Hart, the Minister for Overseas Development. The P.M. undertook to consider how poverty overseas as well as at home could be tackled by means of integrated policies.

***

Here, however, one is thinking of "rights" in a more conventional sense and accordingly of such bodies as the NCCL, Amnesty, Justice, and the Howard League for Penal Reform. Only the last two can be touched upon here.[12] How the Howard League goes about things may be judged from its action over the Criminal Justice Bill, 1972. It made use of the press (article in the *Guardian*, November 1971; letter in the *Times* the following spring); with the National Association for the Care and Resettlement of Offenders (NACRO), it issued a statement and so took part in the debate at one remove; it also briefed M.P.s and members of the Lords who were due to take part literally in the Parliamentary proceedings.[13]

From the standpoint of this inquiry, Justice is interesting less for its modus operandi as such than for an insight derivable from its role in one particular issue—that is, the establishment of a Parliamentary Commissioner for Administration, a species of Ombudsman. The idea for this possible mode of redress for administrative injustice is believed to have occurred to several scholars at Oxford and the London School of Economics in the mid-fifties, but its penetration of Justice may perhaps be dated from a memorandum, published at the time, by a new member of the Council, the Oxford law don, F.H. Lawson. In any event, a Justice research project produced, in 1961, the Whyatt Report (after chairman Sir John Whyatt, a former Chief Justice of Singapore). The point for our purpose here is the extent (disclosed by William B. Gwyn) to which the variations from the proposed Scandinavian model were incorporated in the very drafting according to the rule of anticipated reactions usually associated with the name of Carl Friedrich. In other words, the predicted (hostile) reactions of civil servants to having to disclose departmental minutes, and of M.P.s to being bypassed if the public were allowed the great privilege of complaining directly to the Parliamentary Commissioner, nipped such proposals in the bud. Similarly, the Minister was to be given a veto on whether allegations of maladministration in his Department were to be investigated. As Sir John Whyatt remarked: "What we put forward will have a good chance of succeeding if it means that the Minister will have the last word and there is some sort of filter" *by M.P.s of* complaints from the public.[14]

The question then, however, was whether the so-called success (an Act) would be worth having. A well placed observer, Geoffrey Marshall, politics don at The Queen's College, Oxford, characterized the withholding of direct access as castration, adding that if the proposals were not bold on the subject of ministerial veto and the exclusion of internal minutes, the scheme would be "hardly worth fighting for."[1][5]

In this emasculated form, compared not only with Scandinavia but also New Zealand, the idea was taken up by the National Executive Committee of the Labour Party in 1963 and found its way into the manifesto for the General Election the following year:

Labour has resolved to humanize the whole administration of the state *and to set up the new office of Parliamentary Commissioner with the right and duty to investigate and expose any misuse of government power as it affects the citizen.*[16]

Gaining office then, Labour had the proposal on the statute book by March 1967. That was but a few months short of the tenth anniversary of the publication of Professor Lawson's original proposal.

Little more than three years after the Act, Tony Smythe was writing as general secretary of the NCCL to the incoming Conservative Home Secretary to say that the "Ombudsman [had] made no more than a marginal improvement in the balance between individual rights and the power of the executive."[1][7] As part of a Campaign for a Bill of Rights, both he and Lord Shawcross (chairman of the Council of Justice) called for extensions to the Ombudsman system; in effect, for some of those features excluded by the Whyatt Committee's self-denying ordinance nine years earlier.

What is interesting here is the relationship (in the sometimes unavoidable technical language of system analysis) of *input* to *withinput*, raising questions about the *conversion* of these into policy *output*. Such issues cannot be pursued here,[1][8] but Part II of this book is of course organized around inputs. In this case of the Parliamentary Commissioner, the input from Justice might be usefully interpreted, in part, as a withinput, but one of a rather special kind. It might be called a withinput in disguise.

Morals and Politics

Anxiety about morals is of course by no means new. It sometimes seems, in fact, that every generation on the wane regards the morals of the rising generation with incredulity and even horror. But it appears that such anxiety took organizational form more frequently during the period under review. When the 1960s were reached, two bodies in particular stood on guard: the interdenominational Public Morality Council, a turn-of-the-century foundation, and the Moral Law Defence Association (MLDA) launched in 1959 by three PR men. Two of them were already experienced in pressure-group operations: John Connell, secretary of the Noise Abatement Society, and Richard Clitherow, national organizer of the League Against Cruel Sports. The third, Dillon MacCarthy, a Catholic who had once aspired to the priesthood, ran the new Association.[19] From the early 1960s, however, these two associations had company (whether they wanted it or not): Youth Impact (founded by a young man, also Catholic, from Newcastle-on-Tyne); the Glasgow-based League of Women (critical of "TV plays which have one foot in the kitchen sink and one in the double bed"); and the Women of Britain Clean TV Campaign (started in the Midlands and particularly critical of BBC Drama, for much the same reason: the "habitual game of coital consequences," as a Birmingham councillor [male] would put it).[20] Founded by two women who had been associated for many years with the Moral Rearmament movement (Mrs. Mary Whitehouse and Mrs. Norah Buckland),[21] the Clean-Up TV Campaign quickly acquired national importance as (from 1965) the National Viewers' and Listeners' Association (VALA).

By then the London Campaign Against Obscenity was under way. Founded in 1963 by Edward Oliver, a Catholic, it soon attracted all denominations, including Jewish, and representatives of the teaching profession and the National Council of Women for the purpose of amending the Obscene Publications Act of 1959, described (February 1964) as having "several serious flaws." Thus, to win a conviction, the prosecution had to prove that a book was sold to a particular person and that it tended to deprave and correct him (or her). But police evidence on that point had been ruled inadmissible, which was rather a snag because the actual purchaser was not terribly keen to testify to purchase and to his having been in consequence even a little bit depraved and corrupted.[22]

As the seventies opened, the war on pornography was still being waged. Returning in 1970 from missionary work in India, Peter and Janet Hill took steps that led in September 1971 to the inaugural meeting of the Festival of Light movement, addressed then by such luminaries as Malcolm Muggeridge and Bishop (Trevor) Huddleston, if stridently opposed in person by Women's Lib and the Gay Liberation Front. For a later mass rally in Trafalgar Square (estimates range from 35,000 to 60,000), Arthur Blessit arrived from the United States to speak in the name of the Jesus People, and Mrs. Whitehouse (an Anglican) brought a message from the Pope. "Pornography in the media and on display at the news agent' " was what the Festival of Light movement first went after.[23] But by the mid-seventies it was also casting a beam on the cinema, supporting a Salvation Army social worker's private summons against the distributors of one production. By now (1974) VALA, too, was on the same tack, having made a strategic decision "to widen the scope of its moral crusade."[24] In 1974 Mrs. Whitehouse brought a private prosecution under the

Vagrancy Act (of 1824) against a London cinema for "allegedly allowing 'indecency in a public place' by showing" a certain Franco-Italian film.[25] In 1976 her pressure on the Home Secretary to prevent a film about Jesus from being shot in England by a Danish director led to his being turned back, complete with script, at Heathrow Airport. She is also credited with keeping *Deep Throat* out of England by the simple device of tipping off customs officials that a copy was about to be brought in.[26]

That reads like influence. Certainly the National VALA perturbed the BBC: In 1965 the Director-General himself, Sir Hugh Greene, denounced it vigorously, if not under that name,[27] in the BBC's own journal, *The Listener*, which, four years later, also carried a more specific and extensive attack by Alisdair Fairley.[28] In between (1967) a BBC writer, speaking on the BBC radio programme, *World At One*, allegedly called the movement "fascist," and both he and the BBC were successfully sued by Mrs. Whitehouse. Their chagrin would have been all the greater had they known that the damages they paid went towards the purchase of a car that was put at the service of the movement.[29] Librarians, too, had been put on the defensive. In April 1964, the editor of *Books and Bookmen*, addressing a conference of librarians, had appealed to them "to resist pressure groups which did not want them to stock certain books. . . . pressure groups, like the 'cranky' ones in America, were tending to become more active in Britain and were springing up all over the country." That was some two months after the London Campaign Against Obscenity had started, but the speaker also referred to TV and "such groups as the League of Women. . . ." These were "in a minority [but] their voice was loud and there was the danger that their influence might persuade the television authorities to produce programmes like *Mrs. Dale's Diary* all day long."[30]

Still, reviewing the efforts of the groups as a whole from about the mid-sixties, one observes that not every ploy succeeded. Certainly these new groups proved powerless to prevent in the late sixties a batch of bills that together constituted the most fundamental changes in the realm of "morals" ever enacted by a British Parliament, notably the legalization of abortion, of homosexual relations between consenting adults in private, and of "no fault" divorce. As the secretary of the MLRA had put it in 1964, "The real enemies are the people who want to change the divorce laws or the homosexual laws."[31] Within only a few years the enemies as thus identified had carried all before them, while others had legalized abortion.

What exactly these apparently conflicting tendencies really signify must be left to the social historian. Here one attempts only to tease out the nature of the group-government interplay leading to such profoundly important legislative changes.

***

The most striking feature of that interplay is the weight (or salience) of the withinputs—that is, of Cabinet assistance (not merely drafting, which is common enough with private members' bills, but also the provision by the Cabinet of Parliamentary time at crucial stages and even advice on tactics), without which the originally private initiatives would not have succeeded. And, as with the Parliamentary Commissioner, although directly and not vicariously by way of the rule of anticipated reactions, these were withinputs in disguise—that is, which the Cabinet and so the Government as a whole never acknowledged publicly and for which, accordingly, they could not be held accountable by the electorate. Our concern here, however, is not with the issue of accountability (or with the closely related doctrine of mandate) but with the interaction of groups and government. This may be illustrated from the Sexual Offences Act of 1967.

Homosexual Relations and the 1967 Act

Homosexual relations do not necessarily entail sodomy (or buggery), but their equation in the popular mind seems to be of long standing, assisted no doubt by the record in Genesis of the unhappy fate that befell those two sinful cities of ancient Palestine, Sodom and Gomorrah. In any event, in England it was originally an offence that brought the luckless offender before an ecclesiastical court. In Tudor times, however, "the abominable Vice of Buggery committed with man or beast" was removed from the ecclesiastical jurisdiction and made a statutory offence punishable by death. Whether this transfer merely reflected Henry VIII's quarrel with the Pope and successful assertion of Supremacy or whether it partly meant that the Tudors (if not Henry himself) were more susceptible, the law lasted until mid-Victorian times, when penal servitude for life was generously substituted for the death penalty. A generation later, however, the law was widened (1885) to include any "gross indecency" between males, even in private, punishable by up to two years in gaol[32] (soon to be visited on the head of Oscar Wilde).

In introducing such a criminal provision, England was clearly out of step with the general European tendency of the age. Under the impact of the *Code Napoléon*, the traditional attempt "to suppress sin of every kind by judicial action"[33] was being gradually abandoned as unworkable. This included homosexual behaviour unless a participant had not consented, or were under the age of consent, or the act had been committed in public. Whether England did not know what Europe was doing in this respect or, if knowing, did not care, possibly for good reason, is far from clear. It is well known that the relevant clause was tagged on to the Bill very late in the day (judged both by the clock and the progress of the Bill), and with virtually no discussion. But that might merely have reflected the Victorians' (verbal) incapacity to cope with sex combined with a perturbing perception that homosexual practices were growing more rife (which may well have been objectively true).

In any event, the law was set in a mould that would survive unscathed for the greater part of a century. It began to be challenged, however, in the 1950s.

In the run-up to the 1967 Act, three phases may be distinguished from the vantage point of the group and its principal activity: dissemination (the seed is spread to nongoverning elites), engagement of a section of the governing elite, which in turn engages the Cabinet. In support of this patterning, one can offer here only a bare outline.

Dissemination: 1952-1960. Church of England Moral Welfare Society set in motion investigation of the problem, undertaken by ad hoc group of clergymen, lawyers, and doctors. After its liberal report came out in 1954, the Howard League for Penal Reform as well as the Society proposed an official inquiry. Government appointed (Sir John) Wolfenden Committee, August 1954 to consider "law and practice" of both homosexuality and prostitution (a revealing juxtaposition). With one dissentient, the Wolfenden Committee recommended (1957) that homosexual acts by consenting adults in private should no longer be adjudged criminal.

That recommendation was supported, on balance, by religious opinion. Howard League and the Institute of Social Psychiatry advocated implementation, as did letters to *The Times* from men and women of distinction, many of whom were carried over by one of them (Oxford don, A.E. Dyson) into the titular governing body of a new association (May 1958), the Homosexual Law Reform Society (HLRS).

The HLRS now took up the running, sending copies of a pamphlet to all M.P.s, before the Commons debate on the Wolfenden Report (November). Since, unknown to HLRS, M.P.s also received from other hands two books intended to persuade in the same sense, a "backlash" resulted (pressure from "a rich and powerful lobby of perverts" was alleged).[34] M.P. on executive committee (Kenneth Robinson) warned Society off Parliament until further notice. Society heeded advice, and "concentrated upon the Press and the public,"[35] including churches, student groups and youth organizations—that is, nongoverning elites. This phase of activity may be said to culminate (there is of course always likely to be overlap between phases, as indeed within them) in a well-attended meeting at Caxton Hall in May 1960.

Engagement: 1960-1965. Private members' motion (Kenneth Robinson) to implement Wolfenden Report went down by more than two votes to one, although 99 *for* was higher than might have been predicted (June 1960). In 1961 another Labour member, Leo Abse (also on HLRS executive committee) drew ninth place in the ballot. He toyed with a bill to make the consent of the Director of Public Prosecutions (DPP) a necessary condition for police prosecution of consenting adults whose acts had been committed in private.[36] This idea remarkably anticipated the possibility, given a liberalizing DPP, of getting the Wolfenden results by administrative rather than legislative action. His subsequent bill was talked out, but in July 1964 a new DPP did request chief constables to approach him before prosecuting such cases.[37] Earlier that year, the Conservative M.P. and Father of the House, Sir Thomas Moore, often dismissed as a backwoodsman, urged the Government to implement the Wolfenden Report. He had been influenced by a local case but also apparently by case histories submitted to him the previous year by the HLRS.[38]

Reinforcement: 1965-1967. In May 1965 the Earl of Arran introduced in the Lords a private members' bill to give effect to the Wolfenden policy: that homosexual behaviour between consenting adults in private should not be a criminal offence. To the surprise of many, it obtained a second reading in a vote of almost 2 : 1. The third reading in October was even more decisive (more like 5 : 2). The Arran Bill was then directed to the Commons, where Leo Abse had failed to get a second reading for a carbon copy of it (introduced under the Ten-Minute Rule). The Arran Bill was lost with the ending of the 1964-65 session, and the next session was itself virtually lost by the calling of a "quickie" General Election in March 1966. This also cost the Conservative member, Humphrey Berkeley any hope of progress with his Bill on the same lines (carefully discussed in advance with the HLRS), which, against the odds, had easily obtained a second reading. (The difference between that vote and the vote on the Abse version of the Arran Bill has been explained—by Peter Richards—in terms of attendance, not of a change of mind.[39])

Momentum was quickly regained, however, in the new Parliament. In the Lords, the Earl of Arran repeated his earlier triumph. In the Commons, Leo Abse was poised to strike again with an almost identical bill, the most important difference being a stricter definition of "in private."[40] That was not what HLRS wanted, so here we pick up the trail of withinput. Even earlier, with Lord Arran's original Bill, which had enjoyed drafting help from the Government,[41] the HLRS had learned to its cost that on several important points the Government's version differed from what it would have liked. The upshot was (as HLRS Secretary, Mr. Grey would later ruefully record) that "the Government got its way in a somewhat backhanded manner (especially as it was officially 'neutral' towards the Bill)." Similarly, Mr. Abse did not prove biddable, although he was on the HLRS committee, as Lord Arran was not. He not only narrowed the concept of "in private," but also went his own way on other points; for example, in refusing to attempt to lower the age of consent from 21 to 16 to bring it into line with the law for heterosexual relations. In fact, HLRS was never invited by Lord Arran or Mr. Abse to attend a drafting session with the Parliamentary draftsmen.[42] Again, Mr. Abse agreed to exclude merchant seamen from the benefits of the Bill. Pressure from "sea-going families" to exclude the Merchant Navy had been exerted, as by Mr. Abse's Labour colleague, Simon Mahon (Bootle), even before the Second Reading, when James Margach (political correspondent of the *Sunday Times*) was forecasting defeat if the sponsors refused to make concessions. But the HLRS was left "a passive and somewhat bemused spectator of this seafaring skirmish, which was conducted virtually singlehanded by Mr. Abse."[43]

Somewhere along the way we also come across withinput in a related but not identical sense. It is most obvious from mid-1966 onwards after Leo Abse had again raised the standard in the Commons. By the time he had tested the water in the House (in July) and got ready for another plunge, the balloting for private members' bills in the 1966-67 session was over. The alternative was to have a go under the Ten-Minute Rule, but this would have little chance of success unless the Cabinet helped.[44] In late October, Home Secretary Roy Jenkins, asked the Leader of the House, Richard Crossman, for half a day. Mr. Crossman would have been sympathetic. Apart from the P.M., who may have been trapped because he had been answering Questions, Mr. Crossman and Mr. Jenkins had been the only frontbenchers to attend Mr. Abse's testing of the water back in July.[45] So they took the issue to Cabinet on 27 October, and got away with it, using what Mr. Crossman in his diary called "a highly tactical argument" (that Parliament had voted in favour; better now than nearer the Election).[46]

So Mr. Abse was vouchsafed time, but not an easy passage, for even some of the Labour Whips "were determined [Mr. Crossman would write] not to miss the chance of being violently partisan"—that is, take a different view from his. He added that many Labour Members from the North strenuously opposed the Bill, which was tending to cost the Party much of its own working-class support.[47] It was a thought that would recur the following summer, when reflecting the Bill might be considered twenty years ahead of public opinion, he acknowledged that working-class supporters in the North jeer returning M.P.s, demanding to know why they are looking after the homosexuals at Westminster rather than the unemployed at home. That the Labour Party should have been involved with such a Bill had gone down "very badly."[48]

If so, Mr. Crossman had been hoist with his own petard, all the more effectively if he really had felt from the beginning the aversion that he now (3 July 1967) expressed. For although Roy Jenkins's was doubtless the most eloquent Cabinet voice in favour of the Bill, the Commons business managers[49] were the ones who made its passage possible—that is, Mr. Crossman himself as Leader of the House and chairman of the Legislation Committee of the Cabinet, backed by the Chief Whip, John Silkin.[50] They gave Mr. Abse a Standing Committee of his very own (so to speak) when he found himself far back in the queue. After that stage was speedily passed (a single sitting), Mr. Abse had to meet a "late run" on Report, which was riven by no fewer than thirteen divisions. Again the Cabinet came to the rescue, agreeing to another day and, when that proved insufficient, yet another.

In the Lords, predictably, it was plain sailing. The Bill received the Royal Assent on 27 July 1967.

The Abortion Act, 1967

The approach to the Sexual Offences Act traced one pattern of group representation in the field. The role of the Church of England Moral Welfare Council was significant, not only for its liberal report in 1954 but also because its submission to the Wolfenden Committee was "by far the most influential" (in the judgment of Professor Richards).[51] That represented, however, only the end of the beginning. Despite the claims sometimes made for it, the role of the HLRS was more restricted. As Anthony Grey of HLRS would say of pressure groups just two years after the passage of the Act: At "most" stages of the Parliamentary "game," they tend to have to look on helplessly, knowing about the "backstage manoeuvring and often hastily concocted compromises which are taking place between sponsors, opponents and interested Government departments, but powerless to affect the timing, details or final shape of what they have laboured for years to achieve."[52] That would certainly seem to fit the HLRS experience. In general, however, one should think of a continuum (or spectrum) because some societies are able to sustain a more creative role for a longer period in the run-up to an Act of Parliament. One such is the Abortion Law Reform Association (ALRA).

Space limitations prohibit anything other than a very slight treatment. One simply notes that the ALRA was launched in 1936 by three women from an office in Piccadilly[53] and that its subsequent natural history, too, would seem reducible to three phases:

1. Dissemination: 1936-1952—spread of ideas to local women's groups and so forth, the nongoverning elites;
2. Engagement: 1952-1965—of a section of the governing elite through private members' bills but also indirectly through a sophisticated use of public opinion polls;
3. Reinforcement: 1965-1967—of that section of the governing elite which is now, de facto, engaging the Cabinet.

Compared with HLRS, the ALRA clearly made a more sustained contribution. It was also surely more creative, as in the use of many kinds of public opinion polling, even to the extent, in the end, of being willing to go broke in the process, and in its resort to political advertising neatly timed to fit the various Parliamentary stages.[54] Its contribution to drafting was far greater than HLRS's. Even after it had come round to sharing the drafting of the ultimately successful Bill (Mr. David Steel's) with a committee of his House colleagues, the "Bill emerged much as ALRA wanted it."[55] Perhaps above all, ALRA *reinforced* far more powerfully right inside the Commons. Indeed, as Standing Committee F began its work in Committee Room 10 in January 1967, four ALRA stalwarts were there—below the bar, but *in* if not, of course, *of.* Two others sat behind the throne (or chair): Peter Diggory, the gynaecologist, and Vera Houghton, ALRA chairman (and wife of the former Chancellor of the Duchy of Lancaster and future chairman of the Parliamentary Labour Party, Douglas Houghton).

Such assessments are relative, as between the groups. It remains true even in this case that the relation of *input* to *withinput* was hardly what it was represented to be. Once again the story opens in the Lords, where Lord Silkin (father of the John Silkin mentioned above) had taken up the cause at the suggestion of an ALRA member, Mrs. Scholefield Allen. Like Lord Arran, this noble lord was successful, but following the March 1966 Election, the ALRA got hold of David Steel (Liberal) after he had won third place in the ballot for private members' bills, thus heading off Lord Arran—originally an Irish peerage—who had failed to persuade Mr. Steel, a Scot, to "legislate Wolfenden" (for England and Wales, to which the Sexual Offences Bill featured above was in fact restricted). But, having to get reelected in Presbyterian Scotland, where homosexuality was no joke, Mr. Steel, like Agag, walked delicately, preferring abortion as a subject for reform. Before the year was out, however, he had the bit between his teeth. Just before Christmas (1966), he suddenly beat a partial retreat in tabling a crucial amendment for the Committee stage. "Many" of the ALRA leaders regarded the "action as a betrayal" because back in the merry month of May he had (they believed) promised them the clause that he now unilaterally repudiated.[56] The Cambridge law don, Glanville Williams, who had been the principal draftsman since the pioneering days, promptly wrote in disapproval. In the end, an obviously aggrieved ALRA Executive Committee swallowed their pride and continued to cooperate with Mr. Steel lest they lose the whole Bill.

Withinput in the other sense was also marked. The Commons business managers had given Mr. Abse his "own" Standing Committee: For the abortion Bill, because the usual route was blocked, they (specifically John Silkin) turned the Bill over to a Standing Committee (F) normally reserved for public business. On the other hand, whereas Mr. Abse had got through his Committee stage in a single sitting, opponents of legalized abortion fought almost with desperation. Despite a great effort, they failed in the end; twelve sittings and seventeen divisions later, the Bill in the cut-down form announced by David Steel before Christmas was still intact. But by now it was April, blossom time, so their virtual filibuster had won precious delay. They were losing this battle but winning the war since only one day, 2nd June, remained for both the Report stage of the Bill and the Third Reading.

So the political correspondent of the *Observer* was on safe ground in confidently reporting that the Bill "will lapse unless the Government finds extra Parliament time for it."[57] Despite opposition in Cabinet, some of it (e.g., Lord Longford's) root-and-branch, extra time was promised and given (29 June), but opponents among backbenchers made it insufficient, taking up well over half of the all-night sitting of almost twelve hours. One resilient member even used up precious time by attacking a group of amendments to which he had put his own signature.[58] Emerging into the sunlight, a journalist who had sat up to watch the spectacle judged that the Bill "may have been stopped for good."[59] But Providence dressed as the Cabinet decided to give the wheel another turn, which produced yet another day (13 July) and a two-to-one majority (167-83) for the Third Reading. As the vote had come after another all-night sitting, the date was now 14 July, an auspicious date if reform of the abortion law is seen, as it was by Christopher Price (Labour) in one of the rounding-off speeches, as an important stage in the emancipation of women.

One way or another, it was only right that Douglas Houghton should send a personal letter of thanks to Richard Crossman for all he had done for the Bill; "certainly [wrote Mr. Crossman] he and his wife, who are virtually the progenitors of the Bill, wouldn't have stood a chance without John and me."[60] Apart from all the help already recorded, they had used the threat of an open-ended sitting to erode the opponents' will power on 13/14 July. The threat had been made without telling the Cabinet because if he had taken them into his confidence, he was sure they would not have approved.[61] That was a reference to the Cabinet of 6 July, when the Abortion Bill had been the first item on the agenda and Mr. Crossman had taken pains not to disclose their tactics for endless all-night sittings. Instead he sought and obtained discretionary power. He well realized that such tactics would remove the Government from the neutrality fence: The Government would be taking sides openly, getting "the credit or discredit for it."[62]

Not quite: even the attentive but nonspecialist public could hardly have known enough to be able to make an intelligent judgment, or, accordingly, allocate responsibility. So one could go on. The Family Planning Act of 1967 authorizing local authorities to give contraceptive advice and devices to women, married or single, was another example. Ostensibly a private members' bill (by Edwin Brooks, Labour), it was in fact "virtually a Government draft," Douglas Hamilton later disclosed.[63] The Divorce Reform Act of 1969 is in some ways (e.g., the significance of personality in high office, or role occupancy), even more interesting. Its proximate source was a report from an ad hoc Church of England group recommending irretrievable breakdown of marriage instead of matrimonial offence as the fundamental ground for divorce. The Archbishop (Ramsay) agreed, as did the Church Assembly and the Law Commission (created in 1965 to propose revisions of the Law where it seems unsuitable for modern requirements, or obscure). In late September 1967 Lord Gardiner as Lord Chancellor proposed such a Bill to the Home Affairs Committee of the Cabinet, expressing the view (perhaps of a lawyer rather than a politician) that the measure would not stir up controversy since it had the approval of the Archbishop's Group and the Law Commission. Hearty laughter from the Celtic fringe (the Welsh and Scottish Secretaries of State) in effect denied his proposition. As Leader of the House, Richard Crossman had a by now ready-made solution: Hand the Bill over to a Private Member and provide Government time.[64]

Some members of the Home Affairs Committee still demurred, however, so the issue was taken to Cabinet, where on 12 October Mr. Crossman got everything that he wanted—that is, the Bill drafted in detail in the Lord Chancellor's office and then given to a private member to take (ostensible) responsibility for it. According to Mr. Crossman's reading of the Cabinet Conclusion, the Government would provide time even if the designated back-bencher were not lucky in the ballot.[65] But someone evidently took overt steps to reach out to a lucky backbencher. On 1 November, Philip Rawstorne of the *Guardian*, reporting that the Government was "smoothing the way for reform of the divorce laws in the next session by preparing a draft bill on the lines recommended by the Archbishop of Canterbury's committee," more or less advertised for a legislator: "The bill will be offered to any M.P. who is successful in the ballot for private members' bills and is prepared to sponsor it."[66] Only a Nelson could have missed such an unequivocal signal, and M.P.s clearly have two of everything. About a week later William Wilson (a colleague of Mr. Crossman's at Coventry) won fourth place in the ballot. Mr. Crossman pressed his claims on the Chief Whip only to be snubbed because he had trenched upon the Chief's domain.[67] However, Mr. Crossman later got his way. As for Mr. (Bill) Wilson, by a happy convergence of intentions, he found he had "no hesitation" about what to do if he won a good chance in the ballot. Divorce Reform was his "first choice."[68]

One high hurdle still remained before the Bill took its chance in Parliament: the Legislation Committee of the Cabinet, where the Celtic fringe would be well represented, not only the Nonconformists but a Catholic, Lord Longford who had run up a forlorn flag in Cabinet on such other moral issues. Anticipating a threat of resignation by Lord Longford, William Ross, Cledwyn Hughes et al., Mr. Crossman dissembled, pretending to be completely neutral.[69] The gambit worked, since the potential opponents did not seem to know what Mr. Crossman acknowledged to his diary—that the Government, far from being neutral, was really providing a great deal of assistance. Their apparent unawareness is surprising. Possibly the explanation is that the Celtic fringe was on the fringe in the other sense. Even so, they had Philip Rawstorne's story, with its transparently clear message, to bite on.

Whatever the explanation, the path was cleared for the Bill. It came up for Second Reading early in February (1968). Confident of the votes, the Leader of the House took himself off to Nottingham University. The majority was indeed comfortable (about 5 to 2). The Standing Committee then took the big hurdle in its stride,[70] not dividing over the basic principle (in clause one) that "the sole ground on which a petition for divorce may be presented to the court by either party to a marriage shall be that the marriage has broken down irretrievably."

But clause two covering the criteria of breakdown stirred up a hornet's nest, especially the "unilateral" provision permitting divorce after five years' separation even against the will of one spouse. It was commonly assumed that the unwilling spouse would be the wife, as in Lady Summerskill's famous characterization of the idea as a "Casanova's Charter." In fact, the evidence from New Zealand, where under this rule some four out of ten petitions had been coming from the wives, suggested that the idea might with almost equal justice have been named after Casanova's contemporary, Catherine II of Russia, aptly known as "the Great" (though not only for her sexual prowess and turnover of husband and lovers). At all events the Committee stage took so long that no time was left for the remaining stages, and the Cabinet chose not to come to the rescue as it had for both abortion and sexual offences. Why the Cabinet chose not to provide extra time despite protests in the Parliamentary Labour Party and a direct appeal by J.J. Mendelson, for example, at the P.L.P. meeting on 11th July, is uncertain.[71] One variable then may have been a change in the Leadership of the House, Fred Peart having replaced Richard Crossman at Easter. Another may have been that this measure lacked an *éminence grise* (or of any colour) to match Roy Jenkin's role in arguing for extra time for the two earlier bills. He had received in time for Christmas (1967) a gift of the Treasury. Whatever the reason, this bill was allowed to die the death.

That summer, however, the Government repented at leisure, or perhaps it was moved, after all, by its backbenchers. By the autumn in any case it was ready and eager to make amends. From the start it assisted the "nearly identical" bill introduced by Alec Jones, a new member up from one of those once-green South Wales valleys, who, drawing ninth place in the ballot, had been seized by Leo Abse (who represents another such blasted heath) and persuaded to make himself the instrument of the divorce law reform. The "few changes" that Mr. Jones's bill incorporated "were drafted by the same Parliamentary draftsman."[72] And when early in December he ran slap into difficulties first time out, he was "privately assured" that the bill would "not again be allowed to fail for want of time."[73] Eleven days later a Government motion allowed the Second Reading to be resumed at a special morning sitting, although the Bill itself was not to be whipped and would have to take its chance. It did so easily (18 : 10) although not as easily as in February (25 : 10). It may not be significant, as to the speculation in the previous paragraph, but Mr. Crossman voted *for*, and Mr. Jenkins did not vote. It was significant that the Solicitor-General, Sir Arthur Irvine, Q.C., the Minister responsible for the bill, voted *for*, since, unlike the Attorney-General, he had abstained in February. Although he seemed to one Opposition member to be now "walking a tightrope," others thought his acrobatic feat was even more remarkable. They saw him as also "inclining benevolently towards this Private Member's measure. . . ."[74]

Indirectly that reaffirmed the Government's assurances of help, which proved to be indispensable. The Committee stage dragged on; so did Report. In the end the Government gave the bill the privilege of a Thursday night start. The sitting carried over into Friday, and despite its being Friday the 13th (of June), the sponsors suffered no ill luck but gained a two-to-one majority. They had to wait, however, until 2.10 p.m., by which time the House had been sitting continuously for twenty-four hours.

The Lords produced a better than three-to-one majority, but among other things delayed the date of the bill's coming into effect until 1 January 1971.[75]

5

Operational Groups: Labour and Capital

Here we come to grips for the first time with groups built upon characteristics that are more or less ascribed or inherited (age, sex, ethnicity, church membership, or connection), or at least given at any particular point in time (occupation, neighbourhood, or propinquity). These are the organizations *of* rather than *for*. The more highly politicized ones (accordingly placed in sector 2) have often been studied, both generally and in their political capacity (TUC and the like). But those engaging in political action only irregularly have been very largely ignored.

Sector 1

The most important subclass is the occupational, or economic, including such professional bodies as the Law Society when they engage the Government, as over VAT in 1972 and, earlier, over the scale of fees payable under the legal aid defence scheme. The Society warned the Lord Chancellor that unless fees were raised, its members would no longer participate.[1] In 1973 the Royal College of Veterinary Surgeons urged Parliament to legislate against the cropping of dogs' tails. Local farmers appear here when acting independently, or apparently independently, of the NFU (which belongs to sector 2). In January 1970, for example, in anticipation of the annual price review, Pembrokeshire farmers brought Haverfordwest, the county town, to a standstill as seven hundred mud-spattered vehicles "crawled in stately rural cavalcade through the crowded streets" (*The Times's* Trevor Fishlock reported). Many vehicles bore placards with the words: "Come on, Cled, cough up" (in English naturally, Pembrokeshire being "Little England Beyond Wales"). Cled was the Minister of Agriculture, Mr. Cledwyn Hughes, a Welshman from an even more remote (but Welsh-speaking) section of the Celtic fringe, Anglesey. Neither the Scots nor the English allowed themselves to be outdone. On the same day, as if in collusion, farmers drove sixty tractors through Kilmarnock; Guildford mustered only thirteen but that procession was not only led by a horse but rounded off by a vehicle and trailer containing a pig. Its appearance was presumably intended to be symbolic, if not of the Minister of Agriculture, then of the Chancellor of the Exchequer (as it happened another Welshman, or at least South Walian, Mr. Roy Jenkins). These were the two Ministers who received the official NFU leaders at the annual price review talks in early February. On the eve of its opening,

51

Westmorland farmers drove their vehicles, including tractors and muck spreaders, along the A6 motorway at five miles an hour for fifteen miles, thus producing a splendid build-up of lorries and cars some three miles long. None of this affected public policy, but it did prove that British farmers were as adept as the French at what is known across the Channel as "artichoke warfare."

Beyond the angry farmers and the suave professionals the massed ranks of (industrial) Capital and Labour are drawn up, at times in battle order. Their engagement of the public authorities at this operational level has been little researched, although it is clearly in the tradition of the Russia Company, the Levant Company, and the trade societies of the eighteenth century.[2] We shall proceed from the apparently spontaneous to the obviously organized.

Workers and Unions

Women at Work: I'm Backing Britain

The "I'm Backing Britain" Movement of January 1968 came from the typist's pool rather than the shop floor. Five typists employed by a Surbiton company offered to work an extra half-hour a day with no extra pay to help Britain out of her chronic economic difficulties. The idea attracted widespread attention and touched public policy when the company asked the Department of Economic Affairs (DEA) to implement it for the nation. Edmund Dell, the Parliamentary Secretary, promptly left for Surbiton to hear for himself, while a representative of DEA and of the company enlisted the aid of the Industrial Society whose forte is the improvement of industrial methods and relationships. Normally geared for quiet persuasion, the Society quickly mounted a campaign only to have it upstaged by Robert Maxwell's "Buy British" movement, which had the advantage of his House of Commons base and many connections in business, TV, the press, and public relations. One of the inevitable clashes between the two groups was patched up at the DEA, with Edmund Dell in the chair on 18 January.[3] The campaigns went on, but provoking discussion rather than achieving their declared objects, and so demonstrating once again the difficulty of giving institutional expression to the public spiritedness of ordinary people.

Women at Work: Equal Pay

In the summer of 1968 women at the Ford plant at Dagenham also struck out on their own, but from the shop floor not the typists' pool. They were the sewing machinists. In an attempt to gain a particular job grade, 187 of them brought the car assembly lines to a halt by refusing to sew any more seat covers, thus giving 5,000 men an enforced holiday. "It was not a great success but it did narrow the gap a little," and later the company introduced full equal pay.[4] Of more immediate significance for our inquiry is that the incident precipitated a new pressure group, The National Joint Action Campaign for Women's Equal Rights, whose secretary-treasurer was the area organizer of the National Union of Vehicle Builders, a spokesman for the women machinists during the dispute. After a meeting in the House of Commons in October, attended by some 250 trade unionists, M.P.s, representatives of the parties and of women's societies, the base was broadened to include men, with the chairmanship shared between a woman member of the Association of Scientific, Technical, and Managerial Staffs and the Labour M.P., Christopher Norwood, who in July had tried to legislate equal pay via the Ten Minute Rule. The new body's opening gambit, in November, was a lobby of M.P.s.[5]

Unemployment

Direct from the shop floor in 1969 came an attempt by men workers to use political influence to protect their jobs. In May, Raphael Tuck, M.P., left a petition at 10 Downing Street asking the Prime Minister to intervene to save the jobs of 500 technicians employed by a firm making gyroscopic and precision equipment at Watford, Hertfordshire, Mr. Tuck's constituency. The State had an interest (it was argued) because the firm had been denationalized by the Conservative Government in 1960 with an understanding that jobs would be as safe as under public ownership. On the same day 300 workers descended on the House of Commons in support of the petition.[6]

More organized was the march of about a thousand miners and railwaymen, supported by some Londoners, through the West End (February 1963) to lobby M.P.s in the Commons as a protest against unemployment and the closure of the mines and railway lines. A deputation waited on the Minister of Housing who also doubled as the Minister of Welsh Affairs (Sir Keith Joseph), and on the Minister of Power, Richard Wood.[7]

Industrial Relations Reform, 1969-1971

On May Day 1969, when the Labour Government was attempting to reform industrial relations law on the basis of the White Paper, *In Place of Strife*, the Society of Graphical and Allied Trades mounted a demonstration in which twenty unions were represented by perhaps 15,000 workers. At Lincoln's Inn Fields, the general secretary of the Lightermen's union declaimed: "We must stop Harold Wilson and Barbara Castle and their right-wing clique from putting the trade union movement back a hundred years." Later about a hundred of the demonstrators, drawn mostly from the National Amalgamated Stevedores and

Dockers, lobbied M.P.s at the House of Commons.[8] In late June, the Prime Minister and the Secretary of State for Employment and Productivity, seeing the error of their ways, turned or staggered through 180 degrees and abandoned to its fate the infant bill to which the White Paper had given birth. But the Conservatives, inconveniently winning the 1970 election, rescued the infant, dressed it up and presented it to Parliament, whereupon the unions exerted themselves to prevent the movement's being put back a hundred years. In November, despite the TUC's express disapproval of political strikes, and in specific rejection of its "sedate" approach, shop stewards in Midland car factories began a series of stoppages aimed at the new Industrial Relations Bill.[9] Early in December some 350,000 workers in car factories and newspaper shops, in shipyards and on the docks stopped work for twenty-four hours for the same political purpose, possibly "the biggest single walk-out since the general strike" of 1926.[10] There were demonstrations in Glasgow, Liverpool, and Manchester. In London, after a march from Tower Hill to Speaker's Corner, Marble Arch, some 10,000 attended a meeting that called unanimously for a special TUC Conference "to decide on all forms of activity, including industrial action, to prevent this legislation from reaching the statute book." Later outside Parliament about 2,000 demonstrators tried to break a police cordon.[11] As "extra contingents of police kept the more militant from storming into the building, M.P.s inside were rapidly working themselves into a high state of emotion."[12] Over a thousand persons were admitted to the House to lobby in the traditional way.

These efforts were timed to reach a climax before the Second Reading of the Bill on 15 December. After the Government obtained its majority, another "national day of demonstration and protest during working hours"[13] followed in mid-January (1971) despite an appeal by the General Council of the TUC to protest "during meal breaks and after working hours."[14] Nevertheless on 24 March the Conservative frontbencher, Francis Pym, was able to give "his ebullient shout of 'Aye' to the Third Reading of the" Bill,[15] which received the Royal Assent in early August.

Business

Compensation from Public Funds

The Burmah Oil Company was nursing a grievance. Having, at the behest of the British wartime government, destroyed its installations in Burma in order to deny these to the Japanese invaders, it felt entitled to claim compensation from that British government's peacetime successors. None of these, Labour or Conservative, would hear of it, but British judges eventually conceded what the statesmen had refused, whereupon the supremacy of Parliament over the common lawyers was again demonstrated, with the incoming Labour Government introducing (1965) retrospective (retroactive, to Americans) legislation to undermine the basis of the company's claim. A furious rearguard action was fought in the House of Lords, where a quarter of those voting against the retrospective clause were said (by a Government supporter) to have been shareholders of the company. Generally their lordships heeded the appeal made by Lord Salisbury, who, anxious to stave off a structural reform of the hereditary Chamber, urged them not to reject a Bill that even the *New Statesmen* would later call "particularly disreputable."[16]

Nationalization

By the time Labour returned to power in 1964, the steel-producing companies had already been nationalized once but then denationalized by the Conservatives in 1953. In 1964 the writing was once again on the wall and in the manifesto: "Private monopoly in steel will be replaced by public ownership and control."[17]

Once again, a major steel company, Stewarts and Lloyds, with other such companies, picked up the gauntlet.[18] Its chairman, Mr. A.G. Stewart, who in 1958 had equated the nationalization of steel and other industries with "a long stride towards the establishment of communism in Great Britain,"[19] now dubbed it "old hat," recalling that the Labour Party had proved unable "after much debate, to cast off the shackles of the famous Clause Four—that is, the Marxist doctrine of 'the common ownership of the means of production, distribution and exchange.' You will recall the failure of Hugh Gaitskill and his followers, despite a determined fight with the Party, to have this clause dropped."[20] That part of Mr. Stewart's speech was promptly reproduced in a series of newspaper advertisements. Another threatened company, Guest, Keen, and Nettleford (GKN), also ran a similar series but addressed specifically to its several constituencies: customers, shareholders, employees, and the general public. In all, nine steel companies trod the PR path, disbursing about £640,000 as they went.

Despite that effort and associated campaigns,[21] which cost in grand total an astonishing £1,290,000, the Labour Party just scraped home, gaining office, if not exactly power (so tiny was its overall majority). Even after the March 1966 Election, some Cabinet Ministers would have been content to reach a compromise with the steel manufacturers, but on 7 April (Sir) Richard Marsh, as the new Minister of Power, intervened vigorously in Cabinet to say that he intended to push the Bill through in the first session.[22] And so he did: with the Iron and Steel Act of March 1967. That brought fourteen companies into forced captivity (one already there), but left a private sector of "some 200 companies accounting for about one-third of the industry's sales,"[23] which the British Independent Steel Producers Association was set up to represent. But of course neither Stewarts and Lloyds nor GKN was among the survivors.

Hopes—and fears—of another act of denationalization did not die immediately, but were sustained by the individual efforts of the steel-using companies, which organized themselves as the Iron and Steel Consumers Council, representing "a minimum 75 percent of the direct steel purchasing power in the United Kingdom." By December 1971 the leader of the steelworkers' union, D.H. Davies, was remarking that "a number of Council members are from companies which openly finance anti-nationalization organizations [and that] some of the biggest customers of the Corporation are among the largest donors to the funds of the Conservative Party, Aims of Industry, British United Industrialists and such like organizations. . . ."[24] But the Conservative Party, in power again from 1970 to 1974, did not oblige, and so steel denationalization gradually faded from the agenda of public policy.

Contracts, Licences, Franchises

The text for this section is taken from a remark attributed to an *Observer* columnist: "Politics and business are nowhere closer in Britain than in the troubled air."[25] He might have been referring to the vicissitudes of the aircraft industry or airlines, but in fact he meant broadcasting. Both subjects, as it happens, are grist to our mill.

In context the broadcasting issue of the early sixties (so far as it concerned business influence for Government contracts, or licences or franchises) was whether sound radio financed by selling advertising time should be permitted. By the early seventies the Cabinet decision had been taken and some of the (maximum of) sixty local radio stations visualized in the 1971 White Paper had already come to adorn the British way of life.

Ideally, to savour that success and fully understand the approach pattern, we should reanalyse what had preceded it: the setting up in 1954 of a TV service financed by advertising, which naturally delighted above all the advertising agencies, the manufacturers of TV sets, and the go-betweens who turned miraculously into programme contractors—that is, the basic interests that had energised and financed the cleverest legislative coup in British pressure-group history. It moved Lord Hailsham on more than one occasion to accuse the Conservative Party leadership of "shoddy, disreputable politics" in *deliberately* omitting from the 1951 Election Manifesto any mention of the possibility of introducing commercial TV: ". . . it is not simply the absence of a mandate; it is a deliberate concealment, so far as one can judge, of a vital element which either was, or ought to have been, well within the contemplation of the leaders of the Party at the time of the General Election."[26] Coming from a Conservative of such distinction, the charge was grave but, so far as one can judge, not proven. In any case, it is clear that the legislative job was done from scratch in well under three years, 1951-1954. By 1955 ITV was in operation. By 1961 almost all the country lay within its ambit.

Here we are interested less in the constitutional issue than in the influence of one campaign upon the other, including the effect of the *output* from a certain time period upon the *input* of a later one. Space limitations (alas!) prevent any such adventures. But the context should be borne in mind.

Commercial Radio

The hunt for commercial radio had started—overtly, at least—in 1961, by which time about a hundred companies had staked a claim to licences in the hope that the BBC's remaining monopoly would be broken in 1964 when its Charter and Licence came up for renewal. Some of the entrepreneurs who had cracked the BBC's short-lived TV monopoly were naturally in the van. Mr. Norman Collins, Sir Robert Renwick, and Mr. C.O. Stanley (on the board of ATV and many other companies) formed independent Broadcasting Services (IBS), which had registered a number of companies hoping to operate eight commercial radio stations in the Midlands and the West. Another ATV director, Lord Bessborough, branched out in the company, among others, of three Conservative M.P.s. Their vehicle, the Southern Broadcasting Company (SBC), with Lord Bessborough in the front seat, intended to set off for the South Coast and Isle of Wight. The editorial director of ATV, however (Arthur Christiansen, former editor of the *Daily Express*) looked east (with the Voice of Essex) to Colchester. But there were new contenders. The Rank Organization alone had registered twenty-nine companies; local newspapers were in total not far behind it. However, the Parliamentary connection remained fairly close. Apart from the SBC, Geoffrey Hirst, a Conservative M.P., spoke for the Radio Yorkshire Development Company,[27] and Woodrow Wyatt, a Labour M.P., chaired a company to bring the good news to Banbury.

In the campaign itself three stages may be provisionally distinguished: late 1960-October 1964; October 1964-March 1969; March 1969-March 1971, although the lines of demarcation are even more blurred than usual and the stages do not correspond to the three phases characteristic of some of the moral issues discussed in Chapter 4. Not only was the type of issue different, but the character of one campaign and the Act (or other decision) in which it culminates tend to shape the character of the later phases or, as here, of closely related campaigns. The securing of the commercial TV ground in 1954 had shown that it is possible to bring about fundamental change in domestic policy by negotiation within the governing and nongoverning elites, virtually bypassing the general public. Apart from that, the commercial radio pressure groups needed to adopt a different style from the one exhibited by their commercial TV predecessors. Referring to them, a campaigner would later tell Harold Jackson of the *Guardian*: "That lobby is tarred for all time with Lord Thomson's 'licence to print money'. It would be disastrous if we were to appear to the public in that light. It could even scuttle the whole thing."[28]

For these reasons alone there was hardly a dissemination phase. Some efforts at public persuasion were made. In November 1960, Pye Telecommunications published its *Plan for Local Broadcasting in Britain*, arguing that the cost of setting up a local commercial radio station was not as prohibitive as critics had suggested. Such a station with a transmitting radius of ten miles could be bought (from Pye, among others) for no more than £20,000. The annual running expenses of a small-town station would range from £20-30,000.[29] Coming from one of the frontrunners in the commercial TV campaign, that may be taken as the opening shot of the campaign. The first general campaign body surfaced the following April as the National Broadcasting Development Committee (NBDC), for which Ronald Simms was naturally brought in as secretary since his PR skill in the service of the PTA had been finely honed in the preceding four years (1957-1961) as director of publicity at the Conservative Central Office. But it aimed less at the broader public than the governing elite, which, as earlier, meant M.P.s and ultimately the Conservative Government. On this occasion, however, despite Mr. Simms's antecedents, the lobby apparently could not look to the Conservative Party organization for help. Headed by Lord Chelmer, chairman of the Party's Executive, a study group sponsored by the Conservative Political Centre flatly rejected commercial radio.[30] So the essential point of access seemed to be the Conservative Party in Parliament. By June 1964 the NBDC was credited by competent observers with having won over as many as seventy M.P.s,[31] mostly Conservatives, presumably. The NBDC's hopes, however, were dashed in October when the Conservative Party was beaten at the post in the general election.

1964-1969. The organizational response to the Labour victory was the Local Radio Association. Founded by John Gorst, advertising and PR manager for Pye Limited (1953-1963) but by now PR consultant to John Gorst & Associates, this body became the voice of a hundred or so companies that had already staked out claims for licences. Its line was that to finance local radio from increased licence fees would be unfair and that an Exchequer grant would undermine the service's independence. That might have been expected to please many of the general listening public, many of whom (if not the half claimed by Radio Caroline, one of the pirate stations operating off shore) undoubtedly tuned into commercial programmes transmitted by the pirates, Radio Luxembourg or other Continental stations. All the same, the argument was addressed essentially to the governing elite. In this the Local Radio Association was not left to bear the burden alone. Spokesmen for Radio Caroline urged "their listeners to deluge M.P.s with mail" and took a turn themselves by "assiduously button-holing delegates at the Labour conference"[32] of 1966. The Institute of Practitioners in Advertising and the Incorporated Society of British Advertisers held "conversations" with M.P.s on both sides of the House, "but hardly on a level classifiable as intensive lobbying."[33] By 1968 the cause was being sustained by the new

Conservative majority on the Greater London Council (GLC), which promoted a private bill in Parliament to secure the legal authority for a commercial radio station in London. To bolster that, the Free Radio Association was founded, apparently as a listeners' society, under the inspiration of Sir Ian MacTaggart, company director, former Conservative member of the London County Council (predecessor of the GLC), and Conservative Parliamentary candidate. Even with this extraneous help, the Local Radio Association gained little ground. Its lobbying, which was "of a far more genteel type than the pressure for commercial television" (as Adam Hopkins would write in the *Sunday Times* the following year under the heading "Money in the Air"),[34] may well have influenced some Labour members, but not to the extent of moving the Labour Government, against whose door it battered uselessly for five years or more. The Government's supporting constituency had consisted at one stage of a number of unions, including the Musicians' and the National Union of Journalists, and the Committee for Sanity in Broadcasting (under way in 1966 and apparently comprising several show-biz personalities). The BBC's own defence was indirect: its eight experimental local radio stations, an obvious attempt to preempt the commercial ground. The last in that series opened at Durham in 1968. Twelve more were planned, and some of these began to be constructed. Later, plans for a further twenty by 1975 were announced.

1969-1971. Up to this point the commercial lobby could have been forgiven for feeling (with R.L. Stevenson) that "the road lies long and straight and dusty to the grave." Some recruits to the lobby (e.g., Commercial Broadcasting Consultants, chaired by Hughie Green, already a TV personality) were new; others had been on the line of march for years. Suddenly they were in a position (with the aid of A.H. Clough) to declaim: "Say not the struggle naught availeth, The labour and the wounds are vain. . . ." Looking westward—towards the Opposition frontbench—they could see that the land was suddenly brighter. The Opposition spokesman (or "shadow") on broadcasting the postal affairs since 1965, Paul Bryan, director of Granada TV Rentals, 1966-1970, had long favoured the commercial solution. The Local Radio Association had accordingly worked "closely"[35] with him. "It was the Gorst lobby, composed of about 70 hopeful companies, and strongly supported by Mr. Paul Bryan, then Shadow Postmaster General, which swayed the party leadership."[36] In March 1969, accordingly, Mr. Bryan "pledged the Conservative Party to setting up 100 commercial radio stations. [His] enthusiastic endorsement of commercial radio . . . brought a flicker of life to scores of dormant companies set up over recent years ready to jump the moment commercial radio takes to the air,"[37] and must have been greatly encouraged by the Local Radio Association, the Commercial Broadcasting Consultants, and the Free Radio Association. When asked by the Prime Minister whether the statement made by the shadow PMG "carries his authority," the leader of the Opposition, Edward Heath, chose not to answer, prompting the *Times* question in the form of a subeditorial heading to the Parliamentary report: "Public Want Commercial Radio: Does Mr. Heath?"[38] By May, according to the *Sunday Times's* investigative team, "Insight," the doubt was resolved: "Conservative Party leaders have given private assurances to the commercial radio lobby that, if and when the Conservatives are returned to power, they will open the door to local commercial radio." At the Party Conference in Brighton, Mr. Bryan made the commitment public: "We think it right to break the BBC monopoly in radio, as we did in television, as a start by introducing local commercial radio."

Meanwhile, Mr. Bryan's pronouncements, combined with the strong possibility that a Conservative Government would not only open the commercial door but close the other one (the BBC local radio network), had precipitated a new organization, TRACK "to rally those who would like to see community broadcasting permanently installed on the public service principle."[39] Launched in April by Hugh Barty-King through the correspondence columns of *The Listener*, it operated from an address in George Street, within convenient walking distance of the BBC, for which it may have attempted to serve as the functional equivalent of the National Television Council in 1953-54. That summer the Free Communications Group threw its hat into the ring, on whose behalf was not quite clear except that it was not the BBC's. At one of the Group's meetings attended by about a hundred people, "a distinguished BBC producer" told Philip Whitehead (of Thames Television) "quite seriously" that if he were seen there "he would never be admitted to any confidential conclave at the BBC again."[40] In early 1970 the Campaign for Independent Broadcasting also entered the lists: Of obscure origin, it described itself as "a listeners" organization dedicated to breaking the BBC's monopoly in sound radio."[41]

They did not have long to wait. The Prime Minister, Mr. Wilson, decided to go to the country early, and lost. The Conservatives were returned, having given this undertaking in their Election Manifesto: "We will permit local private-enterprise radio under the general supervision of an independent broadcasting authority. Local institutions, particularly local newspapers, will have the opportunity of a stake in local radio, which we want to see closely associated with the local community." So this time round neither Lord Hailsham nor anyone else could complain of studied omissions from the party manifesto. As if to symbolize the commitment, John Gorst, still secretary of the Local Radio Association, won a seat in the Conservative interest, almost as Anthony Fell, then also a Pye Radio man and already blooded through contact with the Conservative backbench broadcasting committee, had been carried into the House on the Conservative wave of 1951. (Mr. Gorst had been advertising and PR manager of Pye from 1953-1963.)

When it came to the distribution of offices, Paul Bryan, although the shadow in Opposition, did not get the Ministry of Posts and Telecommunications but joined Robert Carr (happily a member of the same Cambridge college) as Minister of State at the Department of Employment and Productivity. That was indeed "one of the big surprises."[42] In retrospect, however, it was less surprising: The reverberations of the commercial TV campaign could still be heard. That may have prompted the P.M., Mr. Heath, to walk delicately, just as the commercial TV companies themselves, in private displaying a keen interest in the possibilities of a link-up with the commercial radio network, refrained from an early approach to the man who actually got the Ministry, Christopher Chataway. As Ross Davies put it in *The Times*: "The contractors, mindful of the fact that a Conservative Government brought in commercial television, are unwilling to embarrass the minister by making it appear as though they are now trying to influence the formulation of radio policy."[43] However, Mr. Chataway naturally proved to be no less eager an instrument of party policy, which reflected the representations of the commercial-radio lobby, than Mr. Bryan would have been. As he told Young Conservatives in London in September, "the further I go with these consultations [about commercial radio] the odder it seems that the monopoly in radio should have lasted as long as it has. This is, after all, an age of increasing concern about the concentration of power over the communications media."[44]

As *The Times*, coming out against a policy "based on a combination of prior commitment and muddled thinking," remarked editorially: "The trouble with this sort of generalized doctrinal comment is that it fails to distinguish between the case for local radio and the case for breaking the BBC's monopoly. . . . If local radio were to develop at the expense of the local press it could result simply in the exchange of the monopoly of radio in local communications for the monopoly of the BBC in the provision of radio services."[45] The irony soon deepened. Faced that autumn with "the worst advertising recession for many years" and the perennial problem of a shortage of suitable radio frequencies, the Minister considered two principal ways of carrying out party (originally pressure-group) policy. One was to stop the BBC local radio development in its tracks and even to obliterate all traces of it. This the Government would have been entitled to do, having as a party held out the possibility at least since the 1969 Brighton Conference. But of course the policy would have required one to interpret "competition" in an Orwellian sense: competition = displacing the local BBC radio monopolies in favour of local commercial radio monopolies. Or, more broadly: competition = changing the base of monopoly.

The other possibility, not necessarily incompatible with the first, was to seize Radio One, the BBC's "pop" counter to such stations as Radio Caroline and Radio Luxembourg and give its medium-wave network on 247 metres to the pressure groups. By the end of the year, Mr. Chataway was reported (by Chris Dunkley of *The Times*) to be "looking for a national medium-wave network to give to the commercial interests."[46] Such a course of action would also have entailed Orwellian refinements. One BBC medium-wave channel devoted to (monopolizing) pop entertainment would be renamed "private enterprise."

In the event, Mr. Chataway tried to ride both horses, leading to a national station and a network of local stations. This intention was leaked to James Margach, political correspondent of the *Sunday Times* (and possibly others) in late February 1971. His story, unequivocally headed "Commercial Radio to Have National Channel," made it plain there would be "no ready-made bonanza awaiting the local companies and the national service." A new central authority would "have power to control the finances of companies given a franchise. To guard against a company operating in a highly prosperous region being able to make high profits quickly, the central authority will have power to divert profits to the poorer areas in order to encourage high programme standards." Here once again the shadow of the commercial TV campaign lay over this kindred one: "The Government does not want to risk being accused of providing a licence to print money, as happened with the first ITV franchises."[47]

That was a prudent and even a proper stand to take, but hardly calculated to endear the Government to the interests, especially as the BBC would probably keep both Radio One and its twenty local radio stations in operation or in the making. Up to this point, as we would expect from some of the moral issues campaigns, the election in June 1970 of a Government committed to one's cause had cast the commercial radio lobby for a subordinate role. In October the Local Radio Association, armed with technical reports from the Marconi Company, had published its views of "the shape of independent radio." In mid-January David Prewett, chairman of the Campaign for Independent Broadcasting (by then 700 members paying a modest annual subscription), advanced its views at a crowded press conference held at the St. Bride's Institute just off Fleet Street. But essentially the groups were flying a holding pattern until they caught a glimpse of that ministerial kite. As Mr. Margach had forecast in his February story, they were "disappointed by the proposal for a national service." That was perhaps an understatement. They feared that such a national network would attract the national advertising, leaving them with the local scraps and accordingly too undernourished to do battle with the BBC. "Angry and bitter" (as Mr. Margach would write five weeks later), they promptly carried the fight to the Central Office of the Party, and even to the Cabinet via, in particular, the Chief Whip, Francis Pym, and the Leader of the House, William Whitelaw. "This campaign of angry protest finally succeeded in the Cabinet by a majority; the White Paper was rewritten, and the national network and national station were written out."[48]

Talked about in September, expected in December but put off until the New Year, then until February, then until early March, the White Paper at last appeared at the end of that month. It authorized a network of up to sixty commercial radio stations that "must be firmly rooted in their locality, and this should be reflected in the choice of station operators and subsequently in output." That partly anticipated the question raised in the House by the Liberal, Jo Grimond: whether the new radio contracts would be distributed in the "most extraordinary" way that ITV franchises had been awarded. However, the agency charged with distributing franchises (the Independent Broadcasting Authority), that is, the former ITA renamed and given wider functions) would not necessarily prevent a company from operating in more than one locality, although "an excessive aggregate interest" would not be allowed. A television company would be allowed an interest if not a *controlling* one in the area of its television franchise. As for BBC local radio, the development of the additional twenty stations was prohibited but the existing twenty were permitted to continue. These, however, were clearly intended by the Government to cater to minority tastes, leaving "the masses" to the care of commercial radio, which, as essentially a vehicle for advertising not broadcasting, was naturally eager to assume the burden.

TSR-2

Advised by the Treasury to expect a balance-of-payments deficit of some £800 million in 1964, the incoming Labour Government (returned in mid-October) sharpened its axe and looked around for victims. Two obvious possibilities were the Anglo-French supersonic Concorde and some of the military aircraft projects, among them TSR-2. Almost the very first subject at the very first meeting of the Cabinet, Concorde would doubtless have been abandoned had the agreement with the French not been cast in the most unusual form of a treaty with no escape clause. By January a compromise was being worked out: to handbuild two prototypes and not lay down the jigs for quantity production until later.

In that situation of uncertainty, so full of foreboding for the companies and workers, Denis Healey held his first press briefing as the new Minister of Defence. Speaking of the industry, he pronounced: "It is not the duty of the Ministry to wetnurse overgrown and mentally retarded children."[49] Although off-the-record, Mr. Healey's apparently off-the-cuff characterisation was soon reported by both BBC and *Daily Telegraph*, for which breach of ethics he later upbraided the media as a whole. That brought the airframe companies into play as active pressure groups, and a colleague, presumably Ministerial, tartly commented: "Bungled. Shooting his mouth off."

Unfortunate no doubt, but the airframe companies' pressure would soon have been exerted in any case. For the compromise over Concorde at once endangered the TSR-2 and two other projects that the Government had inherited. These were a supersonic vertical takeoff fighter and a jet transport, both allocated to Hawker Siddeley Aviation (incorporating among others, such well remembered entities from an earlier era as Armstrong-Whitworth and Avro, Hawker and de Havilland). BAC (basically the offspring of Vickers and English Electric) had the major project, the TSR-2, which the Conservative Government had decided upon in 1959, partly under pressure, at one stage publicly expressed, from the Air Staff itself.[50] Originally conceived as a tactical fighter-bomber for flying at great speeds below the enemy's radar screen, the TSR-2 had become strategic and nuclear by the time the design contract was placed with BAC. The cost was to have been of the order of £200 million. By the time Labour had regained office in 1964, a quasi-official estimate put the cost at £500 million. Assuming a hundred aircraft were thus produced, that would mean a price of £5 million for one, as compared with £2 million for an American TFX (later known as the F-111),[51] for which the Royal Australian Air Force had plumped a year earlier. Moreover, the TSR-2 had virtually lost the two years' lead time it had until then enjoyed. But the immediate and crucial issue was the cost, which inevitably entailed a reexamination of Hawker's contracts as well, so both airframe companies were in danger (not to mention the makers of the engines, Rolls-Royce and Bristol Siddeley).

The future of these three types of aircraft was one of the four main items on the agenda for a weekend meeting of Ministers and others at Chequers on 21-22 November, at which the Minister of Defence at least was ranged against his Service Chiefs. In his disposition to cancel the contracts, he doubtless had the backing, on other occasions if not then, of the Chancellor of the Exchequer (James Callaghan) and the First Secretary of State at the new Department of Economic Affairs (George Brown), who also had their pruning knives at the ready. But the Ministers attending the Chequers session evidently did not think, "If it were done when 'tis done, then 'twere well it were done quickly . . . " because no decision was then taken.

By early New Year the hour was drawing near. The Cabinet needed to reach a Conclusion in time for the Defence White Paper to be prepared and published in mid-February. On 8 January the Minister of Defence made the remark quoted above, mistaking an off-the-record briefing for the confessional box and finding that *its* seal did not hold. On Monday, the first working day after Mr. Healey's briefing, the heads of BAC[52] crowded in on Roy Jenkins, the Minister of Aviation, fundamentally to use him as a stepping stone to the Prime Minister later in the week. By contrast it was "noticeable" that Hawker had "not so far used the same formal lobbying technique."[53] That was consistent with the different conception of pressure-group tactics attributed to Sir Arnold Hall, head of Hawker Siddeley: "Hall is a profound believer in making no public fuss. The Hawker technique is one of 'fighting like hell, but in the inner councils'."[54] It is known that he had already seen not only the Minister of Aviation and the Minister of Defence but also the Minister of Technology (Frank Cousins, the union leader) and the Chancellor of the Exchequer. But he "never asked for an interview, let alone soup, fish and meat, with Harold Wilson," the Prime Minister (a succulent reference that will be rescued from obscurity as this account proceeds). On 13 January, however, Sir Arnold did wait on the Minister of Defence as one of a representative team from the trade association, the Society of British Aerospace Companies, which had been anxious to bring its quota of pressure to bear.

Meanwhile the unions had again (as over Concorde) made common cause with management. On the Tuesday, at Weybridge, Surrey, the main BAC plant, some five to six thousand manual and staff workers (i.e., a half or more of the total number employed) downed tools and held a roadside rally to discuss their tactics. They cheered loudly when the vice chairman of the shop stewards' committee proclaimed: "If Britain is to have military aircraft then they should be British made."[55] An official of the Clerical Workers' Union asked rhetorically: "If we are going to use foreign aircraft, what is going to happen to our best designers? They will go to America...."[56] The meeting decided to demonstrate in London two days later. About five thousand turned out then and marched to a rally in Hyde Park, where Clive Jenkins of ASSET "clearly spoke for them all when he said: 'We want to build big, big, big, big jets'."[57] Appropriate resolutions were passed with unanimity and gusto, including one requesting a meeting with the Prime Minister and the Minister of Aviation. The P.M., however, was closeted with the Turkish Ambassador, having earlier chaired the Cabinet, at which the TSR-2 was not discussed. The burden of receiving a deputation of about ten, representing BAC workers at Preston (whose M.P.— Peter Mahon—was present) as well as Weybridge was put on the broad shoulders of John Stonehouse, Parliamentary Secretary to the Ministry of Aviation, who stuck it out for two hours, during which time his Minister (not a member of the Cabinet) made a brief appearance before beating a smart retreat.

Not everyone could demonstrate in London, especially on a Thursday (pay day, an important factor in the calculations of the shop stewards in Weybridge at least, even though management was willing to make special arrangements on Friday). But even stay-at-homes could and did exert themselves to keep their jobs. On the day before, about a thousand workers from the BAC factory at Preston, where many thousands, variously estimated, stood to lose from the cancellation of the TSR-2 contract had braved the wind and rain to make their protest. They agreed to set up a fighting fund from an hour's pay per head and to send a strong contingent to join the Weybridge demonstrators in London the following day, when they also planned a brief token strike in Preston itself. Peter Mahon sent a telegram to the Prime Minister saying "Preston seething cauldron of rumour and discontent. Members and Prime Minister accused of foresaking October ideals"[58] (referring to the recent British general elections, not the October Revolution in Russia). Nor had the Hawker workers been dragging their feet. The TSR-2 was not in their stable, but in the competition for resources they might well suffer too. So workers at a Coventry plant within the Hawker family, fearful of the cancellation of the jet-transport contract, dispatched to the House of Commons a delegation also representative of their comrades on the TSR-2. There they saw their local Member, Maurice Edelman, who undertook to convey their views to the Prime Minister and the Minister of Aviation.

On Friday, 15 January, BAC got what it had asked for on the Monday—that is, a meeting with the Prime Minister, which took the anodyne form of a dinner at Chequers to avoid the publicity surrounding No. 10 Downing Street, without Denis Healey, the Minister of Defence, but with Roy Jenkins, the Minister of Aviation. But, apart from a brief pre-dinner chat, Sir George Edwards, who naturally attended for BAC, had to share the P.M. with Hawker's Sir Arnold Hall, Sir Reginald Verdon Smith of Bristol Siddeley, Sir Denning Pearson, the 1930s apprentice from a Cardiff secondary school who had made it to the top of Rolls-Royce, and Cuthbert Wrangham, chairman of Short Brothers and Harland, Belfast, the largely government-owned firm that had harboured expectations of getting work on the jet transport from Hawkers. By the time the meal was over at midnight, the atmosphere should have been improved by the victuals but the guests left without "any reassurance on the question of"[59] the three type of aircraft whose future was at stake. The Sunday papers must have added to their gloom and despondency. The *Observer*, for example, carried a long piece on "the aviation crisis," perhaps further illustrating Mr. Wilson's later reflection that "aviation questions almost invariably leaked. I had always suspected Conservative ministers, but when I found how prone our own decisions and discussions were to get into the press, I revised my view." In any event, a diagram now showed the cost of TSR-2 soaring up to and even beyond £750 million, which would be "the absolute minimum total cost."[60] Whatever the precise figure, there seems little doubt (as would be said three years later) that TSR-2 was an "extreme example of a project that had soared out of control—a failure of project management . . . . the thermometers were rising but nobody was opening windows, is how one industry man puts it."[61]

On Friday, 29 January, the Overseas Policy and Defence Committee (a standing committee of the Cabinet normally chaired by the Prime Minister) met for over two hours at Downing Street to complete arrangements for the Defence White Paper due in mid-February. All the Ministers known to have been directly involved in the TSR-2 controversy were present.[62] Some of the dozen or so attending went straight on to a second, briefer meeting at which a few fresh faces appeared, among them Barbara Castle's, Lord Gardiner's, and Anthony Greenwood's. On the Monday 1 February, perhaps alarmed by the implications of the confident story in Saturday's *Sun* ("TSR-2 Wins Reprive—But Order is Slashed"[63]), some two hundred shop stewards and other workers were sent from Coventry to demonstrate support for Hawker Siddeley's jet transport project. Accompanied by the Reverend Simon Phipps, an industrial chaplain at Coventry, they marched to the Commons and passed a resolution asking the Minister of Aviation to maintain the contract.

All to no avail: The Cabinet met—unusually—that morning, and presumably agreed to abandon both the jet transport and the vertical takeoff fighter developments, although Richard Crossman, a Coventry M.P. himself, did not record it, mentioning only a postponement of a decision on the future of

TSR-2.[64] In any event, in Parliament the following day the sword of Damocles fell on Hawker (including Armstrong-Whitworth in Mr. Crossman's constituency), proving the keenness of its edge as it chopped off both the jet transport and the vertical takeoff fighter developments. For BAC's TSR-2, however, "that brilliantly conceived flying weapons system" (almost, for the P.M. "not so much an aircraft, more a way of life"),[65] there would have to be further technical evaluation as well as study of alternative aircraft.

Now it was Hawker Siddeley's turn to let fly. The "separate and different lobbying techniques adopted by the two big airframe groups"[66] had been noted by more than one observer. But, apart from Sir Arnold Hall's own conception of "lobbying technique," a company's dedication to quiet persuasion probably varies inversely with the extent and immediacy of the threat to its interests. With the incoming Ministers stunned by the cost of the TSR-2 (as, earlier, of Concorde), that seemed in the greater danger. Now it was reprived if only temporarily, and two of Hawker's basic projects were stone dead. A day after the announcement in Parliament, Hawker issued a statement apparently claiming that the Government by its decision had made 14,000 jobs redundant (a more considered figure being of the order of 3,000).[67] Sir Arnold Hall went off to lunch at the Commons with a group of Conservative M.P.s, whom he tried to interest in a reach-me-down alternative—that is, Comet wings on the fuselage of the jet transport just discarded. This cannibalization the Minister of Aviation undertook to think about, but it failed to win approval.

By contrast, it was now BAC's turn to display coolness under fire, dispensing hospitality to a dozen Labour M.P.s at their Weybridge command post. They needed all their courage. The estimates were agreed and published and the main lines of defence expenditure even debated and approved but by late March the future of TSR-2 was still unsettled. The crunch came at the Thursday Cabinet (1 April)[68] before Budget Day the following Tuesday. Failing to reach agreement within the normal time, and then having to attend the Princess Royal's funeral, the Cabinet adjourned and resumed at 10 p.m. (a most unusual occurrence). The divisions had not vanished in the interim. The cost was weighed against the loss of jobs and the retardation of technical development if the project was cancelled. Some favoured postponement until the Plowden Committee on the aircraft industry had reported (it had been set up the previous autumn). As the discussion crystallized, the Cabinet split three ways: (a) cancellation without replacement, (b) cancellation with the option of replacement by American F-111-A, the policy of the Minister of Defence, and (c) continuation until the strategic review then under way had been completed. At midnight the P.M., who had to fly off the very next morning to see President de Gaulle, broke the stalemate apparently by consolidating (a) and (b) and proposing (after a head count) that there was "a clear majority" for cancellation, to which the Cabinet agreed. The issue of replacement was passed to the Defence Committee, subject to final Cabinet approval.[69]

Only the announcement remained. As agreed at that Cabinet, it was made during the Budget speech. The Corporation protested and the Opposition moved a vote of censure (13 April), but these actions were only reflexive. By early June the project was so dead that the Minister of Aviation was refusing to authorise a further programme of research flying time (150 hours) for the three TSR-2 aircraft actually completed. That, the Opposition complained heatedly, would have cost only £2 million or so. The expenditure on TSR-2 up to the time of cancellation was (later) estimated to be of the order of £195 million, on the vertical takeoff fighter, £21 million, and on the jet transport, £22 million. Between 1951 and July 1967 cancellations of military aircraft and missiles cost the nation some £430 million.[70] Once again, either Britain had taken on too much, as a *Guardian* leader writer had anticipated in 1959 when discussing "A New Bomber,"[71] or there had indeed been a failure in project management.

Whatever the correct interpretation may be, it is important to note the limitations to even the combined influence of big business and big unions when matched against big government. Despite company denials, business and the unions were hand in glove on this issue. At Weybridge, management was willing to switch pay day to Friday for those who chose to demonstrate on the Thursday. True, the company did not pay the men for that day, but that loss was made up by a whip-round for their brothers who had stayed on the job. At Preston, the men had to meet out in the wind and rain to avoid compromising management. However, they were not docked for their brief but essentially political strike. In short, it seems plain, as a union leader remarked, that "the management were practically helping the workers into their coats" for the march against the TSR-2 cancellation.[72] Or, at the very least, as another such TSR-2 demonstrator is reported to have said in Whitehall, "when we told management we were coming to London, the dogs didn't bark."[73] So workers and bosses were indeed united in a "demo," even if the company did not pay for the buses. In any case, they all lost.

Who, then, would win? The favourite was the American firm General Dynamics, which had wrested from the Boeing Company the contract for the TFX (later F-111), the alternative to the TSR-2.[74] But it had opponents at Westminister among those reluctant to buy American, either on general political grounds or because (in a sense perversely) they recognized the variable geometry principle of the TFX (i.e., foldback wings) as a British invention (by the designer of the wartime dam-buster bomb, Dr. Barnes Wallis) that Britain did not choose to develop. Others simply did not wish to spend the money on either the TSR-2 or the TFX, a sum put at £200 million.

By May the Cabinet was reported to be still "deeply divided,"[75] with the Chancellor and the Ministers presiding over the social service departments against taking up the option and with the Foreign Secretary (Michael Stewart), the Minister of Defence, and the Navy, Army and Air Force Ministers ranged against them. The upshot was that a contract was placed with General Dynamics. The victory, if not exactly Pyrrhic, was one from whose gingerbread the gilt was before long removed. In June 1968 the Government cancelled its order for fifty F-111s. The penalty for cancellation was initially put as "something under $150 million," in addition to which the United States would refrain from placing defence orders in Britain to the tune of $129 million (out of $325 million originally planned).[76]

So as to the TSR-2/TFX issue, it was not "All's Well that Ends Well," yet with so much at stake hardly "Much Ado About Nothing" either. Full of errors indeed, but scarcely a comedy. For the Air Staff, some civil servants and politicians, management and workers, it was more like "Love's Labour Lost."

6

Representative Groups (I): Third London Airport and Equal Pay for Women

Sector 2

Still organizations *of*, these pressure groups are more specialized politically than those in sector 1. Foraging within two subclasses (locality, sex), we return with the Third London Airport case and with Equal Pay for Women.

The Third London Airport

Stansted

The Stansted policy was a Conservative gift horse into whose mouth Labour would have been wise to look long and carefully. Towards the end (as it turned out) of the Conservatives' long postwar reign (1951-1964), the Cabinet chose Stansted to relieve Heathrow and Gatwick in the mid-seventies. Created in 1942 by a United States Air Force that eventually went home but later returned long enough to extend the runway to an extraordinary 10,000 feet before leaving again, Stansted airfield had since 1953 been kept up the Ministry's sleeve as a potential third airport for London. But the cost of maintaining it perturbed the Select Committee on Estimates. This precipitated an interdepartmental Committee on the Third London Airport, which, in 1963, acknowledging that Stansted was "not perfect," recommended it as apparently "the only suitable site." With this, the Minister of Aviation (Julian Amery) and apparently the Cabinet agreed. Work on the site, however, was not to begin for about two years, which gave time for the ground to be prepared in the other sense as well. In order to explain the reasons for choosing Stansted, the Report itself was published in March 1964. That, however, had the effect of making the decision less, not more, acceptable to the local public, and in July the North-West Essex Preservation Association was formed to mount a counterattack. With "East Herts" added later to its already cumbersome title, it became the centre of a resistance network of thirty societies and of forty villages and towns, although the greater local authorities as such, notably the Essex County Council, continued to fight the good fight on their own account, contributing substantially to the final result.

No doubt they fought with greater zest after the general election in October when Labour just pipped the Conservatives at the post. It was not that

North-West Essex or, still less, the Essex County Council warmed to a Labour Government as such but that they must have seen the advantage of a new ministerial team apparently uncommitted to the Stansted policy. The change did bring the promise of an inquiry as well as Mr. Roy Jenkins to the Ministry of Aviation, which would prove as significant for this issue as his later translation to the Home Office would be in the passage of the morals legislation. For he was soon on record as saying that if the inquiry disclosed that another site was preferable to Stansted, "This will be followed up and it will not be ruled out for lack of time to study and survey the site."[1] That was not for him to promise, and later the Ministry responsible for the inquiry (Housing and Local Government) issued first a statement and then a clarification.[2] But it looked as if the Stansted objectors would have a friend at court.

The inquiry did not open until early December 1965. Conducted by the senior partner in a Kensington firm of surveyors and estate agents as inspector, with an air transport consultant as technical assessor,[3] it ended in early February 1966, having taken about a month in actual working days. As far as the inquiry went, the upshot was a victory for the Stansted groups, and such outsiders as the Town and Country Planning Association, which in a memorandum to the Government had rejected the plan root and branch. It was hardly the total victory that the co-chairmen of the Preservation Association would later claim.[4] The inspector gave it as his opinion that "it would be a calamity for the neighbourhood if a major airport were placed at Stansted. Such a decision could only be justified by national necessity. Necessity was not proved by evidence at this inquiry." On the other hand, he had been asked in the terms of reference "to hear and report on local objections relating to the suitability of the choice of Stansted for an airport and the effect of the proposed development on local interests." So he was reporting, not recommending. Nor, evidently, was he convinced by the alternatives proposed, which included the Isle of Sheppey (to the dismay of the Sheppey Rural District Council) and Padworth in Berkshire (to the dismay of the Berkshire County Council). He also expressed his opinion that the whole problem should be reviewed by a more broadly based committee in the light of both military and civil aviation needs. But no doubt that committee, too, like the Stansted inspector, would have been enjoined in the terms of reference *not* to question the need for a third major airport to serve London, so even that procedure might still have led back to Stansted in the end.

What the objectors had won, although they could not know it, was time, and that proved to be crucial. Standard public inquiry procedure was geared to *local* planning projects; there was no such procedure to inquire into "undertakings of *national* importance involving assessment and comparison of alternatives in a number of different areas."[5] Legislation designed to remedy that defect was already being considered by a Cabinet Committee, but no decision had been reached when the issue of a third London airport thrust itself to the fore. So the inspector's report in May to Richard Crossman (as Minister of

Housing and Local Government) compounded a problem already perceived but not resolved.

So: what should be done *now*? A reexamination was undertaken, in which "other experts" were consulted. This confirmed the choice of Stansted. As the principal item on the agenda, the question reached the Cabinet (for the second time) on 9 May 1967. The fight against the policy was led by Roy Jenkins (now Home Secretary and so in the Cabinet), supported by Anthony Crosland and about half-a-dozen others. But there seems to have been about a dozen ranged against them, including Douglas Jay (now at the Board of Trade and responsible for civil airports), although several or even many of these may have been very reluctant suitors, unable to see a way out in the circumstances.[6] Whatever the truth of that, Mr. Jay announced the decision to proceed with Stansted Airport on the very day that the House of Commons was dispersing for the Whitsun recess and therefore "half-empty."[7] This had apparently been preceded in Cabinet by what Mr. Crossman would call "a snap decision."[8] As the policy-makers prudently retreated under cover of the recess, a "grumbling row" (the Prime Minister would later call it) was about to erupt.

Some of the Fleet Street's most powerful guns erupted first, but the local opponents were scarcely less quick to follow. The local M.P., Peter Kirk (replacing Mr. Butler, who had been translated to the House of Lords) promptly announced a fight to the death, to share in which he invited twenty organizations to Chelmsford on 24 May. This precipitated the Stansted Working Party, made up of Mr. Kirk's Parliamentary (but Labour) colleague, Stanley Newens and representatives of the Preservation Association, the National Farmers' Union (Essex), and the local authorities of Hertfordshire and Essex, with the then deputy clerk of the Essex County Council as secretary. A public meeting at Dunmow two days later attracted some 3,000 people and 500 telegrams of support. The Essex County Council issued a writ against the Ministry of Housing and Local Government (under whose auspices the inquiry had been held). Accompanied by two church wardens, the Vicar of Thaxted (the Reverend Jack Putterhill) spent thirteen minutes at No. 10 Downing Street trying to persuade the Prime Minister's principal private secretary that the proposed development might damage the fabric of his church (the "Cathedral of Essex" dating from 1340). In particular, it put at risk the tall spire ("the only medieval stone spire in Essex"), with which the original runway had been deliberately aligned by the American Air Force as a landing guide. He pleaded as a minimum for a realignment of the runway of eight to ten degrees.[9]

By chance, the Vicar's plea acquired an importance that could not have been foreseen at the time. But the second phase of the post-White Paper campaign was essentially Parliamentary. The Opposition put down a motion for debate that did not actually mention Stansted (unsurprisingly, since it had been their choice when in office) but called for an independent committee of inquiry into national airport policy "in the context of which a decision on a Third

London Airport could be taken." Until the Committee reported, the final decision should be put off. What the Stansted Working Party did was to reinforce that characteristic Parliamentary ploy. As soon as the debate was announced in mid-June, they set out their arguments in a substantial document circulated to all members of Parliament, who were later invited (by Peter Kirk and Stanley Newens) to a meeting in Westminster Hall (20 June) to hear expert witnesses for the defence. How many turned up is not clear, but in due course 260 signed a motion calling for a Royal Commission before irrevocable decisions were taken. Some of the hundred or so Labour Members who signed were presumably among those who asked for the special meeting of the Parliamentary Labour Party that took place the following day, but they seem to have been unable to convince the two Ministers responsible (Douglas Jay at the Board of Trade and Anthony Greenwood, now at Housing) of the errors of their ways. According to Charles Pannell, a former Minister, the decision in favour of Stansted was pushed through with the use of "the payroll vote," meaning that the Government had mustered all senior and junior Ministers and even Parliamentary Private Secretaries to ensure that it carried the day. The whole business had been dealt with in "the most uncomradely way."[10]

On 28 June, the eve of the debate, a wider appeal was attempted. About four hundred "demonstrating countrymen" otherwise members and supporters of the Preservation Association, arrived in London by special train. Some of the more photogenic of them, wearing sweaters emblazoned with "No Stansted" but smiling despite their grim errand, were photographed on the arrival platform, and the resulting picture formed a pleasing introduction to the accompanying story in the morning papers. Coaches then whisked the demonstrators to the Commons "for two hours of lobbying"[11] before the debate, but in fact "very few of those who got into the outer lobby were successful in seeing members."[12] A group of ten, led by Sir Roger Hawkey, joint chairman of the Preservation Association, did manage to beard Mr. Jay in his den, but Sir Roger afterwards declared that "it was a waste of time talking to him." As Sir Roger had gone in "an angry man and came out a more angry man," he may well have wished to emulate what an intrepid contingent of the four hundred actually did for the Prime Minister—that is, leave at No. 10 "a letter and wreath of Essex weeds, suitably dedicated. . . ."[13]

If a hundred Labour Members had been in favour of a Royal Commission, they mostly vanished under the hot sun of a three-line whip. In the debate on 29 June, just ten abstained and the Government secured a comfortable majority of over sixty for its amendment to the Opposition's motion. Of course, the amendment as drawn was rather difficult to oppose, welcoming as it did Government policy "to plan airport requirements in the light of all the relevant factors, including the effect on the local population, the needs of the travelling public, safety, agriculture, and the protection of amenity." In any event, the vote sustained Government policy towards Stansted, whose fate seemed finally sealed, despite a brave show of resistance at a large and lively meeting at Bishop's Stortford on 12 July, by the failure of the Essex County Council's legal action against the Ministry of Housing about two weeks later.

The gods, however, were kind. Before the month was out, J.W.S. Brancker, who had been the technical assessor at the original public inquiry, was writing to *The Times* in terms that cast doubt upon the Stansted policy, which in his opinion even the 29 June debate had still not finally settled. Above all, Prime Minister Wilson used the summer recess to reshuffle his Cabinet pack, as a result of which in late August Douglas Jay found himself on the backbenches[14] and Anthony Crosland at the Board of Trade, and as such the Minister responsible for the Stansted policy. (The Minister of Housing had been in the picture mainly because the law required the public inquiry to be held under his Department's flag.) Possibly because of that switch (compounded by the larger musical chairs movement of which it was part), the development order enabling the British Airports Authority to get on with the work, which had been promised for the recess, was not forthcoming. Evidently Mr. Crosland was prepared to think again and as it happens he was given much to think about. Approached by Sir Roger Hawkey and Mr. John Lukies (joint chairmen of the Preservation Association), Mr. Brancker elaborated upon his letter to *The Times*, producing reports that were published in October as *The Stansted Black Book*. At the end of that month, the Noise Abatement Society published a report it had commissioned (at a cost of £20,000) from a team of architects, airport planners, and consultants. This purported to show that the best choice for a Third London Airport would be on the sands off the coast of Foulness Island in Essex. Speaking for the Society, John Connell, exulted: "This is the final nail in the coffin of Stansted."[15] Within a week the Fabian Society published a pamphlet on national airport planning by Dr. Rigas Doganis, that rare bird, a university lecturer in air transport economics. He condemned the procedure adopted in the Stansted case because the proposal had never been discussed in the context of regional or national planning.

By now, the beginning of November 1967, Mr. Crosland was beginning to tack. On 1 November, Arthur Reed, air correspondent of *The Times* was wondering whether the Government would reconsider its Stansted decision.[16] Five days later came an unmistakable signal from a leading political correspondent, Francis Boyd, who wrote (probably with more confidence than he expressed) that Mr. Crosland was "understood not to share Mr. Jay's conviction that Stansted is necessarily the best site."[17] At some stage, accompanied by Stanley Newens, he paid a visit to the site, unannounced and not even advertised later. Then, after the Home Affairs Committee had wrestled with planning aspects of "the Stansted mess-up" (Mr. Crossman's term),[18] the issue reached the full Cabinet again on 9 November. What he sought was another inquiry: What he seems to have come out with was a decision to realign the runways. This would serve two purposes: noise would be reduced at Bishop's Stortford, and, most conveniently, the decision itself could be brandished as a reason for the delay in tabling the (development) order.[19]

Was that a sleeper, a delayed time-bomb, meaning that the decision to realign buttressed as it was by another to increase the number of runways to four, would inevitably produce a new situation, or at least one that could be dressed up as such, ultimately necessitating a new inquiry after all? Many M.P.s would take that view later. A leading political correspondent (Ronald Butt) cast doubt upon that interpretation, which he regarded as "devious theory,"[20] but it would have been acceptable political tactics and not even immoral. Some years later, certainly, Mr. Crosland would recall the days when, braving "the relentless opposition of civil servants, . . . I determined to revoke the Stansted decision."[21]

In any event, the consequences of the changes were predictable. The airlines would not be overjoyed, for the change from the usual north-east to south-west alignment to one more or less north-south would spread out the noise at the expense of losing the prevailing-wind advantage and introducing some cross-wind disadvantage. The Preservation Association could now claim with justice, as Mr. Lukies did on 12 February, that since "this is a new proposition affecting new people," a new inquiry should be held.[22] It could also appeal, as it did, to the Council on Tribunals, founded in 1958 to oversee that part of the public domain implied in its title. Endorsing the appeal for a new inquiry, the Council published its report (to the Lord Chancellor) on 22 February. The effect of that, however, was muffled by the Cabinet's own action that very day. If only two Ministers were armed with copies of the Council's recommendations and if the Cabinet reached its decision without mentioning the report,[23] it may nevertheless have concentrated their minds wonderfully. In any event, but no doubt with several considerations in mind, perhaps especially the underlying weakness in the existing planning procedure then in the process of being remedied in the Town and Country Planning Bill, the Cabinet reversed itself on 22 February and agreed to a new and broader inquiry on the siting of the third London airport. Two of the arguments used by Mr. Crosland in making his announcement to the House that afternoon were exactly what one would have expected from November onwards: Realignment "would affect many people who had neither the occasion nor the opportunity to object at the original inquiry"; moreover, the expansion to a four-runway airport was such "a radical departure from the earlier proposals as to constitute virtually a new project."[24] That was the local view, but the President, who had after all initiated both these changes, advanced it as part of the argument to justify the new inquiry. The Opposition cheered but some Labour backbenchers were angry. At a meeting of the Parliamentary Labour Party that night, they complained of "incompetence" and of the Government's "giving way to pressure"[25] after having produced a three-line whip to put the policy through originally. Others found it in their hearts to praise the Government's decision, which also received an excellent press. The Stansted groups were naturally delighted. Unconsciously echoing John Connell the previous November, Sir Roger Hawkey cried: "another nail in the Stansted coffin." But the Preservation Association did not rest on its laurels (shared in any case with the Essex County Council and other local authorities): Knowing that it had spent £23,000 at the previous inquiry, it promptly launched an appeal for £15,000.

Some three months later, the President announced the terms of reference of the inquiry, which was to consider the timing of the need for the airport as well as the various alternative sites, as to which it was to make a recommendation. The chairman would be the High Court Judge, Sir Eustace Roskill, presiding, as it turned out, over a team of six experts, of whom Professor Colin Buchanan, of Imperial College, London, and author in the early sixties of a celebrated Government Report was the best known.[26] Getting under way on 25 June, the Roskill Commission set about making a list of possible sites, which eventually produced a grand total of almost eighty "conceivables." By a meandering process that total was whittled down to Cublington (Wing) in North Buckinghamshire, an old bomber base; Silverstone, just over the Bucks county boundary into Northamptonshire; Nuthampstead, Herefordshire, another former bomber base; Hockcliffe and Thurleigh, in Bedfordshire; and eventually to three as Silverstone and Hockcliffe were discarded. But a *démarche* by Professor Buchanan made it necessary to include Foulness, backed for some time as a long shot by some very shrewd punters and which had indeed appeared on the various Roskill lists until fairly late in the day. So, finally, there were four on the list submitted to Mr. Crosland at the Board of Trade in February and made public on 3 March.

No Stansted! That called for a celebration locally, although Nuthampstead was only ten miles away, and some other experienced punters had early on (even pre-Roskill) made *it* the favourite; for example, a *Guardian* columnist's note arrestingly headed:

"Per ardua ad
Nuthampstead."[27]

Apart from that, the book was still not quite closed. Local groups kept a suspicious eye on development even within the existing airport, fearing that "they," especially the British Airports Authority (BAA), might try to get their way by the back door. Thus in October 1970 the Essex County Council made a protest to the Minister of Housing about BAA plans to increase the size of the terminal buildings. As the year ended, the Preservation Association was preparing to seek a High Court injunction to stop night flights and further training flights and even claim damages for excessive noise levels in recent years. But for Stansted the great battle was over. On the face of it, "a victory" indeed "for local pressure groups," as the *Observer* remarked,[28] in line with a local judgment: "In planning history it will go down as a famous pressure group victory."[29] *The Times* read it somewhat differently: "a happy ending to one foray in 'participating democracy'."[30]

Cublington (Wing)

At that stage there was no happy ending in sight for the other four places, only toil, tears, and sweat, with here and there some hint of blood (or coming to the surface of that latent violence of the rural areas, which one has encountered, for example, in Oxfordshire even when homes and land were not at stake, "only" the ploughing up of an ancient footpath by some overbearing farmer). The Foulness situation was peculiar. Later a Defenders of Essex Association would appear, but to begin with, the Foulness Island Residents' Committee stood almost alone against enemy hordes, including not only the Roskill Commissioners but also the NFU and the Country Landowners' Association and even some commercial interests, such as the Thames Estuary Development Company, which, suddenly surfacing four days after the Cabinet decision on 22 February, proposed to finance and construct an airport on Maplin Sands, off Foulness Island, by private enterprise.[31] The Residents' Committee even had to suffer a Trojan horse, since the Essex County Council, which for Stansted had fought so valiantly and spent so freely without counting the cost (to the ratepayers),[32] promptly came out in favour of Foulness for the third airport, a stand later supported by a number of other local authorities, including Southend. Local people could have been forgiven for feeling sold down the river, even though, geographically, they were already there (on the north side of the Thames Estuary). So many turned up at Shoeburyness on 17 March that the residents' association had to turn people away from the old council chamber.

The three other localities enjoyed, if not unity (since there were those—pariahs, almost outlaws—who actually wanted the airport), then a working consensus. Their societies were created in the image of Stansted's. The Nuthampstead Preservation Association echoed the name and reproduced the militant spirit. On 17 March, as excitement was mounting at Shoeburyness, over seven hundred people descended on Barkway, a village near Nuthampstead, to listen to Shirley Williams, the M.P. for Hitchin and a junior Minister in the Government. They made threatening noises[33] and launched an appeal for £30,000 to finance their resistance. The Bedfordshire Airport Resistance Association at Thurleigh was evidently a chip off the not-so-old block. So was WARA (= "wearer"), son of SARA, the Silverstone Airport Resistance Association, formed in November 1968 to defend that territory from the depredations of the vandals. With the reprive of Silverstone, SARA herself vanished only to rise from the ashes as WARA, the "W" standing for Wing, another village and the common local name for the old aerodrome officially identified as "Cublington" or "Cublington (Wing)." The centre of gravity of SARA had all along tended to be less in South

Northants than in North Bucks, which was still very much in danger. Put into orbit at a parish meeting at Cublington on 8 March, WARA inherited not only SARA's rule book and money but also some of her leaders, notably Desmond Fennell, a barrister, as chairman; Nevile Wallace, also called to the bar but employed by the NFU, as vice-chairman; and David Robarts, chairman of the National Provincial Bank, as president. But WARA found a local solicitor, John Pargeter, for the secretaryship, and even received a dowry from him in the form of free office space for the administrative headquarters. WARA also captured two local notables: Lady Hartwell, wife of the chairman and editor-in-chief (a Berry, still) of the *Daily Telegraph*, for the executive committee, and Evelyn de Rothschild for the treasureship.

The strategic situation in which they found themselves was fundamentally different from Stansted's. The key to that strategy had been the demand for due process, or proper procedure. Since at the public inquiry into the second London airport at Gatwick in 1954, it had not been possible to suggest alternatives, Stansted set out to remove that limitation. Having secured an assurance from the P.M. himself (thanks to the good offices of their M.P., Mr. Butler) they then sought out the incoming Minister, Mr. Jenkins, and were encouraged to find him sympathetic. After they had, as they thought, won the public inquiry, its apparent overriding by the Cabinet could be and was represented as improper, which by the series of steps recounted led the way eventually to the new inquiry under Sir Eustace Roskill.

By contrast, Cublington (Wing) was on the short list of four, precisely because the initial sifting had already been done by the Roskill Commission as the first stage of its proceedings at which, as arranged by Mr. Crosland, there was no right of representation. This was not of course denied, merely reserved in the first instance for Stage II, when onsite hearings would be conducted by a senior planning inspector (who, as it turned out, was also a Commissioner). Stage III would be taken up with technical and other studies by the Commission's own full-time staff and consultants, who would then, in Stage IV, be questioned by the Commissioners. In Stage V, the grand climacteric, "interested parties" would be able to scrutinize the data already gathered and, "by leave of the Commission," brief counsel, who would be able to cross-examine witnesses.[34]

It was this procedure, in whole and in part, that created for WARA an entirely new strategic situation compared with Stansted's. If it really wished to engage the enemy, its strategy would have to bend to this extraordinary overall pattern. No doubt some of the Stages (e.g., II and III) could be (and were) worked concurrently rather than consecutively (making the scheme analytical, not strictly chronological). Even so Mr. Crosland anticipated that the business might take two years. Would WARA be able to sustain and finance such a long haul? After the Stage V climax, would WARA be able to muster its tired troops to fight an adverse finding by the Commission? In other words, given a five-stage procedure not expected to be completed for two years, would the work of opposition have to be left to the local authorities, particularly the Bucks County Council (as the one mainly concerned)?

If the five-stage procedure and its extension over time represented a general challenge to WARA, Stage II implied a particular one. Since it would not entail a public inquiry in the technical planning sense, it would be open, if the Commission agreed, to whatever pro-airport forces dared to show their faces. (The complaints about "intimidation"—ranging from abusive telephone calls to threats of physical violence—made to Mr. Justice Roskill are discounted by David Perman, who says flatly that they were "unfounded."[35] But that High Court judge believed the complainants, and anyone who has lived long in central rural England and had experience of even a lesser dispute than Cublington's, would have learned to expect it.) In any case, at Stansted the pro-airport forces had undoubtedly been stifled. These forces had not been inconsiderable. Workers at the existing airport had formed a Stansted Area Progress Association as far back as February 1965. They got out car stickers ("YES to Stansted as the Third London Airport") and they got up a petition, signed by 5,000 persons, favouring the development. Four trade unionists wrote to *The Times* from Saffron Walden itself to say that they were "enthusiastically for the airport . . . as surely all modern ambitious people must be. . . ." As another such letter writer put it, many Essex people welcomed the Stansted decision, but they were not so well organized or articulate as the opposers. Rural Essex had always been the Cinderella of the south-east, with lower wages and fewer job opportunities. Great seaports of the last century were neither beautiful nor silent, but they brought trade and prosperity. In similar vein, the Young Socialists of Saffron Walden complained that the opposition to the airport development was conducted by "people who are glad to accept the benefits of living in a modern industrial country, but who are loath to put up with any disadvantages."[36] The Harlow Trades Council (i.e., the trade unions organized on a territorial basis) voted five or six to one in favour of the development.

For one reason or another, however, this potential support had not been effectively mobilized. Labour was itself divided, the Harlow Urban District Council, on which the party had a majority, being strongly opposed. Some of the workers backing the Progress Association tended to be peripatetic, moving from one airport to another and so not available for sustained action. Above all, supporters of the development were not permitted to speak at the inquiry, a restriction left unrecorded by Olive Cook, though not surprisingly since in her *ex parte* account she failed to detail any of the support mentioned in the previous paragraph other than the letter to *The Times.*[37] Their exclusion from the inquiry is surprising, however. Mr. Perman believes the exclusion to have followed from "normal planning practice."[38] But one recalls a statutory inquiry in South Bucks in which local supporters of a housing development were allowed to talk their heads off—that is obviously the language of an objector—and in any case the Stansted inquiry was nonstatutory, held indeed at the discretion of the

Minister, at which local *supporters* could perfectly well have been heard. In any event, supporters were not going to be "gagged" at the Roskill Inquiry: During Stage II, which of course was the first stage for the locals, those in favour, soon to be organized as the Cublington Airport Supporters' Committee, would be heard as well as objectors. So WARA had to devise tactics to neutralize whatever support would be mustered and at the same time demonstrate the extent and depth of the opposition.

That implied resorting to a PR policy, a tendency reinforced (apart from the prompting of local activists) by at least two other factors, the first of which also derived from the nature of Stage II. Since its hallmark would be hearings, not concrete proposals (which of course were not being presented), there would be no courtroom clash or dramatic confrontation. So WARA would have to reach out to its constituency on its own initiative in what Mr. Perman aptly called this "phoney war" stage. Secondly, it seems very likely that WARA would have perceived the Stansted result as a PR victory and drawn the obvious inference.

These factors were not determinants but rather circumscribing tendencies leaving WARA some room for manoeuvre. It decided to rely upon its own energy and resourcefulness rather than on the Bucks County Council. There seem to have been two main reasons for their choice. Residents of South Bucks tend to think that the County Council in Aylesbury dances to a tune played by the "county people" in North Bucks. But these apparently believe that the boot is on the other foot; that the County Council looks South, perhaps especially to Slough and district, whose numerous citizens would suffer less noise and especially sleep more soundly, the more the nearby first London airport (Heathrow) were relieved by a third. Besides, the Council stood to gain materially, in rateable value and jobs, from a Cublington development. In the event, the Council fought the good fight as defined by its North Bucks minority but, having got up a head of steam, WARA continued to move along its own tracks.

That took money, which was the keynote of the speech by William Manning, a local farmer and member of WARA's executive committee (later vice chairman), at a Cublington parish meeting on Saturday night 8th March 1969. At least £50,000 would be needed, he declared. Within twenty-four hours, £16,500 was collected. As Mr. Manning reported: "People have been ringing up all day with offers of monetary support."[39] Naturally they were not all physically able, even if financially, to pay up immediately, so the total announced included promises. However, these seem to have been substantially redeemed, since £19,000 was collected by the end of August.

It would not be a penny too much, for WARA retained Mr. Niall MacDermot, Q.C. (a clever stroke since he was not merely a Labour M.P., but a recent [1967-68] Minister of State at the Ministry of Housing and Local Government). But his brief would doubtless be marked up for many guineas. Moreover WARA would also have to pay for junior counsel in accordance with the profitable self-imposed rules of the greatest of Britain's closed shops, the English Bar. Legal and technical costs at that stage ran away with about £7500. Since it was estimated that Stage V in London would cost between £20,000 and £30,000 (which proved to be about right), a new appeal was launched in September.[40]

To some extent that second appeal reduced the problem presented by the long haul. Stage II opened at Aylesbury on 14 July and lasted eight days. Expert witnesses such as Tom Hancock, the urban planner, came and went, supported by two literary knights, Sir Arthur Bryant, who lived nearby at Wootton Underwood, and Sir John Betjeman, who, in the language of Henry James, characterized the scenery of the area as "unmitigated England." For WARA he turned his views into verse, fearing the time when:

... The birds are all killed and the flowers are all dead,
And the businessmen's aeroplane booms overhead,
With chemical sprays we have poisoned the soil,
And the scent in our nostrils is diesel and oil. ...[41]

At the time WARA kept Sir John's verse in reserve. But it did circulate in pamphlet form its comments and glosses upon the evidence given at the Roskill hearing. Local residents then exerted themselves in various enterprising ways to raise the further money that would be needed. In due course, the fighting fund received, in all, about £57,000, over half as a result of collective efforts locally and some of the rest from personal approaches made by Mr. de Rothschild, as treasurer, to friends and acquaintances.

Since no one doubts that the great majority were opposed to having the third London airport planted on top of them, the extent of local opposition was easily demonstrated. A petition of over 61,000 signatures, authenticated by local bank clerks and even indexed by locality, was presented at the inquiry. Depth of feeling demonstrated itself at the hearings as witnesses insisted that they would never leave their homes, but was mainly expressed in the field. One of the villages, Stewkley, with its homes and Norman church threatened with demolition, hurriedly created its own Action Committee, which in late April staged a protest march covered by press and TV. Anti-airport signs burgeoned suddenly. One, depicting a farmer with a pitchfork at the ready and all set to plunge into a jet, was captioned: "Airport? Over our dead bodies and we mean it."[42] On the eve of the opening of the Roskill hearings, overcoming the reluctance of WARA proper, the Action Committee mounted a general demonstration in Aylesbury in which some two thousand marched to the perhaps anachronistic but still rousing strains of "Land of Hope and Glory." The march would "further demonstrate that we are not going to take anything lying down," one of the organizers declared.[43] In the autumn, as the second financial appeal was under way, an exotic sign appeared in Stewkley's vicarage garden. Linguists identified it as written in Russian, Chinese, and Urdu. Surmounted by a few bars from the "Red Flag," the message in Russian read: "If it is decided to build the airport here, there will be revolution in Stewkley. We will fight against the government as the Russians did in 1917. It is better to die standing than to live kneeling."[44] On Guy Fawkes' Night, Sir Eustace Roskill was burnt in effigy but did not, on the witchcraft analogy, fall dead in his Berkshire home. Marauders paid him a call there in April 1970, however, after the Commission's cost-benefit analysis of the several possible developments had appeared in the January. Under cover of darkness, they nailed up signs marked "No inland airport." At his Surrey home Peter Masefield, chairman of the BAA received the same treatment, plus a bonus in the form of a more specific injunction painted on his gate: "No Wing—Cublington."

By now the WARA leadership, which doubtless disapproved of all this militancy, was thinking seriously about PR. At an early stage, out of the original £19,000, some £3,300 had been spent on publicity. Of the funds raised by one of the associated bodies, WOW, or Wings-off-Wing (based on Weedon, Oving, and Whitchurch), £1,000 had been handed over to WARA specifically for PR use. But WARA was slow and perhaps reluctant to engage a professional firm in the manner increasingly practised by pressure groups and political parties even in Britain as well as the United States. In April 1970, however, as Stage V was about to open, WARA decided (after trying them out) to engage the "high-powered, American-based"[45] firm of Burson-Marsteller whose North Row office was (and is) headed by a well-known PR figure, Claude J. Simmonds. Exactly what the company did to earn their keep (they were taken on at a special rate for three months) is not clear, but the methods are not esoteric. As seen from Fleet Street itself, their representatives "chatted up" selected Fleet Street journalists, the television companies, Members of Parliament, to create the "right image" of Cublington as "an irreplaceable slice of England's green and pleasant land. . . ."[46] It seems very probable they did initiate some of the coverage in press and TV, including an interview on one programme with John Betjeman and Desmond Fennell. Certainly during the General Election, which came unexpectedly in June 1970, they circulated WARA's views to candidates, apparently taking the line that there should be no inland airport of any kind.

By now WARA itself was moving in the direction of Parliament. At the outset M.P.s of all brands locally available (which then meant four Conservatives and two Labour) had been roped in as vice presidents, although Robert Maxwell, the maverick Labour M.P. for Buckingham (i.e., North Bucks) had later resigned, ostensibly on the ground that WARA was class biased. In the House a little later, on the initiative of Stephen Hastings (Conservative, Mid-Bedfordshire), and so with a close interest in Thurleigh as well as Cublington), those vice presidential M.P.s had formed the nucleus of an informal group that seems to have done little, however, except hold a watching brief. Still, that was probably all that WARA and the other resistance organizations had required of them. But by the summer of 1970 WARA at least was getting the wind up, fearing that the Commission was *en route* to recommending Cublington. So it began to manoeuvre. Acting on the precept *sauve qui peut*, WARA approached two of the new M.P.s (Timothy Raison, Aylesbury, and William Beynon, who had knocked out Robert Maxwell in Buckingham) for help in turning the Roskill guns on Thurleigh. Undeterred by a cool reception from them for such a desperate save-himself-who-can manoeuvre, WARA went on to instruct its counsel, Niall MacDermot, Q.C., to argue before the Commissioners in London that Thurleigh was more suitable than Cublington for the third London airport. His advocacy on WARA's behalf gave Mr. Crosland the opportunity to say in the House that it was running the risk of seeming not to "care tuppence for anybody else's noise and environment."

Meanwhile WARA had been gathering more M.P.s into the vice presidential fold, thirteen of them in all, mostly (reflecting the area) Conservative. In the House itself in early July, following a meeting between WARA, three of the local M.P.s and Burson-Marsteller, the informal group dating from the spring of 1969 was rejuvenated as the all-party Third London Airport Group for which the former Labour Minister and M.P. for Hitchin, Shirley Williams, was later recruited as vice president to balance Stephen Hastings in the chair. (By 1973 their roles had been reversed, though presumably the group rarely met.) With William Beynon as secretary, all three inland sites were thus covered by officeholders. That symbolized what an all-party group would have in any case entailed: a policy of *sauve qui peut* at the expense of Foulness for *all three* inland sites, not simply Cublington, as WARA even then was trying to get away with. Later, when WARA believed the tactical situation to have changed to its disadvantage, it tried to make common cause with the Bedfordshire Airport Resistance Association, outraged of course by the cool attempt at the London hearings to palm off the airport on Thurleigh. But for a time the right hand at Westminster was not doing what the left hand at Cublington was doing, although neither suffered from ignorance.

All-party groups, which number about eighty, do not have an easy row to hoe, even when the referent enjoys ready sympathy, such as the British Limbless Ex-service Men's Association (BLESMA) and its constituency. Accordingly, for a particular campaign and favourable decision still ruefully recalled in Whitehall from the mid-fifties, the BLESMA Group went a long way beyond the usual Parliamentary routines.[47]

The Third London Airport Group seems to have been more orthodox but little less efficient, or at least energetic. They invited WARA's chairman and vice chairman to address them: the chairman, Mr. Fennell, spoke up on 2 December, 1970. WARA officers paid a return visit two weeks later, when representatives of other resistence organizations were also brought in. Meanwhile the all-party group had been canvassing support for one of those motions ("Early Day") that serve as a mode of expressing backbench opinion. The movers opposed building the third London airport on any inland site and pointed a minatory finger at Foulness. So they were ready to strike back if the worst came to the worst.

Come it did on Black Friday, 18 December when a summary of the Roskill Commission's Report was published, complementing an announcement in the Commons by John Davies, Secretary of State for Trade and Industry, that new Departmental conglomerate that included the old Board of Trade under whose auspices the inquiry had been held. With one predictable exception, the Commissioners chose Cublington. Evidently they had neither been persuaded by silver-tongued advocates, nor moved by the PR campaign, nor deterred by the extent and depth of local opposition, never less than vigorous, sometimes tending towards the violent. As Professor Buchanan would say later, "They were not prepared to be influenced by any surmises on how the public might react. They regarded that as political. I was quite prepared to say: 'What is likely to be the public reaction to this site or that site?' To me that is not being swayed by 'politics' but simply a way of doing public consultation in advance."[48] What had influenced them, fundamentally, was a cost-benefit calculation, the technique designed to secure an efficient allocation of resources by taking into account in principle and for the life of the project, all the costs to be incurred, indirect as well as direct, and all the benefits, similarly allowing for the externalities. In principle a prudent procedure, it is obviously difficult and may be impossible to apply in practice. But on some such basis the Commission, eliminating Nuthampstead on grounds of noise and regional planning, found that Thurleigh would cost £86 million more, and Foulness £100 million more, than Cublington.

So the later comment by the lone dissenter, Professor Buchanan, seems perfectly apt: His fellow commissioners had seen the "question as an economic problem to which there was an important planning side, whereas his own view was that it was par excellence a planning question, with an important economic aspect." He himself had naturally approached the issue as a planner. At an early stage in the Roskill proceedings—some five or six months after their inauguration—he "had developed the gravest doubts about the inland site," bringing on in his mind "a great red warning light." He also diverged from his fellow Commissioners in his sensitivity to public opinion: "In a lifetime of planning experience, I developed a nose for the kind of decisions that will 'run with' the public, and the kind of decision that is going to be troublesome. I knew in my bones that a decision for an inland site would be very troublesome indeed, if not impossible, to get accepted." But what he knew in his bones took rather a long time to reach his lips. While his colleagues wrestled with the cost-benefit analysis, he apparently nursed his doubts: "I sat through this," he would tell *The Times*, "with this horrible doubt in my mind about the outcome. I had to wait. But I was pretty certain that I had reached a conclusion independently of this exercise."[49] Or, as he would confess to his fellow specialists in the hearing of the same man from *The Times*, "I hate to say it, but I think I reached my conclusion not on the evidence at all, but on the basis of my experience in land use planning."[50] That conclusion, expressed in a note of dissent to the majority Report, was: "It would be nothing less than an environmental disaster if the airport were to be built at any of the inland sites, but nowhere more serious than at Cublington, where it would lie athwart the critically important belt of open country between London and Birmingham. . . . the best site in the interests of the country as a whole" would be at Foulness, which would play a vital role in reducing the social imbalances between the eastern and the western sides of London."[51] That referred in part to the declining importance and even closing of some of the London docks and the comparative impoverishment of most of that eastern side of the London area.

Evidently WARA and the Third London Airport Group in the Commons had lost a battle but not necessarily the war. When the chairman of a Commission fails to hold his team together, there is always hope for the status quo; and Professor Buchanan, although he stood alone among seven, happened to be known to the attentive public everywhere for his *Traffic in Towns* report. Nor was the incoming Conservative Government, only six months old, in any way committed. That, curiously enough, was something that WARA had been anxious about. If it really had feared that the Government might "accept Roskill" in advance of debate in Parliament and even of publication,[52] it must have been developing the paranoia that may perhaps strike any group of beleaguered persons. It is true that, under a previous Conservative administration, Julian Amery at Aviation had placed his imprimatur in the front of the report recommending the choice, or rather the development of Stansted as the third London airport. That, however, had been first time round: This was second time round, in the wake of a Commission that had laboured for over two years in the public eye. There could have been no question of jumping the gun. So the notion that the WARA chairman made the Leader of the House (William Whitelaw) commit himself to a Parliamentary debate by telephoning a question to the BBC radio programme *This is Your Line* when Mr. Whitelaw was on the air (12 January 1971)[53] is just a romantic myth. In fact, almost a month earlier, apparently on the very day of Mr. Davies's announcement, his Minister of Trade, Michael Noble, assured Stephen Hastings "that the Government was in no way committed to the recommendation and that there would be a full debate in the Commons before any conclusion was reached."[54] On the Sunday following (20 December) Peter Walker, Secretary of State for the Environment, a brand new office, said that the Government would carefully examine the environmental issues when it came to decide upon the airport site, and that he was setting up a "small working party" to scrutinize "all the factors in the Roskill Commission report."[55] Obviously he was not proceeding without Cabinet authority, and *The Times* story was correctly headed: "Minister Gives Pledge on Third Airport."

It was the job of Mr. Hastings's own small working party—the Third London Airport Group—to prepare the ground in every possible way. By early afternoon, 18 December, his Group had already secured no fewer than 160 names nailed to the mast of an Early Day Motion "totally opposed to the choice of an inland site or to the extension of any existing airport" for the purpose of making London's Third (whose need, however, they acknowledged) and "strongly" advocating "the selection of Foulness or another suitable coastal site."[56]

Back home the Thurleigh Emergency Committee for Democratic Action, the trade union pressure group that would have preferred Thurleigh itself, nevertheless asked the Government to accept the Roskill Report since the "recommendation had been made in the national interest. A decision in favour of Foulness, the most costly site, would demonstrate the Government's policy of restraint to be hypocritical, cynical and partisan." Even at Cublington, a housewife could be found to say "I stand by what I have always said: I want the airport to come here." But the response of author Geoffrey Household was doubtless more representative: "You cannot evict 1,500 or 2,000 people. Any attempt to tear down their homes could spark off violence. The Army would have to be called in."[57] Leaflets calling villagers to take up arms and explaining how to make petrol bombs were promptly distributed, probably from a base in Stewkley, where on Sunday night an effigy of Mr. Justice Roskill was burnt from a 20-foot bonfire. On the same night in dozens of villages around Cublington, over fifty fires were lit simultaneously and, as the flames flickered, thousands marched and church bells tolled. Hundreds of the leaflets were consigned to the flames as a mark of the disapproval of their contents by responsible local opinion.[58] Soon the Rector of Dunton (the Reverend Hubert Sillitoe) was forecasting in phrases reminiscent of Churchill's in 1940: "We will fight on the doorsteps of our homes, in the fields of our farms, at the churchyard gates and at the church doors."[59] WARA itself certainly disapproved of and even condemned its petrol-bomb fringe. But it was responsible for the chain of bonfires, which, according to one interpretation (the chairman's), were intended to symbolize "the torch of the environment," or, according to his vice chairman's view, to serve (with the tolling of the church bells) as "a warning of peril" that "we are being invaded" (a "folk-memory" from the days of the Armada of 1588, which he specifically evoked).[60] Perhaps these two leaders, Mr. Fennell and Mr. Manning, had agreed upon a division of labour, and so had different audiences or constituencies in their mind's eye. Certainly Mr. Manning was "provost-marshal" for the "roll on" of 3 January 1971, when, taking a leaf from the book of both French and English farmers, WARA dispatched several hundred vehicles of all shapes, sizes, and uses around the perimeter of what would be the new airport, some twenty-eight miles of it. One of the many slogans carried by the vehicles read: "Don't Foul Bucks, Foulness." On the succeeding Sunday, 10 January WARA mounted a mass rally that attracted contingents even from the reprieved Thurleigh and Nuthampstead. Possibly as many as 20,000 converged on Wing, whose narrow roads and lanes were blocked for miles around. The crowd filled and overflowed The Equestrian Centre (a corrugated, hanger-type structure capable of holding some 5,000), where M.P.s (two of them Labour, Reg Prentice and Joan Lester), and local leaders made the sort of stirring speeches expected of them when facing a large and excited audience and the television cameras. Some 5,000 gas-filled coloured balloons were released, each one bearing a postcard that WARA hoped the receivers would send to Peter Walker at Environment as a mark of their "disgust and revulsion at Roskill's choice." As the balloons "gained height and disappeared into the evening mist,"[61] a large cardboard replica of the Roskill Commission Report (not yet even published) was set on fire to the approving cries of the multitude whose martial virtues Cleo Laine sustained by song, with help from her husband, bandleader Johnny Dankworth and some minstrels who had wandered in from the Oxfordshire town of Thame.

Meanwhile other allies had been throwing down the gauntlet. Lord Molson, chairman of the CPRE wrote immediately to *The Times* to oppose any inland site and "strongly" urge "the adoption of Foulness," promising "to mobilize public opinion in this sense. . . ." The society CPRE itself asked its branches to "support the Cublington protest by emphasizing to M.P.s, Mr. Walker . . . and the Prime Minister the case against building the airport in rural Buckinghamshire." Maurice Ash, chairman of the executive of the Town and Country Planning Association, bewailed "the sorcery of cost-benefit analysis" on which the Roskill Commission had relied. The Bucks County Council expressed "complete and implacable opposition," even to the point of saying that it would refuse to sell to the Government the land it owned in Cublington. A week later the Bedfordshire County Council took the same path, followed by the chairman of the Milton Keynes Development Corporation, the agency charged with creating a new town in North Bucks. The "total concept of Milton Keynes," said Lord Campbell (of Eskan) on 12 January, "is incompatible with a major airport near by."[62] Thus two distinguished Scotsmen (counting Colin Buchanan) opposed the choice of Cublington on planning grounds. Two days later many of the big guns of the amenity realm fired together in the correspondence column of *The Times*, booming out "profound concern": the chairman of the CPRE (again), and the presidents of the Civic Trust, Institute of Landscape Architects, RIBA, and the Town Planning Institute. As characterized later by Mr. Crosland, they "scandalously rushed into print before even reading the Roskill report. . . ."[63] Certainly they wrote without waiting "for the publication of the full report." It was no doubt an effective move, "a high point in the campaign," as Stephen Hastings would remark later. Only the Royal Society for the Protection of Birds then broke ranks to defend "the real peace and richness of Foulness."[64]

At about this time, WARA itself was returning to the high road of argument, which it seemed for a moment to have abandoned for life in a three-ring circus. On 12 January, it came out with its critique of the Commission's summary findings, concluding that the majority's recommendations were "of very dubious validity." When the full report was published on 22 January,

WARA specialists at once set to work on it, and Niall MacDermot, Q.C., even flew back from Geneva to draft the resulting counter arguments, which appeared within three weeks. In mid-February the fifteen-page document was delivered at Westminster (during a postal strike) by local M.P.s, who also conveyed locally produced versions of Professor Buchanan's note of dissent, augmenting a supply already taken earlier that very week by a most unusual lobby of six hundred women and children, armed also with a letter to the Prime Minister.

These efforts anticipated the House of Lords debate that opened on 23 February, when Lord Molson as CPRE chairman led the attack on the Report. Nor did the Commission fare any better in the Commons debate on 4 March. That was only to be expected. By 4 January, the number of M.P.s who had signed the Early Day Motion had increased to "well above 170,"[65] and by the day of the debate, to 218, about three-quarters of whom were Conservatives. Some 10 percent of the 218 managed to catch the Speaker's eye. Replying to the debate, Michael Noble, Minister of Trade, virtually repeated what he had said to Stephen Hastings, of the Airport Group, on or about 18 December—that the Government was not committed and would ponder the views expressed.

Three weeks later after the Commons debate, in the company of Michael Heseltine of Environment, Michael Noble paid a visit to all four sites; later his Secretary at Trade and Industry, John Davies, slipped down to Cublington unannounced to see for himself.

Had one known of Mr. Davies's visit at the time, one would have taken it as a sign of which way the wind was blowing. One such warning or alerting sign did appear in the press. On 5 April *The Times* ran a front-page story headed: "Foulness Was Backed by Big Money Lobby." WARA, wrote John Clare, had mounted an "almost disturbingly professional" campaign, citing Burson-Marsteller and its chairman, Claude Simmonds. Two private consortia (the story continued) were interested in Foulness, one headed by Sir John Howard, a former chairman of the National Union of Conservative and Unionist Associations. He had been one of those who had helped to beat off the threat to Stansted and, living at Thurleigh, had also given money to the resistance associations that were campaigning, in effect, for the selection of Foulness. (That chimed with the suggestion made on BBC TV, but strongly denied by WARA, that the pro-Foulness commercial interests were throwing their weight behind the anti-Cublington campaign.) As Derrick Wood of the Action Committee Against Foulness Airport lamented, they had been able to muster only £3,000; opponents of Cublington or of any inland site (and so, implicitly, proponents of the choice of Foulness) had spent £700,000. Certainly, as John Clare concluded, the anti-Cublington campaign "was not the spontaneous action of the Buckinghamshire peasantry that has been so often suggested."[66]

That almost disturbingly professional campaign must have been in the mind of Conservative M.P., David Crouch (Canterbury) when, declaring himself "appalled," he demanded to know whom the Government listened to: "high pressure public relations groups or engineering contractors" rather than the Roskill Commission, "5 to 1 against Foulness"? The occasion was Mr. Davies's announcement in the House on 26 April to the effect that the Government had overturned the recommendation of the Roskill Commission, "despite the economic penalty involved," which would be "of the order of £150 million all told, discounted to 1982." The basis for the decision was that environmental and planning needs were "of paramount importance."[67] As the Prime Minister, Mr. Heath, would later tell the Country Landowners' Association: "the Government's decision to reject all inland sites for the new London Airport was one of the most important decisions regarding the environment. For the first time a government taking a major national decision has given pride of place to the protection of the environment."[68] On the day WARA's chairman had said the same thing as the bells of six churches in the district rang out the good news. At Stewkley a service of thanksgiving marked the reprieve; they did not forget to pray for the people of Foulness before going out to light another bonfire. At Cublington the landlord of the only public house gave free beer and food to all comers: "It is not every day you are saved from extinction by an airport." Two local activists amended their sign—from "We Shall Overcome" to "We *Did* Overcome."[69]

Did they claim too much? Some observers above the battle, such as Patrick Rivers, have remarked upon the "enormous outcry" from "the people of Cublington," and reached the conclusion that "under sheer, naked political pressure the Government gave in and Foulness was chosen instead."[70] In the judgment of Stanley Johnson, too, the switch to Foulness was not "a major victory for environmental sanity," but rather the result of "pressure mounted on the new Conservative Government to overturn the conclusions of the inquiry."[71] On the other hand, some active participants, such as John Flewin, the news agency man who acted as WARA's Public Relations Officer, deny even now that WARA could be called a pressure group.[72] A planning authority, Professor Peter Self takes a different tack, disputing the claim that the Roskill Report was "a highly rational report overturned by very biased pressure groups. . . ."[73] He recalls that nearly all the local authorities and planning bodies in the region favoured Foulness, which is true, but also believes them "more detached" (than the pressure groups), which is more dubious.[74] To anyone above the Third Airport battle, as Professor Self was not,[75] such authorities as the Buckinghamshire County Council (which spent £40,000 of its ratepayers' money, hardly for the benefit of South Buckinghamshire, e.g., Slough, close to Heathrow) seemed exceedingly biased. For a truly detached view, one might turn to someone predisposed towards the country: "As a professional environmental protester I certainly hope that neither WARA's strategy nor its manners are a blueprint. . . . the Cublington campaign, so far from being a blueprint, should be treated as the last shabby triumph of an outworn ethos"—thus, Christopher Hall in *The Countryman*.[76]

Whom had been overcome *is* clear: the Roskill Commission other than Professor Buchanan, which had spent two and a half years in futile exercise, at a cost to the taxpayer of over £1,100,000 "every penny of it wasted," as Bernard Levin remarked in his column.[77] In that sense taxpayers as a body, of course, had also been overcome.

Foulness-Maplin

Nor was their ordeal over. As Mr. Davies announced on 26 April, the new airport was to be developed within the context of a seaport, "in joint participation with private capital." As the British Information Services ("An Agency of the British Government") would explain the following year to an American public accustomed to thinking big: "Eleven thousand acres of windswept sandbanks northeast of the Thames Estuary are to be reclaimed for the world's first environmental airport . . . the as yet un-named airport" at Maplin Sands, just east of Foulness Island, with its four runways each 2.5 miles long, would entail the "biggest engineering project ever attempted in Britain." It would be part of a "$2.5 billion complex that will include a seaport, new road and rail links, and an airport city for at least 250,000 people which will be built some 15 miles away."[78] For Prime Minister Heath, Peter Walker, and others (including James Prior and Geoffrey Rippon, who would soon replace Mr. Walker at Environment when he took over Trade and Industry), Maplin Sands would be the British answer to Rotterdam as a first-class facility for the late twentieth and twenty-first centuries.[79]

Once again the Government proposed, and some entity other-than-the-Government disposed. That deliberately vague phrase is used because one is too close to events to be sure of one's ground. It does not seem that the disposition can be attributed to a local resistance movement. Foulness Island is too small in population and too working-class in social composition (compared with Cublington) to provide the sinews for such a long and costly war. Through Derrick Wood its chairman, the Defenders of Essex complained (e.g., about inadequate consultation) and wrote to *The Times*,[80] but looked beaten before they started.

If heaven did not protect the helpless, time proved to be on their side. Lord Balfour of Inchrye, formerly both a member of the board of BEA and a Conservative Minister, came out against the Maplin concept. By 1973 Lord Molson, who on behalf of the CPRE had stoutly defended Cublington at the expense of Foulness, was having second thoughts, wondering whether a third London Airport would be needed after all. That was in the Opposition's mind too: In the Commons in May, Anthony Crosland, generous with his metaphors, said that a report from the Civil Aviation Authority about air traffic and capacity in the London area had driven another nail in the "enormous coffin of this absurd white elephant of Maplin."[81] By the report stage in June, some

Government backbenchers were also aroused. Fifteen of them defied a three-line whip to vote with the Labour Opposition to insert a clause imposing delay on the start of the construction. Five or ten others abstained. Most of these critics wanted to see the project abandoned, being worried, above all, by the mounting cost projections. Two runways at Maplin, said Winston Churchill, would *each* cost £500 million. To spend that "would be nuts." By contrast an extra runway at Gatwick "would cost only a few million pounds."[82]

Figures published the following year did not entirely support the sharpness of that contrast. It was then calculated that two extra runways at Heathrow (not Gatwick certainly) would cost at the outside £90 million, whereas to create two *de novo* at Maplin would cost at least £850 million. So Mr. Churchill had the right order of magnitude for Maplin's cost, and it was staggering. However, the criticism of these backbenchers, which doubtless pleased the Treasury, seems to have found its mark: In an interview with a Minister a few days after their defiance, it was cited as an example of backbench influence as against the commoner view of backbenchers as lobby fodder.[83]

In the end, the Government got its way. In October the Maplin Development Act authorized in one fell swoop reclamation from the sea of certain land for an airport and seaport and planning permission for it. All the same the Government also agreed to delay the project, which meant (wrote Terence Bendixson) that "there are two extra years to get it right."[84] Within months rather than years, Labour was back in office (February 1974). As with Concorde and the TSR-2 in 1964, it decided to review the Maplin scheme. Ominously (to proponents), the Department of Environment withdrew the consultative documents put out on the subject of alternative road and rail connections.[85] Sure enough, the Maplin scheme was soon consigned to that special Valhalla reserved for public projects, heroic but dead, that Britain has eventually discovered she cannot afford or cannot stomach. This particular abandonment came some ten years after the original Government commitment to a third London airport at Stansted; six from the time when the Roskill Commission was appointed; three since the Government had abandoned the Roskill Commission to its fate and plumped for Foulness-Maplin.

From that apparent speeding up of the rate of abandonment, one might perhaps extract some comfort, taking it as a measure of the improvement in self-knowledge or self-perceptions. Up to 1972 the Port of London Authority alone had apparently invested over £500,000 in "research and field studies" at Maplin.[86] The Treasury was spared the £430 million's worth that went on military aircraft and missiles between 1951 and 1967 before these were put on the scrap heap. Even so it tends, somehow, to be rather cold comfort.

Equal Pay for Women

"Equality for Women—Is 1975 the Year?" asked the editor of *British Record* in January, addressing America's attentive public.[87] What prompted the question was that, late in 1972, the UN General Assembly had designated 1975 as International Women's Year. For Britain, the answer to the question was certain to be a full-throated "Yes." The Equal Pay Act of 1970 was due to come into full effect soon after Christmas. It would be buttressed by a new Sex Discrimination Act, foreshadowed by the White Paper *Equality for Women* published in September 1974. The Act would make it illegal to discriminate on grounds of sex in the domains of education, training and employment, housing, and the provision of services.

The legislative victory had been a long time a-coming—that is, two generations, even if we count only from the acquisition of some electoral power in 1918-1928, the period when British women were deemed to come of age politically. The concomitant Joint Committee on Women in the Civil Service (1920) sought equal treatment as one of its objectives. The Status of Women Committee (1935) had equality as its central preoccupation. Confining ourselves here to the equal pay issue, we perceive at once that the advance to 1975 was made in two stages: 1944-1961 and 1961-1975. In the first, women captured the redoubt that was essentially the Civil Service but also included local government, hence schoolteachers and the general and clerical grades (higher grades were already covered) as well as the nationalized industries.[88] In stage two, the inner citadel that was private industry fell to the insurgents, many of whom were indisputably male.

In retrospect, success in the public services marks the beginning of the end of wage discrimination in private industry as well. At the time, however, it must have seemed little more than the end of the beginning. In the week in January 1961 when women in most of the public services gained parity, Geoffrey Goodman of the *Daily Herald* was pointing out that, "No major industry had yet agreed to pay its women workers the *same rate* for doing the *same job* as a man." "It is incredible—but true—that the average national weekly earnings for men are £14: 2: 1d but for women the figure is only £7: 5: 0d. Engineering, by far the biggest single industrial group, pays unskilled men a basic rate of £8: 4: 10d and women £6: 13: 6d."[89] Altogether there seemed *prima facie* to be another "just case," as Bill Carron of the Amalgamated Engineering Union but speaking for all five engineering unions with women in membership, had in fact tried to persuade the engineering employers in 1958, drawing on the principles of natural justice.[90] But the walls of this Jericho were less likely to fall, especially as the Government would not go out of its way to help. As the Minister of Labour, John Hare, would tell the TUC in December, the Government was "not prepared to take any steps on" equal pay in private industry "because it does not wish to interfere with wage negotiation through collective bargaining."[91]

In October 1964, however, the Government changed hands, Labour having been returned to office on a manifesto that promised a Charter of Rights for all employees, including among the seven specified "the right to equal pay for equal work."[92] It hardly had time to settle in before the General Council of the TUC in November was writing to the Minister of Labour to remind him of the election undertaking and the ILO Convention.[93] Whether or not in response, an interdepartmental committee proceeded to examine the issue in terms of the prices and income policy, but its work, the Minister warned the TUC, would naturally take time. Unwilling to assume that no news was good news, the 1965 Congress pressed the Government to redeem its election pledge. This view was relayed to the Minister in January 1966, but before any concrete result could be expected, a general election unexpectedly supervened.

As it turned out, all was not lost. Labour was again returned, having confirmed in the manifesto that "we stand for equal pay for equal work and, to this end, have started negotiations."[94] Exchanges, certainly, there had been, and these were resumed on 21 April at a meeting between the Minister of Labour and representatives of the General Council. Confirming that the Government accepted the principle of equal pay, he quickly added that in the circumstances its implementation would have to be gradual. For the Government, he also turned down the deputation's request for ratification of the ILO Convention and matching legislation. On the other hand, ratification might be considered if agreement could be reached on "a broad plan of action"[95] by way of tripartite discussions between Government itself, the TUC, and CBI. Under the chairmanship of the Parliamentary Secretary, the three sides met in mid-July, when after "a general exchange of views" a representative working party of officials was set up to examine the problems[96] in depth and detail.

About two months later, a spokesman for the General Council expressed the view that the delegates who had met the Minister in April "did a good job. . . . They have got the caravan moving."[97] In Whitehall, however, caravans tend to move slowly even when the brake is off, and especially if the travellers are not of one mind. Between the CBI and TUC there were differences of opinion, principally over the very meaning of equal pay. The TUC sought the broad definition used in the ILO Convention ("equal pay for work of the same value"), but eventually accepted "equal pay for the same work" simply to allow a study of the costs to be undertaken on a common footing. Subject to the TUC's reservation about certain minimum conditions, the working party agreed that voluntary methods were to be preferred to legislation (unless Britain joined the EEC). After three meetings they submitted a report to the Minister containing those (and other) recommendations. It was discussed and approved at another tripartite meeting, when the Joint Parliamentary Secretary reaffirmed the Government's commitment to equal pay but regretted that it could not be fully implemented "in the present economic circumstances."[98] By now it was near Christmas 1967, not 1966.

Still, 1968 augured well, assuming that history and governments have some sense of the fitness of things: Human Rights Year, jubilee of the enfranchisement of women (so much for the power of the ballot box), and, for good measure, the centenary of the founding of the TUC. In late June, as if in acknowledgment of the ripeness of the time, Mrs. Barbara Castle, who had just emerged as First Secretary and Secretary of State for Employment and Productivity (the old Minister of Labour writ large and renamed partly (as to First Secretary) to confer status and partly to head off barroom jokes about her derived from the conjunction of Labour and Productivity), told the House that she proposed to start discussions with both sides of industry to have equal pay introduced in stages over an "appropriate period," tentatively defined as "a limit of seven years." Start she did the following month, receiving the CBI and TUC in separate deputations.

As agreed at those meetings, the study of the cost of introducing equal pay in the several sectors was now intensified, a joint study group relieving the working party of officials of the burden. Already, in May, the TUC had made one survey of its 118 unions with women members (one and three-quarter million of them, but concentrated—some 85 percent—in twenty unions) in order to elicit some facts and attitudes about equal pay. Now with the detailed prior agreement not only of the TUC but of the relevant unions and employers' organizations, the CBI submitted questionnaires to companies in thirteen or fourteen industries asking them to estimate the cost of introducing "equal pay for equal work."[99]

All this, of course, took time. It had been December before the CBI could even get the questionnaires out to the companies. While these three teams were thus travelling "along the cool sequester'd vale of life" in the classic consultative manner, others were far from keeping "the noiseless tenor of their way" (echoing Thomas Gray's *Elegy* written in a more leisurely age, the eighteenth century). In March 1968 the National Union of General and Municipal Workers (NUGMW), having the largest number of women members, went so far as to announce an equal-pay campaign. "We will press the Government," the general secretary, Lord Cooper declared, "for positive action to give fair pay to the women it employs."[100] That summer (as recorded in Chapter 5) the women sewing machinists at Ford's Dagenham plant took some positive action on their own account, stopping the job in process.

At the annual TUC meeting that soon followed, as if in retrospective endorsement of positive action, an amended resolution was carried against the platform stating that "the General Council shall call upon affiliated unions to support those unions who are taking industrial action in support of this principle" of equal pay.[101] Bloody but unbowed, the General Council held up its head and dug in its heels. A memorandum prepared by its Women's Advisory Committee for a conference at Congress House in November (200 representatives of sixty unions with women members) stated without equivocation that "representations to Government, advice and guidance to affiliated unions, is as far as the TUC itself can go in the campaign for equal pay. Negotiations with employers are matters for individual unions and only the members of those unions can determine the policy to be followed by their negotiators."[102] This line the General Council itself endorsed.

The Conference proved to be lively. If, as the General Council would later claim, no opposition to the memorandum was expressed,[103] the dominant note struck by the delegates was (as the *Guardian* reported) "strongly" critical of the TUC "for the sort of faintheartedness which has kept the issue on the resolution list for eighty years. . . . By the end of the day the platform partly looked almost part of the historical retrospect it had gently offered to open the affair." The subeditor surely caught the spirit of the occasion: "TUC Receives a Beating over Women's Pay."[104]

After the last speech was made, delegates (without the blessing or at least the official support of the TUC) joined in a lobby of M.P.s organized by a new arm of the movement, the National Joint Action Campaign for Women's Equal Rights. This had emerged as an unintended consequence of the women's strike at Ford's. Their action evoked such sympathy—"hundreds" of supporting letters reached their spokesman, Fred Blake, area organizer of the National Union of Vehicle Builders (NUVB)—that "it was realized, for the first time, that there was an enormous, unbridled pressure group for equal pay."[105] This crystallized as a formal organization at the House of Commons in October at a meeting attended by some 250 enthusiasts from the unions, parties, and women's groups, as well as the House itself. Made up of men and women equally even to the joint chairmanship (Christopher Norwood, M.P., and Mrs. Audrey Hunt) but with Mr. Blake as secretary, the Campaign Committee (NJACC) was now trying itself out for the first time.

It had something specific as well as general to lobby for. During the summer Mr. Norwood, with the support of such other Labour M.P.s as Mrs. Anne Kerr, had published a private members' bill to make a start on establishing equal remuneration for work of equal value within a year of enactment, by Orders in Council or regulations, by collective bargaining, or by some combination of the two. Lobbying for the bill, the NJACC marked down about a hundred members as potential allies, but by April Mr. Blake was expressing disappointment that those members "had not been able to win active Government support." A meeting with members in the House later in the month in an "attempt to reassert pressure for legislation"[106] seems not to have been productive. The bill failed, in any case, to get a Second Reading.

The pressure was sustained on a broader front—that is, a rally in Trafalgar Square in the latter part of May. Judged by the 30,000 once anticipated[107] (surely in a fit of euphoria), the turnout was poor: A thousand or so marched from the Victoria Embankment to the traditional meeting place, where their steadfastness was rewarded by speeches from Lady Summerskill, "Ernie" Roberts of the Engineers, and Christopher Norwood, M.P. They may also have felt rewarded by the publicity engendered for the central claim of their five-point charter: "equal pay for work of equal value."

What value should be attached to the campaign's own efforts or those of others is difficult to judge. Certainly, like the ILO vote and Convention in the early fifties, an external factor now impinged upon this domestic policy. In 1967 the Labour Government had sidled up to the EEC only to be immediately rebuffed by de Gaulle who again set his face against British membership. But in March 1969 he himself suffered something of a rebuff at the hands of the French electorate, and he chose to make it the occasion for another retreat to his village home, ceasing to exercise his functions as President of France. That at once improved British prospects of joining the club (or, as some said, cartel), and the club's charter—or Treaty of Rome—contained an equal-pay provision.

Internally, the Cabinet and the General Council of the TUC had by now locked horns over the reform of industrial-relations law. Since the First Secretary was herself deeply engaged in that trial of strength, she must surely have wished to satisfy the TUC on at least equal pay. But the key to that, within the context of whatever remained of an incomes policy, was obviously the cost of implementation, which was still being inquired into by the working party drawn from the TUC, CBI, and the Department of Employment and Productivity (DEP). What the Parliamentary Under Secretary at the DEP would soon say to the TUC, rather tartly, might have been applied to the Campaign as well: The Government accepted "full responsibility for discharging their commitment to equal pay, irrespective of any responsibility which may be accepted by trade unions to promote it."[108] By agreement, however, progress towards equal pay was on the basis of tripartite discussion and consultation.

From that meeting of minds there now came a report estimating that when equal pay (for equal work) was fully operative it would add 3.5 percent to the country's total wages and salaries bill. Taking that in her stride, the First Secretary announced to the annual Labour Party Conference in late September 1969 that in the forthcoming Parliamentary session she would introduce a bill to implement equal pay fully by the end of 1975. Early in October the DEP resumed consultations with both TUC and CBI, although of course at a different level, submitting "some tentative proposals about the form and content of the proposed equal pay legislation."[109] Already the CBI's nose had been put out of joint by the announcement at the Labour Party Conference: They thought that the policy should not begin to be implemented until the balance of payments had been held at £300 million for two years and even after that applied only gradually over at least seven years. In responding to the consultative documents, the CBI (inter alia) still objected to the timing and asked for some flexibility; expressed anxiety about the definition of equal pay (for the same or broadly similar work) as well as the hope that the concept of similarity would be very strictly interpreted; and opposed the stipulation of a single intermediate stage since an acceptable formula for it would be difficult to devise and the imposition of even one stage might prejudice negotiations with the unions.

On the other hand, the TUC itself was not overjoyed. Like the CBI, it disliked the basic concept, but for different reasons. Except perhaps where there had been job evaluation, women (it judged) would not get the equal pay for work of equal value that it had advocated. And the implementation of equal pay in the other sense—1976 was to be the first full year for it—was too far off. Having aggregated opinion within its own ranks, the TUC made representations along those lines, and submitted a new three-phase timetable designed to reach full equal pay by the end of 1972. By the end of 1971, even, women should have at least 9.5 percent of the comparable male rate of pay.

Remaining unconvinced, the First Secretary invited representatives of the General Council to a meeting "to discuss points of detail in the consultative document," which meant that she was not prepared to go over the basic principles again. But as a suitable date could not be found she went ahead and published the bill towards the end of January. Within two weeks she was opening the second reading debate with what *The Times* called her "pane-gyric. . . . The sun is shining from these benches this afternoon."[110] Apart from some small clouds of criticisms and doubts, the sun shone throughout the chamber until after ten o'clock, when the bill obtained an unopposed second reading. In one respect, at least, the bill undoubtedly justified the lyrical language of the Minister in charge: It provided a "means of redress" through the Industrial Tribunals Board that would be "speedy, informal, and accessible," whereas other countries ratifying the ILO Convention (as Britain herself soon would) typically left aggrieved women to fight for their rights through the courts.[111]

If the First Secretary was giving the TUC less than it sought, she was giving management in the relevant section of industry rather more. Through an executive council member, the Clothing Manufacturers Federation promptly uttered a two-pronged warning. The industry would experience great difficulty in deciding which jobs were to be covered. Of the work force of 460,000, 85 percent were women, so equal pay would cost a minimum of £50-60 million a year. The director of the Multiple Shops Federation who doubled as honorary secretary of the Retail Consortium also drew attention to the impact of equal pay upon the retail trade in which almost two out of three employees were women. Payrolls would be increased from 13-30 percent.

Bearing such remarks with fortitude, the Minister quickly resumed her discussions with the TUC, holding one meeting nine days after the second reading and another on 18 May. Again she held her ground but agreed for the sake of clarity to redraft the section of the Report stage, when an amendment was also passed enabling, but not requiring, the Secretary of State for Employment to make regulations that would give women 90 percent of comparable men's rates of pay by the end of 1973. That, obviously, bore some relation to one of the TUC's proposals. She was also "pressurized" (her own word)[112] by the TUC to bring occupational pensions schemes within the scope of the Bill. This, however, she resisted, not on principle but because she feared that the introduction of such "a highly complex subject" would delay her Bill. On that issue the TUC did not give way, and a suitable amendment was moved as late as the Report stage. It was withdrawn when the First Secretary agreed to have further talks with the TUC, though without commitment to its views. The upshot was a pledge to the House on 27 May to legislate in the next Parliament. When the General Council was officially informed, it "welcomed the Employment Secretary's response to their representations."

The CBI had not been inactive. During the Committee stage it briefed the Conservatives on various points the CBI considered should be raised and held talks with members of the Opposition in the Lords, but to no avail. Its only hope came in late May with the unexpected announcement of a June election. The bill was then "waiting to enter its committee stage in the Lords," where a bill to nationalize the ports was promptly abandoned when news of the election was received.[113] By agreement between Government and Opposition whips, several other measures were also abandoned in order to clear the decks for the Finance Bill (embodying the Budget) and the Consolidated Fund Bill before Parliament was prorogued on 29 May. The Equal Pay Bill, however, was spared. It received the royal assent on 29 May, with its provisions to come into effect on 29 December 1975.

For the TUC the only move left was to attempt to exploit that concession it had won late in the progress of the Bill empowering the Employment Secretary to make an order conferring 90 percent of the comparable men's rates on women workers by December 1973. In May 1972 the General Council made its opening gambit, which the Secretary countered by saying that before taking a decision he would have to await the report of the Office of Manpower Economics on the progress so far achieved. After it was published in August, the General Council found "no reason" to change its view that the order "needed to be made."[114] Time, however, was running out. In July, at the Prime Minister's invitation, tripartite talks (Government, TUC, CBI) had opened in the hope of forging a common policy against the serious inflation. After ten sessions between principals at Downing Street and Chequers, the talks collapsed on 2 November.[115] Four days later, the Prime Minister announced a ninety-day freeze on prices, dividends, and pay, and the corresponding Counter-Inflation (Temporary Provisions) Act received the royal assent just before the month was out. In those circumstances, obviously, the Government would not be making the 90 percent order, even if the CBI had supported the TUC, which it did not, arguing that such an order would create difficulties for employers and would in any case have to wait until stage two of the new incomes policy had been determined. With the White Paper on stage two in mid-January 1973, the Government made it plain that the order would not be made, although some adjustments would be possible so as to secure orderly progress towards the December 1975 objective. In a letter to the Employment Secretary, the General Council expressed extreme concern about that policy and asked for a meeting. This was held on 4 May, but the Secretary held out for fear of "inflationary repercussions."

So December 1973, with its hope of 90 percent comparability, came and went. The unexpected General Election of February 1974 then brought a new Government and Employment Secretary (Michael Foot) into play, but, as General Council representatives acknowledged when they met him on 10 June, any attempt to catch up on that comparability "would probably require new legislation." Despite the "current strains on Parliamentary time," however, since a Labour Government had put the Equal Pay Act on the statute book they expected "the present Labour Government to implement the intentions of its own Act."[116] In reply, Mr. Foot reaffirmed the Government's commitment and expressed its determination that there should be no backsliding: Any employer in breach of the Act when it became fully operative on 29 December 1975 would suffer "disastrous consequences."

When the time came, no one had to be sent to the guillotine. The Act was even complemented by another—the Sex Discrimination Act of 1975—making it illegal to discriminate on the basis of sex in training and employment, housing and the provision of services (and, from a later date in 1976, in education). This was a Labour measure but one to which the Conservatives had been committed since 1973, only they had run out of time and office. Such consensus may have been a special case of a carryover of legislative output from one time period (the Equal Pay Act) as input into a succeeding period (the Sex Discrimination Bill). No doubt there is nothing automatic about it. In this instance private members' bills in both Houses kept the wheels turning, aided, as in January 1972, by the Women's Lobby, apparently a coalition of forces and such journalists as Mary Holland of the *Observer*.[117] The efforts of Lady (Nancy) Seear, the Liberal economist, were important because her Anti-Discrimination Bill precipitated a House of Lords Select Committee, which recommended in its favour, which precipitated a Government decision to do the job itself. All the same the 1970 Act evidently carried over, and it was appropriate that both Acts should come into force (with that one exception) on the same day in December 1975.

It was also appropriate (if accidental) that the important new mechanism against sex discrimination, the Equal Opportunities Commission, with its staff of some 400, should have opened its doors in Manchester. It was there, perhaps even before the middle of the last century, that women seem to have first stirred themselves to overcome discrimination in electoral life. To it, in any case, belongs the great tradition, from Lydia Becker's Manchester Women's Suffrage Committee (1866) to the Pankhursts and beyond.

7 Representative Groups (II): Trades Union Congress

Sector 2

This is the land of the more highly politicized producer organizations. It is, as even the mere outline in Chapter 1 revealed, very densely populated. We confine ourselves to the TUC and, on the other side, principally to the CBI, hoping that what is lost numerically may be partly made up in political significance.

In the period under review, three types of approach patterns (or modes of representation to government) may be distinguished: (a) straightforward consultations, as in the exchanges leading up to the Race Relations Act, 1968; (b) consultations conducted against a background of public campaigning on the very same issue by some affiliated unions, as in the Equal Pay case just reviewed; and (c) consultations accompanied by public campaigning in which the General Council of the TUC itself is out in front, whether of its own volition or pushed there by a vociferous and angry membership. The outstanding example is the struggle against the reform of industrial-relations law within the period 1968-1974. It will be seen that (a) and (c) represent something like polar extremes of a continuum, and (b) some position in between.

Race Relations Act, 1968

This Act made "fresh provision with respect to discrimination on racial grounds, and . . . to relations between people of different racial origins," but here we concern ourselves only with the employment aspects, which is what concerned the TUC too. On that subject its representations were made within the framework of "the consultation of interests," which, if not yet a constitutional convention in the technical sense,[1] is of course a well established constitutional practice. Obviously, no Government would have dreamed of legislating on such an issue without initiating talks with the TUC and CBI, so the consultations were straightforward in that limiting sense of being initiated virtually automatically. The consultations were also straightforward in following a common pattern of letters and deputations, the exchanges extending over a considerable period (in this instance, more than a year and a half) before Parliament obtained sight of the Government Bill. But above all the consultations were straightforward in that, on the side of the consultees (authorised, perhaps to one's surprise, by the Oxford Dictionary), the General Council made the running, without the benefit of, or hindrance from, overt campaigning by individual unions. In short, the classic consultative mode in this sector: cool, unhurried, quietly disputatious, and essentially pre-Parliamentary.

Two phases stand out: August 1966 to April 1968, and April 1968 to October 1968.

Phase 1

At first the argument turned on what the consultation was and should have been about. When, in August 1966, the Treasury told the TUC (and CBI) that the Government had decided to insert in government contracts a clause to discourage and prevent racial discrimination by the firms contracted with, it did *not* invite "comment on the substance of the matter but only on the form of the clause, which would apply to engagement, upgrading, short-time working, dismissals, and selection for training, among other things." That displeased the General Council, who argued in some detail that "the practical implications of the proposed clause had not been fully considered." It concluded that "a conciliatory approach rather than one based on statutory provision was likely to be more successful in resolving cases."[2]

That policy the General Council pursued up hill and down dale as the Government's own intentions broadened into legislation against the problem in general. The journey, which was mostly up hill, included: (a) deputations to the Chancellor of the Exchequer, Ministers from Home Office and Ministry of Labour and Home Office spokesman (10 May 1967), attended also by CBI men; Home Secretary and Minister of Labour (June 1967 and March 1968); and (b) making common cause with the CBI, whose policy matched the TUC's. They held a joint meeting in January 1967 and speaking for "the interests primarily involved," produced a joint statement, which they sent to the Chancellor and also pressed on the Minister of Labour at a meeting of the National Joint Advisory Council later that month. He undertook to sound the Ministers concerned about holding a joint meeting, which they, however, proved reluctant to arrange. In April, after discussions with the CBI, the General Council specifically requested a meeting with the Minister of Labour and the Home Secretary, but at neither of the May meetings did the latter make himself available.

By April, both TUC and CBI had come around to a cautious contemplation of some legislative action. Whether, as one close observer apparently believes, they were influenced by the proposal made at the NCCI Conference in February by Oscar Hahn, president of the Birmingham Chamber of Commerce and chairman of the West Midlands Conciliation Committee of the Race Relations Board, is uncertain.[3] No doubt his proposal of new independent committees for voluntary conciliation within a statutory framework did precede the change of position, but as it happened the General Council denied that the Conference (or the PEP Report) gave grounds for modifying its policy.[4] It is possible that Mr. Hahn influenced the CBI's April proposal for further discussions about adding to the existing voluntary machinery some new component, but the CBI had been impressed by the PEP Report, which "indicated that discrimination in employment might be more widespread than employers had generally believed."[5] Certainly both peaks were acutely aware of the mounting outside pressures for legislative action. Hence even a comprehensive voluntary scheme might have to be supplemented by legislation.

In line with that most tentative decision, the General Council representatives at the May meeting asked that if legislation had to be framed, it should be "with the intention of supporting and extending voluntary procedures," to which the Minister of Labour sounded very sympathetic. When, on 19 June, the Home Secretary (Roy Jenkins) at last made himself available to the TUC and CBI, he informed them in his opening remarks that "the Government had so far taken no decision either individually or collectively" and also disclosed that "he was inclined to the view that the Government should declare discrimination illegal and that some form of ultimate sanction was necessary. . . ." He assured them, however, that "Legislation–if any were finally decided upon–would certainly allow industry the first opportunity to deal with the issues involved and would lay stress on the use of voluntary machinery." With that, the TUC and CBI had to be content. On 19 *July*, at the Home Affairs Committee of the Cabinet, Mr. Jenkins stated his case for legislation the following session, and easily obtained approval.[6] Soon he was telling the Commons that employment (and such services and facilities as housing and insurance) would be brought within the scope of the 1965 Race Relations Act.

In making his announcement, the Home Secretary naturally undertook to consult those concerned, including the TUC and the CBI about the terms of the amending legislation. At the end of the year the CBI "was still waiting to be consulted," as it would itself, perhaps reproachfully, remark.[7] The TUC fared little better. October saw preliminary informal discussion with civil servants at the Ministry of Labour, but that yielded so little that in November the General Council decided to try to find out, in the light of Ministers' previous undertakings to consult, what the Government had in mind. Neither the Council's nor the CBI's curiosity was satisfied until late January 1968, when a memorandum containing outline proposals for legislation arrived from the Minister of Labour. Discrimination on grounds of colour, race, ethnic, or national origin was to be unlawful not only in engagement, conditions of employment, promotion, and dismissal but also in admission to trade union membership and action by a trade union on behalf of its members. The only exception possible would be that (in the TUC's paraphrase) an employer should be allowed to refuse to engage a person on grounds of race or colour if his purpose was to preserve a balance between different racial groups in his labour force. Complaints would be passed by the Minister of Labour to whatever conciliation machinery existed by virtue of agreement of both sides of industry. In doing so, he would apply certain criteria, particularly that the machinery "must be open to all workers" (i.e., not only to union members). Complaints that remained unsettled, or were simply beyond the scope of the existing machinery, would be passed to the Race Relations Board. To this court of appeal, the Home Secretary would appoint the president of the Industrial Court as ex officio vice chairman and at least two other members after consultation with the TUC, CBI, and Minister of Labour. In the last resort, the Board would be able to start civil proceedings in the ordinary courts of law. The NCCI would be replaced by a Community Relations Board to work for harmony in the localities.

Discussing the memorandum in February, the General Council decided to hold informal talks with the CBI at office level and to seek a meeting with Ministers, which took place—Home Secretary and Minister of Labour—on 14 March. The thread running through the representations made on that occasion was (still) the desirability of assimilating the new machinery to "the system of industrial relations generally." Up to a point the Home Secretary proved responsive. Disclosing that the Minister of Labour would now enjoy discretion in the disposition of unsettled cases, enabling these to be referred back to the industry machinery rather than to the Race Relations Board automatically, he undertook to prepare a revised version of his proposals. Both Ministers were left with a TUC memorandum making various submissions, including the counter-proposal that the exceptional case visualized should not turn on the maintenance of an existing racial balance but on the "needs of a particular undertaking, its nature and circumstances."[8]

Whatever the rationale, the possibility of making an exception was one of the issues about which "a furious, though necessarily silent, struggle" was even then "taking place behind the scenes in Whitehall" (as Malcolm Southan of the *Sunday Times* reported).[9] "Necessarily silent" was used no doubt because the Bill was still being drafted. That did not prevent the leaking to the *Sunday Times* of the memorandum from which the Parliamentary draftsmen were presumably working, but the very fact might be taken as an index of the fury. Equal Rights, a successor to CARD (Campaign Against Racial Discrimination), led the opposition. It wanted to eliminate the racial balance clause—the exception to the rule—and sought some other changes especially to strengthen enforcement.[10] A week after the Bill was published Equal Rights sent a ten-page commentary to 200 M.P.s of all parties, some 50-60 of whom were believed to be already on the side of the angels.[11]

This clash of opinion evidently made the Government think again on at least the racial balance clause. On 8 April the Parliamentary Under-Secretary of the Ministry of Labour told General Council representatives that "the original proposal allowing an employer to maintain a racial balance amongst his workers had been reconsidered, and it was now proposed that some limitation might be allowed on the proportion of employees who had not been wholly or substantially educated in this country, but no limitation would be permissible on grounds of race" (i.e., on the indigenous colored). The TUC request for consultation could be satisfied by six monthly meetings with the Minister of Labour and by the nomination with TUC endorsement of trade union members to the local committees of the Board. In other respects the Departments stood pat. Regretting that, the deputation "otherwise welcomed" the revised proposals "as a very great improvement on those put forward earlier."

Phase 2

The Bill itself was published the following day 9 April, inaugurating what we have here identified as the second phase. It followed the lines made familiar over a year and a half or more of private discussions and to some extent agreed, but made one important departure about which the General Council had not only not been consulted but not even informed.[12] The Race Relations Board would have the power to initiate an investigation even where no complaint had been lodged; where a complaint related to a breach of an undertaking previously given, the Board would be able to withdraw the case from industry for its own consideration. At its meeting later in the month the General Council discussed the terms of the Bill in the light of the meeting at the Ministry of Labour. Still apprehensive, it expressed various reservations, but relying upon assurances about regular consultation and review, decided to accept the Bill as "broadly satisfactory."

What, however, was the view of the official (as against the private) Opposition? It came out against the Bill. Hardly news, except that, in keeping with the Leader of the Opposition's (Mr. Heath's) earlier pledge that "race relations must not become a party issue," he and his principal colleagues in the Shadow Cabinet had originally intended "to give the Bill an unopposed second reading, and then to seek to improve it in committee stage." They fell victim, however, to a "Westminster version of gunboat diplomacy" played out initially in the Home Affairs Committee, a component of the 1922 (or Conservative backbenchers') Committee.[13] Learning that the Bill was due to be published at 4 p.m. on Tuesday, 9 April, the Committee's officers put off the usual Monday meeting until 5 p.m. that afternoon. Whether as a result of an autonomous groundswell or of vigorous whipping by the rapidly formed anti-Bill lobby, 150 members squeezed into Committee Room 14 for an unusually well attended meeting under the benevolent guidance of Quintin Hogg, the Shadow Home Secretary. Although no vote was taken, he reported the following evening the impression (not confined to him) that the Party wanted a reasoned amendment, not an unopposed Bill. Meanwhile Ronald Bell (South Bucks) had drafted such an amendment, for which, according to the Whips, eighty Conservatives stood ready to vote even if the Shadow Cabinet stayed neutral. Cornered, the Shadow Cabinet had little option but to give way, and before Mr. Bell tabled this amendment (if he had really intended to go so far), it authorized another version from the hands of Anthony Barber (the party chairman) and Sir Michael Fraser (of the Conservative Central Office). Unlike Mr. Bell's motion, the Shadow Cabinet condemned racial discrimination but declined "to give a second reading to a Bill which, on balance, will not in its practical application contribute to the achievement of social harmony," which really set the cat among the Labour pigeons.[14]

On the day for the Second Reading (Shakespeare's birthday), the immigrant community, for which Equal Rights did not speak, made its displeasure known. The West Indian Standing Committee, for example, placed pickets outside the Home Office with placards reading "Race Relations Bill Is a Toothless Tiger" and "Race Relations Bill Is A Farce: Strengthen It or Scrap It!" The Government went on, however, to an easy victory, all the easier because some 20-25 Conservatives gallantly abstained from voting for the Shadow Cabinet's instant policy.

That was a victory for the principle of the Bill; it did not mean that the Government (or the TUC) was home and dry. The divisions between Government and Opposition and within the Opposition foreshadowed for the committee stage that possibility of penetration by pressure groups to which Professor Samuel Finer long ago drew attention in discussing the conditions of successful group influence in Parliamentary proceedings.[15] At the committee stage of the 1965 Bill, backbench critics, partly reflecting CARD's policies, had tried hard but in vain to move the Government. Four times they "pushed their amendments to a division . . . but on each occasion they were defeated by an alliance between the Front Benches."[16] That was over the scope of the Bill: a victory as to the method of enforcement—conciliation instead of criminal sanctions in dealing with discrimination—was consummated at the committee stage but already secured beforehand precisely as a result of an unusual alliance of pressure group/backbenchers and H.M. Opposition, who squeezed the Home Secretary/Government into submission.

The 1968 situation was more complex, especially for the TUC (from whose vantage point this sketch is being mainly written). Throughout the long first phase, the TUC had worked hand in glove with the CBI, who deemed it prudent to leave the tactical execution mainly to those enjoying a special relationship with the Government. But the CBI had naturally had detailed consultations with the Department during the drafting of the Bill and had been pursuing some goals peculiar to it; for example, that "an employer should not be held liable for the unlawful acts of his employees if he could show that he had taken all reasonably practical steps to prevent them from doing such acts."[17]

So as the Bill reached Standing Committee B in early May, the peaks are resuming their traditional connections: the TUC gravitated towards the Government team of ten or eleven, led by James Callaghan, who had replaced Roy Jenkins at the Home Office. For the employment clauses, the TUC's link was Eric Heffer, the Walton (Liverpool) member sponsored by the Woodworkers (now in the Union of Construction, Allied Trades and Technicians). The CBI reached out to the main Opposition team of seven, led by Quintin Hogg, the link being especially Eldon Griffiths, the former *Time* magazine man returned to his native land. Beyond them stood the five-man Radical Right, including Ronald Bell and Sir Frederick Bennett who would carry their root-and-branch opposition to the Bill as far as the Third Reading. Straddling the scene was an all-party group: nine Labour (four of them lawyers), two Conservatives, and one Liberal. Out to widen the scope of the Bill and strengthen the enforcement powers of the Race Relations Board, they constituted Equal Rights's point of access. Before each of the thirteen sittings, Equal Rights's legal advisers briefed the Labour and Conservative members in separate sessions and helped them to prepare amendments.[18]

This symbiotic relationship proved to be productive. Thus section 2(2) of the Act, which enumerates examples of the facilities and services in which discrimination would be unlawful, now specifies the services of "local and other public authority" as well as of "any business, profession or trade." That specification of local and other public authority was the handiwork of one of the Labour lawyers in the all-party group, Ben Whitaker, who took up an Equal Rights amendment.[19] Other ground, too, was gained and held, but not in the field of employment. There the exceptional racial balance provision, Section 8(2), already much discussed in phase 1, precipitated a battle royal. Equal Rights (and other bodies) had made forceful representations against it and now, working through the all-party group, tabled an amendment to delete that section. This seemed certain to prevail because the Opposition Front Bench also had an amendment in the same sense, which altogether tended to produce the Finer conditions for successful group influence in this setting: *Equal Rights/all-party group + Opposition vs. Government*. In anticipation of defeat, the Government revealed a disposition to compromise, but apparently then learned, just before the section was debated, that the Opposition Frontbench was going to withdraw its amendment. And withdraw it did, thus destroying the conditions for a successful squeeze. The spokesmen for the TUC and the CBI spoke up, and the all-party (Equal Rights) amendment went down to defeat.

Even on this ground of employment, not quite hallowed but carefully prepared during phase 1, some changes were made. Section 8(1) of the Bill provided for a transitional period: Employers of not more than ten people would be exempt for two years, after which employers of not more than five would enjoy a further two-year grace period. Reflecting CBI policy, the Opposition Frontbench tried to secure permanent exemption for employers with a work force of not more than twenty-five. Since that would have driven a coach and horses through the Bill, the Government resisted the amendment, but Roy Hattersley (DEP) did undertake to consider raising the temporary exemption level from ten to twenty-five and then from five to ten. In due course that was in fact done. Again, the CBI wanted to eliminate the liability of employers for their employees' acts of discrimination. Mr. Griffiths "failed to convince the Committee"[20] of the wisdom of that, but the CBI later made a point of claiming that "in particular a proviso was secured that an employer should not be held liable for the unlawful acts of his employees if he could show that he had taken all reasonable steps to prevent them from doing such acts."[21] This is covered by Section 13(3) of the Act, which provides that an employer who has taken such "reasonable practicable" steps can indeed offer that as a defence in civil proceedings.

In general, however, Anthony Lester (who, as legal adviser to Equal Rights observed the proceedings as closely as any outsider can) is correct in his judgment that "the employment provisions were scarcely changed by the Committee. . . ." But his explanation requires some refinement. The employment provisions were scarcely changed (he wrote), "probably because the Government had become so firmly committed to them in the course of its negotiations with the CBI and the TUC."[22] But those provisions would not have been left largely unchanged had the tactical situation been different—that is, had the all-party group (Equal Rights) been able to line up with the Opposition in a squeeze of the Government. As Mr. Lester knows better than most, even the crucial racial balance exception to which the Government had long been committed, almost reached the point of being defeated by such a combination of forces.

We should also beware of reading too much into an explanation expressed in terms of a Government commitment reached after negotiations with CBI and TUC. The implied attribution of power to these bodies, which were naturally seen as adversaries by Equal Rights, might have been intentional or unintentional. Either way, we have to recall that the legislation itself was imposed on both bodies, which had made common cause against it, to no avail. So "negotiations" is not very apt if it means what Professor Harry Eckstein meant in his well-known study of the British Medical Association: "Negotiations take place when a governmental body makes a decision hinge upon the actual approval of organizations interested in it, giving the organizations a veto over the decision. . . ."[23] In race relations the Government had decided what it wanted to do and did it; what the others did (CBI and TUC) was to make the best of a bad job. Of course, once that position was reached, all three entities would try to keep the basic arrangement intact. That is the extent to which the prior discussions of Government and TUC/CBI explain why the employment clauses emerged more or less unscathed from the committee stage.

From that stage, the Radical Right emerged more dissatisfied than ever, since, as Sir Frederick Bennett would say later, "no substantial improvements" had been achieved.[24] Still unreconciled when the Report stage was reached in early July, they prepared to attack the immediately following Third Reading, on which, once again, the Shadow Cabinet decided to abstain. With others, Ronald Bell, architect of the Second Reading coup that forced the Shadow Cabinet into a vote, put down "a wrecking motion on which they intend to mount a straight vote against the measure." But, to make the confusion worse confounded, a number of Conservative backbenchers, including nine of the eighteen members of the executive of the 1922 Committee (among them, Sir Frederick Bennett), tabled, without giving the whips advance notice, a reasoned amendment virtually identical with the one that the Shadow Cabinet had been forced to adopt for the Second Reading.[25]

Meanwhile, also with an eye on the Parliamentary timetable, another component of the Radical Right had taken to the streets. As the critical week approached, members of the Immigration Control Association (a motley crew of Smithfield and other market workers, Right-wing militants, and leaders of tenant organizations) carried "ban immigration" petitions into Downing Street. Anticipating and perhaps hoping for a counterdemonstration, one of the leaders told a reporter: "We won't attack them with the alien methods of the knife, bludgeon, and cosh. We will defend ourselves with our good old Anglo-Saxon methods—knuckles."[26] But the need for bare knuckles did not arise, nor did the direct action darkly hinted at for the following Sunday materialize. By then the Parliamentary struggle had been, to their way of thinking, lost. For the Third Reading, the Shadow Cabinet was not caught off balance: It kept control of most of its army (i.e., most of the Opposition abstained). As many as forty-five of its troops did disobey orders and vote for the Bennett amendment. But that "trauma" (as David Wood of *The Times* called it) soon passed. At a quickly summoned meeting of the 1922 Committee executive, the rebels made their peace: "Their apologies and explanations [were] then accepted with almost too much eagerness by the full 1922 Committee that later crowded into a Commons committee room to hear the closing chapter of the revolt. . . ."[27]

That was almost the closing chapter of the Bill, too. Its passage through the Lords was by no means uneventful, but it received the Royal Assent on 25 October and came into force on 26 November. Both sides of industry then proceeded to assist indirectly in the administration of the Act. Affirming that "it was in the interests of industry to see that the Act operated effectively," the CBI undertook to keep in touch with the DEP and the Race Relations Board "so as to provide a channel for advice between industry, the Government and the Board." One immediate result of this cooperation was the publication by the Board of an employers' guide to the Act.[28] In the New Year, the General Council of the TUC reviewed a note of guidance prepared by the Board on the application of the exceptional racial balance clause. The final draft "embodied some modifications" it had suggested.[29] This was some two-and-a-half years after the TUC had first been consulted on the issue of racial discrimination in employment.

Equal Pay Act, 1975

The long revolution culminating in this Act was sketched in the previous chapter essentially from the point of view of women's organizations. We return briefly to the subject in order to illuminate another facet of the TUC's approach to government.

For the race relations measure, the TUC not only had the trade union field to itself but, by tacit agreement with the CBI, championed industry as a whole. For equal pay the TUC shared the field with some individual unions. If they did not exactly march shoulder to shoulder, they heard the same drummer and moved in the same general direction. In explaining the differences between the two situations, one variable is as obvious as it is fundamental. In the first, the TUC was reacting to something that the Government proposed to do: It was being consulted about Government policy. In the second, the Government, having steeled itself to make (in its election manifesto) a commitment for which it had never shown much enthusiasm, needed to be kept up to the mark. In other words, in the case of equal pay, the unions had to show initiative. That was all the more necessary because on this issue they could not expect even moral support from the CBI, which naturally worried about how employers would foot the bill.

Up to a point, such differences did not divert the General Council from the classic consultative mode: correspondence with Ministers, face-to-face discussions with them, research, conducted in this instance by a tripartite working party and then a special study group, and so on. But then other subgroups within the TUC began to assert themselves. Thus, in July 1966, the Women's Advisory Committee of the TUC "expressed its concern that no woman had participated in the talks with the Minister," especially as the General Council had two women members. It "also expressed the opinion that the General Council's representatives attending the tripartite talks later in the month should include a woman."[30] But, as delegates to the September Congress would complain, the General Council "saw fit to ignore this expression of opinion by its own Advisory Committee." In the same year the TUC Women's Conference resolved that "some action . . . be taken in order to impress the Government with the urgent need for legislation on equal pay"[31] (i.e., the "Conference called for the lobbying of members of Parliament to put pressure on the Government.")[32] As the women activists readily acknowledged, that body did not constitute a policy-making conference and so any decisions they took would not be binding on the General Council. However, the decisions and the whole tendency constituted pressure on the General Council from within, building up the head of steam released at the Women's Conference of November 1968 (as already recorded). By then the women sewing machinists at Ford's had served the cause by stopping sewing, and some individual unions had promised to campaign if not by the same method.

Action by individual unions, especially in the collective bargaining sense, is doubtless what the General Council considered appropriate. General Secretary George Woodcock put it bluntly at the 1967 Congress, in the context of incomes policy but following a debate on equal pay. Echoing in part Frank Cousins, the T & G leader, Mr. Woodcock remarked: "... I should like to repeat on this business of equal pay what he has said: that we do too much talking about what the General Council should do and what the Government should do when a lot of it could be done yourselves without bothering us about it if you really believed in it."[33] For the General Council, G.H. Lowthian spoke just as plainly the following year: "... the means for achieving equal pay are matters for unions themselves to decide, and God knows you will be telling us in various other debates this week how important is the autonomy of the unions."[34] But respect for autonomy was not the only reason why the General Council wanted to keep its distance. Ever since Labour returned to power in 1964, the General Council had been in consultation with the Departments on this issue. Tripartite talks (Government, CBI, TUC) had been held, a working party established. Specialists were even then sitting down together to work out the figures. Now every method of approach to Government tends to have an opportunity cost for the actor: Some other method foregone or underplayed. The opportunity cost of orderly, empirically based exchanges with government tends to be the militancy foregone. So, granted the need to continue the consultation generally and the joint research in particular, the General Council could hardly join in the fray. Nor could it comfortably back unions that went on strike for equal pay, which was what the amendment moved at the 1968 Congress really ultimately meant. ("The General Council shall call upon affiliated unions to support those unions who are taking industrial action in support of this principle.") Accordingly, the Council refused to commit itself in advance to automatic support of industrial action irrespective of any other consideration and opposed the amendment only to see it carried.

Still, it's one thing to take a horse to water. ... At the Women's Conference in November (as noted in Chapter 6), it was made clear that the General Council still intended to keep its distance: "Representations to Government, advice and guidance to affiliated unions is as far as the TUC itself can go in the campaign for equal pay." And that, effectively, was that. Aided by such unions as the NUVB, the campaign warmed up in the spring of 1969, but the General Council ploughed its own furrow to the end.

Industrial Relations Reform (Epilogue 1969-1974)

To the First Secretary, Barbara Castle, the attitude of the trade unions to equal pay symbolized one of their fundamental weaknesses. "What had the unions ever done about it at the bargaining tables since the TUC passed its pious resolution in 1888? Now they wanted a Labour Government to do it for them—by law." She began to wonder whether the trade unions were not "chiefly interested in the Labour Party as a cover for their own inadequacies." On the other hand, in return for the legislation they wanted, what were they "prepared to do for a Labour Government? Ruin it with inflation and ludicrously irresponsible strikes and then vote at the polls against the consequences of their own anarchy?"[35] That point of view, echoing in the last eleven words Aneurin Bevan's comment on Labour's loss of the 1959 Election, its third successive defeat, was one element in Cabinet-level thinking that gave rise to the Industrial Relations Bill of 1969, the first legislative step in the contemporary period to reform the law governing industrial relations.

Such were the attitudes and beliefs, obviously highly cathected (or emotionally charged), of the Minister responsible for the celebrated White Paper, *In Place of Strife* and the concomitant Industrial Relations Bill, which probably brought more strife to the Labour Movement in the broadest sense (Cabinet-Parliamentary Labour Party, including the Trade Union Group-National Executive Committee-TUC) than it had ever experienced. This fascinating story of high drama and low politics cannot be reanalysed here. All one can do is to explore the nature of the group-Government interaction at the outset and then after the Bill had been abandoned.

Long before the White Paper was published, the general secretary of the TUC, George Woodcock, had been invited to the Department (of Employment and Productivity) (DEP) to see a draft of the proposals and pass preliminary judgment upon them. According to report, he judged that there was nothing in the draft to which the unions could "fundamentally object."[36] But he also begged leave to tell the General Council, "ever sensitive on the subject of prior consultation," what was in the wind. To this the First Secretary, anxious or even desperate for his goodwill, agreed. So he told the General Council in confidence, apparently at its meeting on 18 December. Far from being won over, the Council expressed concern, and reaffirmed its opinion that "legislation as a method of dealing with industrial disputes" was "inadvisable and inappropriate."[37]

So when, at a one-and-a-half hour meeting with the First Secretary on 30 December, General Council representatives were officially, though still secretly, notified—she "outlined the 17 main points which the Government proposed to publish in its White Paper"—and they expressed "surprise and concern,"[38] that has to be taken as a ritualized response. The concern, however, was genuine. For although the seventeen points included such gains as compulsory recognition of unions and a right of appeal against unfair dismissal, these were in the Council's eyes greatly outweighed by such new-fangled ideas as a conciliation (or cooling-off) period to head off unofficial strikes; a compulsory ballot before major strikes; giving power to a Minister, as a last resort, to settle interunion, especially demarcation, disputes—all of which would carry fines as sanctions. "It is more like a Tory policy," remarked a General Council delegate after the meeting.[39] That is not what it looked like to the CBI at a two-hour meeting with the First Secretary the following day. If that was indeed intended essentially for an exchange of views, it was because the CBI listeners could agree to so little. They thought that the organization might swallow legislation against unfair dimissals provided that voluntary procedures could be tried before the law was invoked. But they pronounced anathema on most of the other proposals, including enforced union recognition. These the director-general, John Davies (who would be transformed into a Tory Minister in 1970) likened to "taking a nutcracker to crack a cannon ball," or, even more unkindly, "imagining you can get rid of a problem by blowing on it."[40]

On 2 January the TUC deputation returned to the scene of the crime, where, guided by Mrs. Castle, they reexamined, in terms of interunion disputes, the conciliation pause, compulsory strike ballots and other obnoxious proposals, what the TUC would come to call the penal clauses. All the deputation obtained was the cold comfort of clarification. That ended the first phase. It had been pre-Parliamentary in more than the usual sense, since the Cabinet as well as mere backbenchers had been deliberately kept in the dark as far as possible. From Congress House in Bloomsbury (the TUC headquarters), the scene had been a simple one: somewhat to one side, the Trade Union Group of the PLP (addressed by First Secretary on 17 December) and the CBI, and in the foreground, the DEP (or First Secretary). That sparsely populated scene vanished on 3 January 1969, when the draft White Paper came before the Cabinet for the first time.

Government spokesmen were by now telling reporters that part of the already developing uproar was really the consequence of the Government's special effort on this occasion to consult interested parties before rather than after the publication of the White Paper. What is true is that the contents of a draft White Paper are not usually disclosed to an outside group in such detail that good accounts appear in the morning papers before the issue has been discussed in Cabinet or even studied in Cabinet Committee. Or rather, such a White Paper would usually pass through or be constructed in a Cabinet Committee, standing or ad hoc. An ad hoc Cabinet Committee was already available, created in 1967 precisely in anticipation of the Donovan (Royal Commission) Report. Instead the First Secretary relied on her own resources— Ministerial colleagues and especially civil servants. Why was the normal procedure not followed? The Prime Minister's explanation for posterity touches only the narrower issue of why the TUC was informed on 30 December and the Cabinet on 3 January: The reason "was the extremely tight timetable on which we were working to bring out both Barbara Castle's White Paper, and Dick Crossman's draft of his revolutionary incomes-related superannuation scheme in good time for Parliamentary discussion, when the House resumed on 20th January 1969."[41] But that does not explain why he agreed to short-circuit the usual Cabinet Committee procedure, which he himself had done much to strengthen since he became Prime Minister, especially since 1967 (when he ruled that in general an appeal to Cabinet from a Committee was to be made only with the agreement of the Committee chairman).[42] There is only one rational explanation of the short-circuiting: The First Secretary and Prime Minister, trying to take a giant's step beyond Donovan, must have feared that they would be tripped up by one or more of their colleagues if they followed the prescribed route.

Nor, for the same reason, could the P.M. and First Secretary make use of the Parliamentary Committee, that inner circle of the Cabinet—about ten in all—which he had created in April 1968[43] to cope with major current issues and to peer into the future. Serviced by the Secretariat, it was no less official than the Cabinet as a whole, which indeed for a time it supplanted, meeting twice a week in the traditional way, thus squeezing the full team of twenty-three into fortnightly foregatherings. Perhaps it did fail in its objective of providing "some of the co-ordination and cohesion hitherto lacking," as Alan Watkins, political columnist of the *New Statesman* would later charge.[44] But his evidence—"the evidence is in Mrs. Castle's White Paper on union reform"—is unconvincing. For that purpose the Parliamentary Committee could hardly have been used. In particular it contained James Callaghan, who had fought the P.M. for the leadership of the Parliamentary Labour Party (PLP) in 1963, coming in third behind George Brown. He had a power base in the extra-Parliamentary Party, being Treasurer, the choice of Conference (i.e., of the unions); that gave him a seat on the National Executive Committee. And the new General Secretary of the Party, Harry Nicholas (like Mr. Callaghan, a former union official) found him *simpatico*, perhaps partly because Mr. Callaghan had promoted his appointment. So, for one reason or another, Mr. Callaghan was expected to oppose the White Paper, and even (in the reformers' judgment) to "tip off" the unions far in advance. All in all, the reformers must have calculated that they would have to do good by stealth.

They failed, overcome by some combination of intense TUC pressure, a revolt within the PLP, and the ready availability, not in the wings but in the Cabinet itself, of an alternative leader, Mr. Callaghan. "Casca with a rubber dagger," the Left had called him,[45] but on the Right Ronald Butt knew better: "Nobody should doubt for a moment his ambition, his political sophistry in Labour Party terms, or his ruthlessness when he becomes convinced that ruthlessness is needed."[46] It seems as clear as anything can be at present that the P.M. stood to lose both the Bill and the premiership.

Whatever the precise weight of these variables, it is certain that the political situation favoured the TUC. By the time the General Council ambled into No. 10 on Tuesday morning, "news had been travelling at an indecent speed." The leaders at least "had a pretty good idea that they had won the battle,"[47] among them, General Secretary Victor Feather. For their part the P.M. and First Secretary of course also had a pretty good idea that those leaders had harboured such a pretty good idea; they suspected that "some of the TUC leaders had been fully briefed about the Cabinet's line before"[48] the face-to-face decision on 18 June. Despite that, they presented a bold front; Mr. Wilson, who naturally bore the burden, seems to have acquitted himself exceptionally well. But the General Council "confirmed that they would not modify their attitude to a change of rule"[49] (i.e., they simply wouldn't do it). They would provide a "solemn and binding agreement," which they did. This the P.M. had to brandish like a trophy to the Party and nation; ostensibly in return he and the First Secretary abandoned the Bill and promised not to do anything like it again in the lifetime of that Parliament.

Epilogue

Bound by that promise, the DEP in the autumn sent the TUC an outline of "a comprehensive Bill which the Government intended to introduce to give effect, broadly, to those proposals in the White Paper *In Place of Strife* which had not been superseded by the agreement reached between the Government and the General Council on June 18th 1969."[50] Perhaps sensitive to charges of inadequate consultation last time round, the DEP offered "consultative documents on each subject to be covered by legislation," of which there seemed to be fifteen. A series of exchanges on the basis of the documents prepared the ground for a meeting of General Council and First Secretary in late March 1970 and a new Industrial Relations Bill, published on 30 April. After scrutinizing it, the General Council submitted "a note of comment" to the First Secretary and asked for a meeting before the Second Reading, expected in early June. Time, however, was running out. On 13 April, even before the Bill was published, the P.M. had virtually decided that a General Election should be held in mid-June. On 12 May, the Management Committee (or Inner Cabinet) "unanimously endorsed" his proposal to recommend a dissolution.[51] It came on 29 May. Unlike the equal pay measure, the Industrial Relations Bill was lost.

In winning handsomely, the Conservatives earned the right to try their hand at industrial relations reform, a fundamental feature of their election manifesto. They showed that they meant business by putting it into the Queen's Speech in July. By early October the basic Conservative approach of encasing industrial relations in law had been turned into one of the most massive Consultative Documents (or Green Papers) of recent times, about 11,000 words of it. Taking up some two and a half pages in *The Times*, it cannot be dealt with here. We may simply recall that some of Labour's hated proposals resurfaced, such as cooling-off periods and secret ballots before certain strikes. Since these were exactly the issues on which the TUC had dug in its heels so successfully, their inclusion alone was ominous, prompting Eric Heffer in the House to wish the Government "the best of luck." But there was much more, including a proposal to outlaw the closed shop (meaning that you can't *get* a job, much less *keep* one, unless you join the union), and above all a Labour Court to adjudicate upon industrial relations through an industrial code. Familiar elsewhere but new to Britain, this would be on a par with the High Courts and so, in the last resort, would have the power not merely to fine but, for contempt, imprison. Unions as such as well as individuals might have to pay up and would in any case have to register (and so have their affairs scrutinized by a newly endowed Chief Registrar) if they were to enjoy their various immunities at law.

In examining the TUC's approach pattern on this occasion, we find a fundamental and startling contrast to that traced in 1968-69. On this occasion the consultative system broke down; for the first time in thirty years, the TUC's access to government at a very early stage in (relevant) policy formulation was denied. The TUC seemed to have embarked on the familiar course in early September, when Victor Feather saw the new P.M., Edward Heath, for almost two hours. According to Mr. Feather, the P.M. told him that a consultative document would be available at the end of the month, "that it will be a genuinely consultative document, and that its proposals will be susceptible to change in response to reasoned argument."[52] But nothing was arranged and when (24 September) the General Council asked the new Secretary of State for Employment, Robert Carr, for a meeting, he declined to arrange one until after the Consultative Document had been published. By contrast the Secretary of State and his officials did receive a CBI deputation beforehand.[53]

This difference in treatment could be defended. The CBI had something specific to discuss other than the Document—that is, the recommendations of the (Len) Neal Working Party, which had recently completed a six-month study of providing a legal framework for industrial relations. So with the CBI there could be a meeting of minds, whereas the TUC simply rejected the approach through law, favouring voluntarism, which others, including Mrs. Castle in 1968-69, identified as laissez-faire.

Still, established expectations were upset at the very start: the TUC had grown accustomed to at least appearing to be in on the ground floor. Two other differences in the process and even the nature of consultation emerged soon afterwards, fuelling the fire. Like the CBI, the TUC received the document on 5 October, with a request for comments within six weeks. Even the CBI called this timetable "extremely tight." So it was for such a massive Green Paper, but Mr. Carr and the new team of party managers had learned something from the seemingly endless comings-and-goings of May-June 1969. They let it be known that they were not "prepared to allow consultations to turn into a delaying action against the Bill."[54] So, evidently, they decided to move the interests along at a brisk pace. The TUC's request for an extension of time was specifically denied on the ground that the Government was not prepared to delay publication of the Bill.

Even more significant was the change in the meaning or nature of consultation, or at least towards making that meaning more explicit. At a two-and-a-half-hour meeting on 13 October with the finance and general purposes committee (the TUC's "inner Cabinet"), the Secretary of State made it plain "that the proposals were based on eight central pillars, which the Government had no intention of removing." These "essentially non-negotiable provisions" (as the TUC would later call them) included not only the various new ideas but also the older Labour ones (cooling-off periods, compulsory strike ballots, and so forth) on which the TUC had already pronounced anathema. Would the Secretary be willing "to set aside his proposals and enter forthwith into discussions with the TUC and the CBI about how best to improve the voluntary system"? The answer, of course, was "No."[55]

The meeting marked a real turning point. As he came away from it, Mr. Feather commented: "I think we are on a loser as a country with this consultative document." As for the trade union movement, it "would not want to talk about details."[56] Since details were all the Secretary was willing to talk about, that foreshadowed the end of consultation as the TUC had come to understand it since 1940. So, what other methods of approach to government were left? Broadly, the TUC could continue as a regular pressure group but trying alternative approaches, or it could mobilize industrial power to serve political ends (the modification of public policy), widely regarded as falling outside the range of acceptable methods.

Both these modes of action were discussed by the General Council at a special meeting on 15 October and again two weeks later. From the first, predictably, the idea of political strikes found no favour, and on the second occasion the Council went further, agreeing unanimously to advise unions not to support unofficial demonstrations or strikes against the Bill.[57] Equally predictably, shop stewards disagreed, proceeding to mount the series of unofficial demonstrations and strikes outlined in Chapter 5. What the Council favoured was something thought up by its finance and general purposes committee even before they dispersed after seeing Mr. Carr on 13 October: a great public campaign, a common enough technique but not practised by the TUC for many a long day. Such a campaign culminating in another Special Congress in February 1971—just before the final Commons vote on the Bill—was approved by the Council on 15 October. As a start about four hundred senior officials from affiliated unions were brought to Congress House on 12 November for a discussion of the strategy to be pursued in this campaign of opposition.

This was to be essentially a "propaganda campaign," as Paul Routledge of *The Times* reported. In other words, in terms of the distinctions developed earlier when discussing propagational groups, the work was to be mainly disseminative, quite uncharacteristic of the TUC in this era. Two variables appear to stand out in explanation. To some considerable degree H.M. Opposition was compromised by Mrs. Castle's own recent attempts at reform, elements of which, including the penal clauses, reappeared among the eight pillars of the new measure. Besides, the Parliamentary attack on it was to be led by none other than Mrs. Castle. "What devotee of black humour dreamed up the idea that Barbara Castle should play a part in opposing the Tory measure?" a 1971 Congress delegate would ask.[58] The question reveals one of the grave limitations that rank and file trade unionists suffer from: they are seldom sophisticated enough to appreciate the resilience and plasticity of Parliamentary Man when switched from Government to Opposition. Of course, the TUC leaders understood that the good Parliamentarian can easily make yesterday's shining virtue seem like today's mortal sin, but they were still sufficiently inhibited to hold back from an all-out effort via Her Majesty's Opposition. On 16 December Mr. Feather did address the Trade Union Group, but mainly to tell them what the TUC had planned and was already doing.[59] In the same month the General Council appointed Mr. Feather and four others to liaise with the PLP (and NEC). But the Liaison Committee met only in January, March, and June, and only the "first two of these meetings concentrated on Parliamentary business." Amendments to the Bill proposed by individual unions were passed on to the PLP, but the TUC made it plain to them that it "was not in a position to be closely involved in the process of amending the Bill."[60]

The other variable was the TUC's perception of what had happened to the consultative relationship: "The Government's wilful denial of the facilities for consultation that had been accorded it for the previous thirty years."[61] In fact, the new Government had not denied such facilities, although it may well have seemed so since at about the time when Mr. Carr was refusing a meeting (until after the Consultative Document was out), Mrs. Thatcher at Education was refusing to receive a deputation to discuss a Congress resolution. What the Government had done was to deny (in effect) that consultation was about substance rather than detail. Deep down that may have been and constitutionally should have been the attitude of all its predecessors, but if so, the true nature of the interchange had often been fudged, and the Conservative Government was guilty of disclosing the reality beneath the ritual. In any event, the TUC-Government relationship had been disrupted. That put the TUC in much the same strategic position as the moral-issue or other propagational groups, except of course that its aim was to veto (i.e., persuade negatively rather than positively).

Thus "conditioned," the TUC set out on a disseminative campaign with two objectives: to inform, inspire, and enlist the aid of "all active trade unionists," "and to win over public opinion generally." Nearly 2,000 full-time officials were briefed in a special training programme, so that they in turn could brief their active members, who were also to read the TUC case in a pamphlet entitled *Reason*, of which 200,000 copies were printed. Nine regional conferences were mounted in early 1971. For the broader appeal, the TUC resorted to some of the oldest weapons in the working-class armoury: national demonstrations (February's—the estimates ranged from the police's 100,000 to Victor Feather's

150,000—would be described by the TUC as "the largest and most representative demonstration against Government legislation to take place in Britain in the twentieth century"), and a national petition, bearing almost 550,000 signatures, presented on 24 March to the House of Commons, whose Members were heavily lobbied on the same day (coinciding with the Third Reading). But the TUC also took up a comparatively new weapon: political advertising. In January and February, with the help of an advertising agency and at a total cost of £51,000, it placed a set of three advertisements in six London dailies, twenty-one provincials, and *Tribune*, spanning the political spectrum.[62] The January version opened in bold type: "It's easy to stop strikes—You just introduce laws to silence, fine and jail workers." After an effectively worded text of almost three hundred words, it ended: "The Trades Union Congress—If it's a crime to fight for a better life, we're guilty."[63]

In Parliament, meanwhile, that other Opposition had also been blending old tactics with new. One day in late January, in an interview room in the basement beneath the Commons Chamber, a *Tribune* Group (including Eric Heffer, now speaking from the Front Bench) decided upon another form of political advertising. That night, just before the vote was due, about thirty of them moved to the centre of the Chamber and stood in front of the Speaker's Mace, which "was almost knocked off its perch."[64] A good time was being had by all when the Speaker suspended the Sitting for fifteen minutes.

Despite these innovative methods inside and outside Parliament, and the vigorous application of more traditional ones, the Government naturally got its Bill, which received the Royal Assent in August. The TUC had mounted a remarkable campaign, at considerable cost (£120,000 *net*, just up to April), but it had lost. Or had it lost the battle but not the war? Already in fact the campaign of opposition to the Bill had been turning into a campaign of non-cooperation with the Act (i.e., a boycott). The ground work for it was laid at the Special Congress at Croydon as far back as March 1971, when the General Council offered seven recommendations intended (as Mr. Feather would say) to "add up to an attempt to ensure that the Act will be ineffective. Not [he hastened to add] because the trade union Movement is above or outside the law. But because we have the democratic right not to co-operate with the machinery of an Act which is abhorrent to all of us."[65]

The key to the boycott lay in the registration provisions: no registration—no protection from liability for inducing a breach of contract in furthering a trade dispute, which meant that the union and its officials would be liable for damages in virtually every strike; damages for unfair industrial practices would have no upper limit; and so on. In fact, unregistered, the union wouldn't even be a union but an organization of workers, which, however, the TUC stoutly refused to acknowledge.[66] Such bodies would also lose tax exemptions (on their sick and other provident funds), estimated by Mr. Feather at about £5 million a year altogether. Nor would they be able to negotiate the kind of closed shop that the

Act allowed, a fatal limitation on such bodies as Actors' Equity. On the other hand, they would gain freedom from State supervision.

Since the net effect would be different for different unions (disastrous for some), the General Council at Croydon proposed a compromise: it strongly advised against registration, and just managed to get that recommendation through (a majority of only 771,000). In September, however, it lost the day. Against its wishes, it was instructed by Congress (a majority of 1,125,000) "to immediately instruct" unions not to register, which meant, as a potential victim said, "No matter what your domestic circumstances may be, you will do as we say or we will kick you out . . . that is really what is behind this word 'instructs'."[67] The Council took its time, first trying suspension, but decided in June 1973 to recommend expulsion, the ultimate sanction. In September, twenty unions (total membership 370,000) were cast into outer darkness, including the Health Services Employees, Bank Employees, and Seamen. Both the National Graphical and the Calico Printers had already anticipated their fate by resigning. The appeals of the five unions bold enough to make them, including the Air Line Pilots and Actors' Equity, were each dismissed by majorities of the order of 7.5 to 8.5 million.

Little sign there of that toleration of nonconformists for which Lord (Ted) Willis had pleaded in his appeal to Congress on behalf of the Writers' Guild.[68] But then a defining characteristic of unions as organizations is that conformity is power, or at least a necessary condition of it. Certainly the policy of nonregistration was immensely successful. Among those concerned with the drafting of the Bill, no one dreamed that unions would decline to register (or, if provisionally registered by the Chief Registrar, promptly take themselves off): In every sense, it would cost them too much. That was a perfectly reasonable assumption but it proved, in the circumstances, to be wrong, and so the whole strategy of reform was undermined.

Eventually the weakened structure would surely have collapsed, but this was hastened by another kind of boycott—of the National Industrial Relations Court (NIRC), which had started work on 1st December 1971—by individual unions. At Croydon in the spring the TUC had undoubtedly used the language of noncooperation with it, too, though exactly what that meant was never defined. When it came to the point, one of the giants, the T & G, interpreted noncooperation to include open defiance of NIRC, a species of High Court. T & G stewards had "blacked" lorries from a St. Helen's transport firm trying to deliver containers to the Mersey Docks. The union was taken to court, but only metaphorically, since it did not put in an appearance on the first occasion (23 March 1972) or the following week at the contempt proceedings, whereupon it drew a fine of £5,000, or three weeks later, when (the "black" still on) the union was hit for £50,000 with the prospect of sequestration,—that is, having *all* its assets seized (some £22 million), too. With financial support from the TUC, the T & G would have been willing to "submit" to sequestration.[69] The Finance and General Purposes Committee (inner Cabinet) of the TUC recommended such support, but the General Council balked, partly because it would put the TUC as a whole at risk, partly because "it would be wrong . . . to deliberately encourage unions to break the law."[70] So the Finance and General Purposes Committee had to recommend that the T & G should pay up, leaving the T & G leader, Jack Jones, fuming and complaining to Eric Heffer of the TUC's "lack of support," or what the Engineers called "its retreat." The Council did, however, back the T & G appeals all the way up to the House of Lords, where the case finally went against the unions. The Council also accepted the burden of legal costs to the extent of some £13,000.[71]

This boycott of the NIRC by the giant unions was as successful in its own way as the Congress-imposed boycott of the Chief Registrar. As late as the beginning of May 1974, three months after a Labour Government had been returned, the Engineers' National Committee (the policy-making body) voted 4 to 1 against paying the £47,000 compensation awarded by NIRC to Con-Mech, a Woking engineering firm, and to continue to boycott court hearings even after Michael Foot, the new Secretary of State for Employment and distinctly a man of the Left, had asked them to call it off.[72] Instead they called a strike. The battle was not joined, however, because some Robin Hood (if he is the right symbol to invoke) mysteriously paid up. But the game had been up for almost two years. In July 1972 the NIRC had put five London dockers in Pentonville for refusing to stop "blacking" a company in Hackney. They had, naturally, boycotted the proceedings. Reg Prentice, representing a constituency nearby, gave them the rough edge of his tongue for acting without "the support of their union. They are even more wrong to defy the order of the Court. They have been looking for martyrdom for weeks."[73] That was not the view of other dockers who promptly came out on strike, followed by other militants. The Finance and General Purposes of the TUC asked for an interview with the P.M., which was immediately granted (24 July). Two days later, the General Council, disappointed with the results of the meeting with the P.M., who of course declined to interfere with the Court, called a one-day general strike for Monday, 31 July, the first such call since 1926.

By a strange concatenation of events, still not fully explained but including the decision of the Law Lords against the T & G in the St. Helen's case mentioned above, the Official Solicitor's visit to Pentonville to talk to the five dissidents and their surprising release, the one-day general strike was avoided. But the calling of it meant that the General Council, too, had become radicalized (as often happens during confrontations, so union district officials are heard to remark).

By now management itself had had about enough. On 2 November, at the final meeting in a long series (forty hours in all) of tripartite talks (P.M., three Cabinet Ministers, the two senior civil servants of the day; CBI; TUC), Michael Clapham and W.O. Campbell Adamson (president and director general of the

CBI), who trying unsuccessfully to prevent a breakdown, said that every point could be negotiated, "even the status of the Industrial Relations Act."That "rather annoyed Ministers because they had no intention of giving way on that at least."[74] But the CBI, if it had not exactly given way, had already given up on the Act. In discussions with the TUC after the railwaymen's strike in the spring, when a cooling-off period and a strike ballot were imposed without changing the outcome, the two sides began to try another tack. On 13 July, after a meeting at the CBI, they announced that "collective bargaining is best brought to a satisfactory conclusion by voluntary means . . . "[75] which the Act had implicitly denied. Accordingly they decided to set up a new conciliation and arbitration system from 1 September. An agreement to use their own specially recruited conciliators was signed on 2 August. As Labour Correspondent Paul Routledge remarked, "an important aspect of the agreement is that it envisages the minimum use of the Industrial Relations Act by both sides."[76] Exactly: management was disenchanted. Early in 1974 Mr. Campbell Adamson would get into trouble for proposing resuscitation with union help or modification of the Act itself. But that was mainly because he chose to say it during a General Election campaign, when it was imprudent for those in public life to face facts and speak their mind.

In "the last scene of all that ends this strange eventful history," Labour returned to office in that election and promptly set about undoing not only what its predecessor had done but in part (cooling-off periods, compulsory strike ballots, fines, and the ultimate imprisonment of workers) what it had itself striven for only five years earlier. The TUC, with the help of the T & G and the Engineers, had lost the Parliamentary battle but won the political war.

8 Representative Groups (III): Business

Sector 2

The subject of business groups in general is substantial enough for a book. Even for the more limited purpose in mind—studying the mode of group representations—the task remains formidable, so rich is the field, not only in species but in varieties, including hybrids. Moreover, new growths keep appearing: the British Nuclear Forum (1964), which represents nuclear-power interests, commercial and industrial, before government (and in Foratom, the peak for such interests in fourteen European countries); the Freight Transport Association (1969), organizing transport interests, both users and operators (companies, trade associations, local authorities); the British Importers Confederation (1972), made up of ordinary members (individuals and companies) and association members (covering the rubber trade; wine and spirits, chemical and dyestuffs, and so forth); not forgetting the London Chamber of Commerce (the Confederation's host and service agent, with its own 2,000 import specialists). The Confederation stands ready to address government on behalf of any of its members. In 1972 another Confederation appeared the British Textile; with five associations and five trade unions in full membership, it looks like a biological sport. In fact the joining of unions and management was arranged so as to "add strength to any representations made to Government" (in the words of the Devlin Report).

Simply to get our bearings from the point of view of modes of representation, we may follow an unusually experienced guide, Mr. T.C. (Tom) Fraser, in identifying

. . . two fundamental and natural tendencies among businessmen. The first is the tendency of those engaged in business in a particular area to wish to come together from time to time to exchange views and information, to discuss their common interests and to take such action as they may decide is necessary to represent those common interests to local and public authorities of various kinds, and to governments at home and abroad. The second is the equal natural tendency for those engaged in the same kind of production or trade to get together to exchange views about their common problems. The one is a manifestation of a recognition of common local interests, the other of the particular industrial or commercial interests of those who are engaged in the same activity.[1]

123

The first tendency has crystallized in two principal forms: Chambers of Commerce and Chambers of Trade.

Chambers of Trade. The terminology is confusing. As a learned official of the National Chamber of Trade explained, "commerce" comes *via* French from the Latin meaning "wares" or "merchandise"; "trade" coming from Middle Low German to mean "buying, selling or exchanging of commodities for profit."[2] Yet, particularly in the Midlands and the North, we come across a Chamber of Commerce and Chamber of Trade in the same place, and elsewhere a Chamber of Commerce that is really a Chamber of Trade. But what is *that*, really? Historically, a chamber of trade organized the local shopkeepers—"the word is as honourable as manufacturers," a journalist thought it necessary to write in 1900,[3] three years after the peak, the National Chamber of Trade (NCT) had got under way—but in the 1970s chambers of trade appear to be rather more heterogeneous. As a past president of the NCT asked in 1973: "how many Chambers would be in existence today if they had all depended on retail traders for administration?" The emphasis, he thought, should be on small business as opposed to big business.[4]

If so, the terminology is less apt than ever. However, we can do no better than follow usage, again following that same learned official of the NCT who quotes from Horace's *Ars Poetica* (in Roscommon's seventeenth-century translation):

Use may revive the obsoletest words,
And banish those that now are most in vogue;
Use is the judge, the law, the rule of speech.

Use makes a chamber of trade an organization of local businessmen, especially the retailers.

Chambers of Commerce. It follows that Chambers of Commerce, too, under that name, are not quite what they seem; functionally, most are Chambers of Trade in the sense indicated. But even about the remainder (88 in the ABCC in 1974) confusion abounds. Historically, these were organizations of merchants, starting in Scotland (Glasgow) in the 1780s and soon spreading to England (Leeds having the first claim there to the title). Functionally, the merchants were often wholesalers, especially dealing overseas, although whether "many" of them rated "themselves superior to their retail-trade brethern," and so "preferred to call themselves merchants, thus sparing themselves and their families the embarrassment of too-direct a connection with trade," as the NCT has claimed, is another question.[5] In any event, the merchants were organized apart from the manufacturers, also trying to get going in the 1780s as a General Chamber. But today of course and long since (granted Britain's industrial transformation and Mr. Fraser's first tendency), manufacturers are found in membership, even constituting a majority in several regions, such as the West Midlands (based on Birmingham), East Midlands (based on Leicester), and the North West (based on Manchester). All told some 750 trade associations, many of them industrial, are members of Chambers of Commerce. In Birmingham, the Chamber both accommodates and services trade associations; in the early seventies, two members of its staff did nothing else but look after a baker's dozen of them.[6]

Such are a few of the organizational complexities of a mature capitalist society. It seems almost unkind to add, having distinguished Trade and retailers from Commerce and wholesalers, that, on average, retailers account for some 10 percent of the membership of all Chambers of Commerce in the sense of the 88. On the other hand, they find the door of the London Chamber of Commerce barred to them, and elsewhere are not encouraged.

Mr. Fraser's second tendency is represented *today* by trade associations (TAs) and employers' organizations (EOs), which together *may* total about 2,000 (1972). *Today* because a high proportion of these bodies were started locally, although their interests would always have been less general than those pursued through the two classes of chambers. *May* is used because even the Devlin Commission "found it impossible to ascertain the number with any exactitude...."[7] Even that gross figure may exaggerate the true situation. Having started with a list of some 2,500 probables, the Commission Staff whittled that down to about 2,000 after discovering that 600 were affiliates of about a hundred major enterprises. But when they wrote to the other 1,800, they received no more than 760 replies. So they could be sure of only 860 (760 + the 100 majors), together with 800 affiliates, making a bedrock total of 1,660 (easy to remember from the date of Charles II's return from his travels).[8]

Functionally, the basic division of course is between the furtherance of a collective trade interest (the TAs) and industrial relations/collective bargaining (the EOs). The shipping industry is one where the line of demarcation is clearly maintained: a Chamber of Shipping as TA (20 associations, mostly based on the ports), and a British Shipping Federation, covering 99 percent of the industry, as EO. Engineering furnishes another and more important example. The Engineering Employers' Federation (EEF) is *the* (pure) EO. It has its weaknesses, in textile machinery and especially in vehicle production, partly because the body builders go their own way but especially because the North American companies (Massey Ferguson, Chrysler, Ford and Vauxhall; i.e., General Motors) deliberately keep their distance. Otherwise the EEF has its roots in 5,200 federated firms organized as 22 local associations (the actual members). Among the TAs relevant to this sprawling industry are the Society of British Aerospace Companies (400 of them in aircraft or component manufacture, space equipment, airfield construction); the Society of Motor Manufacturers and Traders (SMMT), which has 1,600 companies, distributors as well as manufacturers, the British Electrical and Allied Manufacturers' Association (BEAMA), 400 companies reorganized in 1971 as a federation; the Machine Tools Trades Association (MTTA), uniting importers and manufacturers.

This division of labour is quite straightforward, the only problem being acronymic (e.g., the EEF plays EO to the TA of the BEAMA). But simplicity is left behind when we discover that a very considerable proportion of the organizations are neither one thing nor t'other but hybrids. Well-known examples of the EO/TA hybrid include the National Farmers' Union, said to represent 85 percent of the full-time farmers in England and Wales; the Road Haulage Association (RHA), speaking for the operators of goods vehicles organized into a baker's dozen of functional groups—the specialized carriers—and into areas; the British Federation of Master Printers (BFMP), all printing except newspapers (3,800 companies in the British Isles/120 local associations/10 Regional Alliances); the Newspaper Society, the publishers of provincial dailies and weeklies, teaming up with the BFMP for collective bargaining on a national scale; the Publishers Association (370 companies); the National Federation of Building Trades Employers (NFBTE), 12,000 companies in England and Wales/220 local associations/10 regional bodies. Exactly how the EO and TA elements combine is impossible to judge (at present). The Chemical Industries Association (CIA), made up of 300 companies engaged in the manufacturing and processing of chemicals *plus* 15 specialized associations affiliated, presumably represents the limiting case. Hybridized in 1965 from the principal EO and the principal TA in the industry, the CIA permits a member company not to be bound, for example, by wage agreements it has negotiated. Conversely, a company may be glad of help in labour relations while looking elsewhere on some TA business.

It must not be assumed that for every EO there is a matching TA, somewhere. The Newspaper Publishers Association (the national dailies) is an EO; its ten member companies do not seem to arrange themselves as a TA, or to be aligned with one. Conversely, most of the TAs in the distributive trades do not negotiate terms and conditions of employment. Of those that do, only six made compliance a condition of membership; for example, the British Jewellers and the Master Saddlers.[9] For the rest, compliance is no more than voluntary. Nor of course is structure a wholly reliable guide to day-to-day function. The Brewers' Society (90 brewery companies in the United Kingdom) is a TA that not only advises on industrial relations matters but has undertaken some actual negotiations; for example, the wages and conditions of managers of public houses.

***

That all these bodies play pressure-group roles is clear in outline if not in detail. For chambers of trade generally the issues tending towards political action in that sense have included planning and development, shop hours,

Sunday trading, leases, the postal service, car parking facilities, the by-laws governing display boards, street trading, and the like. Some of these concerns naturally impel chambers towards the local council's offices, sometimes by supporting or even sponsoring candidates. Some activity has less to do with public policy as such than its enforcement or policing, as in 1973, when the Taunton Chamber (at a cost of some £400) and the local council went after a wholesaler who was also indulging in retailing. Some local councils operate substantially within a centrally determined framework; the chambers look in London's direction as well, using the ancient device of submitting questionnaires to Parliamentary candidates during general elections. Some issues of national policy are pursued, too. In 1973 the Leeds Chamber on its own initiative helped along a private member's bill to ban the import and sales of *replicas* of .45 Colt automatics made in Japan, or indeed their manufacture in Britain.[10]

Chambers of Commerce

Chambers of Commerce (in the more limited sense) are also "essentially representative of business vis-à-vis local and regional government, and each Chamber is in constant contact with the local authority in its area."[11] But these Chambers of course carry more weight than chambers of trade: some are even heavyweights, the Birmingham Chamber for example, with some 4100 members and an executive staff of 30 (in the early 1970s). Many others are, in comparison, middleweights and to that extent the more inclined to act independently of the national organization (or peak). Some of this individual effort is case work, or intermediary work, as it was called after World War II—that is, after suitable inquiry, writing to "the responsible officer in the Department concerned," or asking for an interview on behalf of a member.[12] But "occasionally" (the Devlin Committee reported) a major Chamber also stakes out its own position on national policy; for example, "taxation, membership of the EEC, decimalization." This is borne out by the unanimous vote, duly publicized, of the council of the Birmingham Chamber in July 1971 in favour of joining the EEC on the terms offered, a ballot having disclosed that all but 11 of its 4,164 members commended that course of action.[13] The Luton Chamber's production in 1975 of "some original ideas on energy conservation"[14] constitutes a post-Devlin example.

Some light on the mode of representation adopted by an individual Chamber may be gleaned from the part played by the Birmingham Chamber in persuading the Board of Trade to approve, with financial support, a new National Exhibition Centre there rather than in London. The idea for such a centre had been talked about for more than a decade, almost invariably on the assumption that it would be located in London, where indeed various sites had been considered by the Greater London Council (GLC) but not developed. In 1968 a Board of Trade working partly under the Minister of State—Lord (Wilfred) Brown—recommended a site near London Airport (Heathrow), but a year later there was still no sign of a sod being turned.

In Birmingham, the Chamber of Commerce had already submitted evidence to the Board of Trade in support of its claim for an industrial centre in the Midlands. Now, in 1969, its President Noel Bond-Williams and Secretary Robert Booth teamed up with Town Clerk Harry Parkinson and the leader of the Council, Conservative Alderman (Sir) Francis Griffin for "an intensive lobbying campaign and found immediate interest at Government level." This meant that they went backwards and forwards to see such Ministers as Anthony Crosland (Board of Trade) and Anthony Greenwood (Housing and Local Government) and civil servants. At one stage the team was ready "at the ring of a telephone to climb into cars and head for London even if only for a 20-minute talk." "It was worth it with £11 million at stake," commented Alderman (Sir) Griffin. "We must have burned up the M1 with the number of journeys we made."[15]

In late January 1970 they got their reward for initiative and effort: the new President of the Board of Trade, Roy Mason, announced that "the proposal by the Birmingham City Council and the Birmingham Chamber of Commerce and Industry offers the best possibility of a viable development within a reasonable time scale...."[16] He promised £1.5 million from Government funds for the development of a 150-acre site some nine miles from Birmingham, reachable in 85 minutes from London by rail. That would leave £9.5 million (£11 million total cost) to be found. Birmingham itself was to lend £3 million and private developers would put up the rest. Within minutes of the President's announcement in the Commons, the President of the Birmingham Chamber was holding a press conference (arranged two days earlier) to give thanks all round.[17]

The London interests were naturally dismayed: they had been caught not just napping but dead asleep. Not only the GLC but the SMMT (responsible for the Annual Motor Show) and the Association of Exhibition Organizers immediately protested. Soon the "London lobby, sensing that it had got to pull something out of the fire if it is to save the day [was] lining up trade associations with the efficiency of a Republican presidential candidate. All of the power and the pull of the City [of London] has been lent to the lobbyists' elbow, rarely can a provincial city have had to face such an imposing army of opponents."[18] It was small as armies go (some 70 organizations), but it outnumbered Birmingham's organizational allies (a total of one) and was indeed imposing (including the CBI, BEAMA, MTTA, British National Export Council as well as the SMMT). Some 27 of these opponents even declared that they would not use a centre located in the Midlands. By March there was "growing evidence that Birmingham has been premature in sipping its celebratory champagne: London may yet win the battle to be home to a national exhibition centre."[19]

Meanwhile, however, Frank Cole (Chamber President) had been "trouping the country drumming up support from exhibition organizers." When he became chairman of the Centre in May, he remarked: "We are so far ahead now that I don't think anybody can catch us." They might have been overtaken in June, when a general election brought the Conservatives back into office, for six months earlier Keith Joseph, the Shadow Minister, had greeted the decision with a demand for an emergency debate, saying it had created a "serious situation." The new Cabinet did indeed discuss cancellation of the Birmingham plan but "firmly rejected" it,[20] enabling Michael Noble, the new President, to make an announcement in mid-July. With some misgivings, a *Times* leader writer acknowledged that "full credit has to be given to the Birmingham interests involved for their display of enterprise and lobbying skill in siting a national showcase in a region that probably accounts for 40 per cent of Britain's exports."[21] But he evidently wondered whether the public interest had been served. Some members of the public were blunter about it: the Labour Government (a reader wrote) had been guilty of "wilting to pressure from the Birmingham authorities to site a "national" centre more than 100 miles north of the capital."[22]

Employers' Organizations

About the pressure-group role of the EOs, local or national, we have little real knowledge. The EEF says of itself that it makes "representations on any matter affecting the industry, a sectional interest, or even an individual member firm." Its approach is essentially "through contacts with Government departments," which in turn consult it about certain legislative proposals.[23] All the national EOs looked at by the Donovan Commission researchers were found to

regard the representation of members' views to Government as an important and growing part of their function. The general importance arises from the fact that much legislation has a direct bearing on industrial affairs, and associations take very seriously their responsibility to seek amendments to existing or proposed legislation, which would have a harmful effect on their members, or to improve the practical execution of the Government's intentions.[24]

But the number of *national* organizations studied was small and the principle of selection unclear, so we cannot safely extend the findings to the whole corpus of EOs.

Trade Associations

The pressure-group role of TAs (in particular) rests on the fact, officially acknowledged by the Herbert Committee in 1950, "that under modern conditions organized liaison between representatives of trade and industry and private individuals on the one hand and Government Departments on the other is an essential and recognized part of the machinery of government. This applies most obviously to the formulation and execution of general policy."[25] But it also applies to case, or intermediary, work, as the Herbert Committee discovered: "We found that intermediary work was being carried out on a great scale by trade associations, trades unions and voluntary organizations. . . . these are the really important intermediaries."[26]

"On a great scale" implies what is technically called a "systemic" point of view, thinking of the impact of the activity on the system of government as a whole. How important intermediary work is compared with policy representation for any one TA or class of TAs, we do not know from published evidence. TAs generally have testified that the former is "quite secondary" to the latter (and to advising their own members),[27] a claim endorsed later by others for the period up to about the mid-fifties.[28] What has happened to the mix since then is not clear. It is clear that since the Restrictive Trade Practices Act of 1956, which outlawed collective price discrimination (or price fixing) by manufacturers, the rationale of many TAs for a hundred years, some important structural changes have been taking place. The Devlin Commission found that 215 of its 865 respondents had been formed in the period 1957-1972, compared with 96 in 1946-1956, and 135 in 1940-1945.[29] The Commission attributed that to an increase in mergers following the 1956 Act.

Sponsorship

The general position, in any case, is that some TAs enjoy automatic access to government and even others, if judged reasonably representative, enjoy a presumption in their favour that can be used as a lever to gain access. In the most symbiotic of these relationships, an industry is sponsored by a department, which supervises it in the broad sense of "watch with authority the work or proceedings or progress of. . . ." The machine tool industry provides an example. Britain had in 1969 the fifth largest machine tool industry in the world, exporting 20 percent of its output to the United States despite America's being no. 1 (output five times as great). So, as Anthony Wedgwood Benn, when Minister of Technology, remarked "There is a continuing Government interest in the machine tool industry, not only as a major manufacturing industry itself but also because of the significant contribution it makes to the general mechanical engineering industries through the provision of modern tools of production." Hence "the machine tool industry was one of the first to come under the sponsorship of the Ministry of Technology." This meant that "throughout its sponsorship Mintech's main efforts have been directed towards stimulating the development and production of advanced machine tools and accelerating their acceptance by user industries." It also meant that Mintech had been providing "research support aimed at preparing the ground for the next generation of machine tools." To W.L. Sims, then president of the MTTA, it meant helping the industry to achieve "government objectives which would be beyond the province of an individual company's normal business consideration."[30]

Mintech was of course the sponsor Department for much else, including computers, telecommunication instruments, electronics, motor vehicles, aircraft and aero engines, and shipbuilding. As such it afforded the TAs (SMMT, Society of British Aerospace Companies, and so forth) *a* natural point of entry into the system. Equally naturally, the precise location of the point of entry varies as the structure varies, which Mintech's own unhappy fate illustrates. Its permanent secretary, Sir Richard Clarke (that man of many talents, all extraordinary) thought that its structure was so logical that the Department was bound to last.[31] Even before he spoke, however, the Conservatives, then in Opposition, were exhibiting dissatisfaction with the existing set-up, in particular tending to the view "that the traditionally powerful fiscal role of the Treasury should be balanced by a stronger Board of Trade, acting with clear terms of reference, as the main sponsoring department for industry and commerce."[32] This concept of turning the Board of Trade "into the main sponsoring Ministry for Industry" crystallized in 1970 as the Department of Trade and Industry (DTI), substantially a product of the Board and the industrial side of Mintech, which died the death a year later when part of its aviation side (the aerospace policy component) also passed to the DTI (the military part going to Defence).

With some exceptions, the way in for most TAs was now (1973) through the Industrial Development Executive (part of a group), and specifically through that part of the field then commanded by Deputy Secretary R.H.W. Bullock, whose span of control entailed the following sponsorships:

Sponsorship	*Via Division/Department (Under-Secretary)*
Films, tourism, timber, board, Printing, publishing, newspapers, books, distribution and service trades; leather and consumer goods industries (such as pottery, glass, cutlery, furniture, and footwear)	Paper, Printing, Publishing, Services, and Distribution (H. Bailey)
Cotton and wool textiles, man-made fibres, tobacco, rubber, chemicals, fertilisers, proprietary medicines, toiletries, and so forth	Chemicals and Textiles (P.W. Ridley)
Shipbuilding and shiprepairing	Shipbuilding Policy (E.V. Marchant)

Sponsorship	Via Division/Department (Under-Secretary)
Nonferrous metals industries and electrical engineering and process plant engineering and contracting industries	Minerals, Metals, Electrical Engineering, and Process Plants (D.C. Clark)
Motor vehicles, metal and woodworking machine-tool, agricultural machinery, construction and mechanical handling equipment . . . promotion of industrial technologies	Mechanical Engineering (P.J.L. Holman)
Electronics . . . and the computer	Computers, Systems and Electronics (J.W. Nichols)
Industries involved in offshore supplies that are not otherwise covered in the Department (goods and services for oil and gas development)	Offshore Supplies Office (J.P. Gibson)

That was by no means all. Within the Aerospace and Shipping Group, J.A. Hamilton (Deputy Secretary) covered four Divisions, two of which were sponsoring Space (J.R. Steele), and Air (D. le B. Jones), dealing with the aircraft and aero-engine industries. A third (T.P. Jones) gave all its attention to Concorde policy and administration, and so might well be regarded as entailing quasi-sponsorship. Sponsorship of the airlines, however (British Airways, with its 220 or so aircraft; the Civil Aviation Authority, responsible for the regulation of civil aviation in Britain; and so forth) was located in another part of the group, run generally (in 1973) by D.F. Hubback and specifically (Civil Aviation 1 or CA1) by P.G. Hudson. Count in such other sponsorships as nuclear design and construction, and the private sector of the iron and steel industry (where about a third of the total work force in the industry is still employed in 110 companies, represented by the British Independent Steel Producers' Association), and it is clear that the DTI did indeed become *the* sponsoring Ministry of Industry. No wonder that the perennial head of the team, the Permanent Secretary, was given an office with a god-like view.

To such a degree have departments come to be regarded by their political masters as fair game for ravishing at frequent intervals that the DTI itself soon became a victim, being split into parts, thus changing (technically at least) the entry points for TAs. For example, sponsorship of the aircraft and aero-engines industries (including dealing with Rolls-Royce Ltd. and Short Brothers and Harland Ltd.) remained with the Air Division, but within the new Department of Industry. So, too, with the sponsorship of the space industry (Space and Air Research Division) and the quasi-sponsorship of Concorde, and so on. On the other hand, CA1, the entry point for British Airways and the Civil Aviation Authority, found itself in the Department of Trade. In due course, a Department of Energy came to sponsor the nuclear construction, and so on.

This could not be entirely a reversion to the *status quo ante*, but it did tend to reintroduce that division between Mintech and the Board of Trade, which many senior civil servants had found "vicious and destructive" because it meant having "one ministry for home business and one for overseas, one to sponsor and protect industry and one to encourage free trade. The prejudices of the two were totally different, and officials tell harrowing tales" of direct confrontations, proposals, and counterproposals that "would all consume time and passion right up to ministerial level," and indeed end up in Cabinet.[33] But the point for this analysis is simply that, despite all the permutations, there is always at least one department bent to the task of sponsoring and protecting industry, which means that the TAs (and of course a great many big companies, such as BAC, builders of Concorde, Dunlops, ICI) would be drawn into continuous relationship even if they did not seek it of their own accord. Of course, they have their own reasons for wanting to be in touch with the departments, so the relationship is reciprocal, the connection being effected typically through a division, though less the Under-Secretary, whose own span of control may be considerable, than an Assistant Secretary.

Because the division is the buckle that binds, such a structural change may not of itself (i.e., unless accompanied by shifts in policy) greatly discountenance the TAs. They may have to track the division down to its new milieu (not necessarily a new home, physically), for example, the Atomic Energy Division (AE) of the DTI to the new Department of Energy. They may find some in old locations as the Society of British Aerospace Companies, BAC, and others would have come across new Under-Secretaries in both the Space and Concorde Divisions. They would also have found that the Deputy Secretary had flown the nest (to the Cabinet Office), and even the Secretary, Aerospace (and Shipping) was off and running (the new Department of Trade). But there was continuity too (as provided by Mr. Hudson at CA1 and Mr. Herzig at AE).

Some brand new creations, too, may cause a blurring of the sponsorship lines. The Department of Prices and Consumer Protection seems to have confused the Federation of Bakers and others in 1974, as it certainly angered the Ministry of Agriculture, Fisheries and Food (MAFF), sponsor of the food and drink manufacturing industries and distribution trades. In April, Norman Buchan, Minister of State at MAFF, insisted publicly at a Federation lunch that "his ministry was the main sponsoring department for their industry."[34] As one has heard MAFF civil servants crisply reply, when asked to comment upon the charge that their Department had been colonized by the NFU, Mr. Buchan went on to say: "There are two F's in MAFF and not one." On the Price Code, he agreed, the Federation should consult Mrs. Shirley Williams, the Minister in charge of the new Department. Otherwise the Federation should "continue to regard our ministry as a basic sponsoring ministry for your industry. . . ."

Every sponsoring Department could be expected to take a similar stand. One of the difficulties Mrs. Castle faced in 1970 in attempting to launch a commission for Industry and Manpower (CIM) as "a single, strong, independent body" was that it would have undermined the whole sponsorship system, which Hugh Stephenson judged "far too strongly entrenched."[35] What this means, made crystal clear by Mr. Buchan's speech in which he was openly enlisting the support of a TA against the claims of another department, is that departments need TAs (and other such groups) in more than the commonly asserted sense—as sources of basic data and advice. TAs may also help them stand their ground in Whitehall and Victoria Street, whose very names as metaphors aptly suggest that departments do not lack a "territorial imperative." This gives the TAs a special status, which may be turned to account not only individually in the one-to-one relationship but as a class. In the 1970 battle to kill the CIM, TAs and individual companies approached all the sponsoring departments for industry to use their influence to block the proposal.[36] For reasons explained above, they would not have been reluctant to oblige (some, notably Mintech, may even have encouraged the TAs to protest), although the relief came in fact through Labour's loss of the election that summer. Since the World War II years, in fact, industries (essentially through their TAs) have come to "regard their sponsor departments as being able to put forward informed views in relation to any representations being made to other government departments," as T.C. Fraser, a former TA chief executive, records.[37] The sponsor becomes the backer—even against departments.

Economic Development Committees ("Little Neddies")

Since 1964 TAs as a class and some particularly have been accorded, in effect, another channel for influencing government: the Economic Development Committees (EDCs, popularly known as "Little Neddies"). These emerged from the surprising conversion of the Conservative Government in 1961 to central economic planning in the loose sense of coordination between sectors and generalized forecasting, itself in part the product of the equally surprising conversion of the Federation of British Industries the year before. That gave rise to a National Economic Development Council (NEDC, or "Neddy"), essentially tripartite (Government, the unions, management) but with independent membership, which met for the first time in March 1962. It was not intended to be just another advisory committee, commenting on decisions already taken, declared the Chancellor (Selwyn Lloyd) but to share from the start in the task of relating plans to resources. A Labour successor, Michael Stewart, as First Secretary of State, put it even more plainly in September 1966 when he said that "we emphatically want Neddy to be a body at which the CBI and the TUC can be there at the formative stages of policy."[38]

If Neddy did not entail Little Neddies, of which there was no "clear-cut" concept (T.C. Fraser has recalled), they were found necessary "empirically" in the course of attempting to do its work.[39] By the 1964 election, nine, all essentially tripartite, had been formed, including chemicals, electronics, machine tools, and mechanical engineering. Another dozen or so were set up between the election and the summer of 1966 (i.e., by the incoming Labour Government). So by then the basic framework had been fashioned (although a couple of EDCs did not actually meet until later).[40]

How then did the TAs relate to this novel structure? With some EOs (and of course the unions, via the TUC), they were in on the ground floor, being invited to nominate representatives in whom they had confidence. These were representatives in the sense of the peas-in-a-pod theory of representation—that is, they were not representative of particular TAs (or EOs) but "the right sort of people," rather like their industrial and commercial constituents in attitudes and behaviour. What happened was that TAs and EOs, ranging from 8 to 50 according to the industry (which in itself ruled out representation in the more direct sense), consulted with one another and agreed on six or seven names. These were then invited by the Director-General of NEDC to accept membership.

All that was in keeping with the design: The industrial members of EDCs were expected to be conscious of the sources of their nomination and of the general attitudes prevailing there. On the other hand, they were invited as individuals, with no provision for alternates. In accepting the invitation, they accepted the goals of clearing away obstacles to growth and of general improvement. By an imaginative stroke the nominees from Industry X were barred from the chairmanship of the EDC covering Industry X: thus Robert Appleby of Black and Decker chaired not Machine Tools but Clothing; Leyland's Sir Donald Stokes presided over Electronics, not Motor Manufacturing, which was in the hands of Sir William Swallow, of ESSO; another ESSO man, Duncan Dewdney had Mechanical Engineering, and so on. According to John Jewkes at Oxford, one of the severest critics of the whole planning tendency, this was an arrangement by which "those who know less are entrusted with the duties of advising, and even controlling, those who know more."[41] Hardly "controlling": the EDCs were essentially advisory, with no executive power whatever. In any case, the arrangement represented an intriguing attempt to transcend the limitations of the TA/sponsored department relationship "where the weight of vested interests must inevitably be great," as Michael Shanks, the economic journalist turned temporary planner in this period (one of the "irregulars"), reflected in 1967.[42] T.C. Fraser, a TA chief executive for more than a decade and a half, has acknowledged the inevitable bias in the representations made by TAs to their sponsor department.[43] As head of the Industrial Division of NEDC, he was a founding father of the EDCs.

So the TA/Little Neddy relationship is difficult to characterize, even after bearding Mr. Fraser, by then temporary Director-General of NEDC, in his tall Millbank tower. It is quite clear that the Little Neddy structure does not afford just another entry point for TA influence on government. Still Neddy and Little Neddy do "filter the facts of industrial life into the Whitehall consciousness and hence into the policy considerations of the Cabinet," as Mr. Fraser has said.[44] In this the unions have their chance, but do they have the expertise? By the time the system was settled, in 1967, virtually every chairman of the twenty-three EDCs was chairman, deputy chairman, managing director, and so forth of a substantial enterprise, or, in one or two instances, recently retired from such a role. One had been a partner in Peat's, the celebrated firm of chartered accountants, with many connections in industry, to which indeed some of its partners moved.

There is nothing Machiavellian in all this: How could it have been otherwise? But it surely does mean that the invention of EDCs has given the TAs, as a class at least, an extra string to their bow. Nor should we forget that the EDC structure as a whole is superimposed on the TA/sponsor department relationship, which still flourishes, as it should, but for which there is no union/department equivalent. So, dialectically, TAs do seem, on balance, to have acquired an advantage in terms of access.

Access does not necessarily spell success, however. What happens when TA and sponsor disagree? "Ultimately," they are "in the position of bargainers with, of course, the possibility of recourse to parliamentary lobbies. . . ."[45] Some TAs do reach for the political level, by letter or memorandum, or face-to-face in a deputation. Some strike the department and Cabinet obliquely, as through evidence to a Select Committee (British Trawlers' Federation arguing for extra subsidies to the trawling industry), or by a memorandum to the Chancellor as well as the departmental Minister. Such efforts and initiatives are commonly publicized, but the black art of Public Relations (PR) is of course practised independently of them. Here the message appears to be directed at the public at large, though not of course to the exclusion of the governing elite.

Though lacking the deep grooves of the sponsored and NEDC relationship, these direct interchanges, too, have a certain regularity and decorum. Even if preceded or precipitated by specific criticism in public, a deputation will be conducted in a civilized way. Thus in May 1974, after Gilbert Hunt, chairman of Chrysler U.K., but speaking as president of SMMT, had warned the Government against "dangerous meddling and obstructive policies," adding that Britain must choose "between nationalized stagnation and a profit-motivated industrial future . . . ," he was able to have an amiable chat with Mr. Wedgwood Benn, the Secretary of State for Industry.[46]

Such structured relationships are of course disrupted from time to time. Trade associations may reach a stage in their organizational life when they decide to keep their desperation quiet no longer, embarking on a lively public campaign that in itself almost constitutes a breach of decorum. Two examples

spring to mind from the areas of steel nationalization and resale price maintenance, where what seemed to the TAs like a declaration of war made all methods
fair.

In a way reminiscent of the treatment meted out to some Government
departments, the steel industry has been turned and turned about since World
War II, with little to show for it (at the end of the day, three men, compared
with America's two, were still being used to produce a ton of steel. *Tribune's*
plausible hypothesis[47] to account for the industry's *relatively* poor prenationali-
zation performance—that "the steel industry is dominated by the gentleman
amateur"—has not (so far) been validated by postnationalization experience). In
any case, faced with the ultimate threat, the companies, especially Stewarts and
Lloyds, took the PR road, which proved (as we saw in Chapter 5) to be long,
arduous, and expensive. But at least they did not travel alone. As travelling
companions, they had not only the ubiquitous *Aims of Industry* but the British
Iron and Steel Federation, with its substantial staff (still 480 as late as 1967).[48]
In the run-up to the 1964 election, for example, the Federation spent on PR
some £650,000, which exceeded the companies' own total expenditure by about
£10,000. Its earlier moves were tentative, more in the nature of prestige
advertising than political. Thus, in August 1963, a half-page advertisement had as
its message "Steel Shows the Way to Build More Homes," concluding with
"British Steel: Strong in New Ideas."[49] In January 1964, steel was still showing
the way (e.g., "To Build for Education"[50]) and still strong in new ideas. But by
then the Federation had been striking a more overtly political note. The BISF,
wrote E. Julian Pode, its president, "did not intervene publicly when this issue
arose earlier in the year, hoping that wiser counsels within the Labour Party
might still prevail...." As they had not, the Federation entered the lists. In
doing so, it virtually invoked the doctrine of an electoral mandate, remarking
that the case it had previously advanced against steel nationalization had been
"upheld in three successive General Elections" by the electorate.[51]

As planned, the PR strategy for the New Year, which had to be a General
Election year, was "to put quite clearly before the public, without slinging mud
around, what the position of the industry is, what its record is and what it is
trying to do."[52] The campaign that opened early in January followed that
specification. In addition to the old *To Build* ... series, which overlapped for a
while, ads were run on the theme of "Steel and the Nation ... British Steel
works well for you," in between which variable messages were sandwiched,
about the dependence of Britain's exports on steel, the complexity of the
industry ("Steel is a dozen industries ... a hundred markets ... a thousand
products"), freedom to buy from "among the 260" steel companies, and the
like.[53] No mud was slung, but the implications were clear and became explicit.
In August: a magnificent sandcastle, Union Jack flying from the highest keep, is
about to be jumped on by an older boy. Daddy cries: "Careful now!" The text
opens: "One thoughtless move could destroy so much good work ...," leading

on through the industry's achievements to "All this would be threatened by nationalization." What had been the final "British Steel works well for you" now had an injunction tacked on: "Leave Well Alone."[54]

Steel: Leave Well Alone was the title of an excellent booklet that readers of the advertisements were invited to write in for; excellent in crystallizing "the emerging areas of debate" and so attempting to engage the general public and indirectly the Labour Party in a rational exchange of views.[55] About three months earlier the BISF president had tried a more direct approach, asking (in a half-page advertisement) "What *is* Labour's case for nationalizing steel?" He went on to urge: "Tell The People, Mr. Wilson" (i.e., explain in detail the reasons for the policy). The failure to argue it out was not good enough for those who worked in steel, for British industry, or "the British people, who have not been schooled to think of democracy as a matter of 'take it or leave it'."[56] But on such grand issues the limits of democracy as discussion are very soon reached and perhaps always tend to be intraparty rather than interparty. In any event, Labour did not heed the appeals, won the election and put steel nationalization into the Queen's Speech in November.

For various reasons, Labour did not get the job done until March 1967 (the Iron and Steel Act). This the BISF had fought in the customary Parliamentary way, apparently using Government backbenchers as well as the Opposition. But, as a new BISF president, A.J. Peech, acknowledged: "Only minimal concessions have been made to the scheduled companies" (i.e., the fourteen to be taken into public ownership).[57] Some concessions were gained, but the Federation had really shot its bolt before the Labour Party returned to office in October 1964.

Resale Price Maintenance

The resale price maintenance issue (fair trade to Americans) arises out of a splendid paradox—that " 'competitive industry' is the home of restrictive practices," as economist Alex Hunter once put it in a British Association paper on the control of monopoly. The point is that competition is extolled by professors (from Adam Smith onwards) but unloved by businessmen themselves, judging by their behaviour rather than their rhetoric. If there are so many of them that they cannot, as in the limiting case of monopoly, control price and output, then they, or some number of them, come (or used to come) to an arrangement for exclusive dealing or price fixing or both. In the good old days, price fixing was often extended to the distributive trades via resale price maintenance (RPM). These devices for avoiding the rigours of competition (in the classic sense that it enforces efficiency) were administered by the TAs, which indeed were often created specifically for the purpose. The sanctions, also administered by the TAs, included collective enforcement (or collective boy-cott), whereby manufacturers cut off supplies to distributors who didn't play the game, and distributors cut out manufacturers who sold to distributors outside the ring.

In 1956, the Restrictive Trade Practices Act—product of a remarkable Conservative initiative—made *collective* enforcement of RPM illegal, and that was supposed to be that. As it happened, RPM in the food trade did begin to be eroded, but that was less cause and effect than the result of aggressive supermarket retailing, a new phenomenon in Britain.[58] Generally RPM survived remarkably well for an institution pronounced dead. The fundamental reason was probably that, during the passage of the Bill, the Government gave an undertaking that a TA would be permitted to help an *individual* manufacturer to enforce *his* resale price conditions, which was still legal.[59] Within a couple of years, an official body pointed out that the Act had indeed increased the power of the individual manufacturer in that sense. This gave successive Presidents of the Board of Trade (BOT) food for thought, if perhaps not enough fuel for action. But in 1961, after an internal BOT inquiry by civil servants had apparently made a strong case for abolition of RPM on *economic* grounds, a new President, Frederick Erroll, put up a proposal to the Economic Policy Committee of the Cabinet. It survived there but not in Cabinet, where R.A. (now Lord) Butler, Iain Macleod, and others opposed on *political* grounds, partly reflecting the influence of Conservative backbenchers generally and the Trade and Industry Committee in particular, which in turn partly reflected the influence of the TAs and of the local shopkeepers. In the following year the P.M. himself (Harold Macmillan) moved tentatively towards abolition as part of a consumer-oriented reform, which, however, failed to move the Cabinet.[60] In the autumn of the following year, Mr. Macmillan was himself on the move, being replaced as P.M. by Sir Alec Douglas-Home (who had quickly disrobed as the 14th Earl of Home). Frederick Erroll was not so much replaced as superseded by Edward Heath in that the Department was up-graded and Mr. Heath became Secretary of State, not a "mere" Minister.[61] And he was a leader of the modernizers.

In terms of RPM, these changes came in perfectly on cue because it was now being gravely threatened by what the *Pharmaceutical Journal* called the "trading stamps tamasha," (an Urdu word apparently used in Britain since the 1880s to mean a fuss or commotion). A great tamasha indeed. Cadbury Brothers, one of the last of the RPM-ers in the food trade, cut off supplies of chocolate and biscuits to shopkeepers who gave away stamps and was counterattacked by Jack Cohen, chairman of Tesco Stores. Business leaders such as Lord Sainsbury of Sainsbury's and Malcolm Cooper of Allied Suppliers (Home & Colonial, Maypole, Liptons, Pearks, and so forth) mobilized the opposition into a Distributive Trades Alliance (DTA), to which "most of the leading" TAs (it was claimed) adhered: ". . . before very long every section of the retail trade and many manufacturers were deeply embroiled in a noisy confrontation over the issue of whether housewives should be allowed to collect gummy-backed pink, green, orange and blue trading stamps."[62] In December the DTA took full pages in newspapers to assert: "It's smart to save money—not stamps!"[63] Full pages were taken in January to claim that, as a result of the first ads, "unprompted and unasked, hundreds of women wrote expressing their indignation against trading stamps."[64]

The whole campaign was political rather than commercial, the January advertisements specifically so: "This important problem of giving the housewife proper information and protection is being discussed in Parliament on 31st January." Two private members' bills had given the Cabinet generally and Mr. Heath in particular "furiously to think": one, by John Osborn (Cons.), to regulate the use of trading stamps, and the other, by John Stonehouse (Lab. and Co-op), to abolish RPM. Introduced on 11 December, Mr. Stonehouse's Bill even required them, and rather too quickly for comfort, to make up their minds on the question of abolishing RPM, especially as the known support of some Conservatives might well give the bill a second reading and carry it through.

Support not so much for the bill as such as for the principle came from an unexpected quarter, the National Economic Development Council (NEDC), which in terms of our typology is neither fish nor fowl, neither a purely private group—because publicly financed—yet not governmental. Consistently with its great theme ("go for growth"), it pressed for the abolition of the RPM as one species of restrictive practice. At its meeting on 8 January, a leading member put the issue squarely to the chairman, none other than the Chancellor, Reginald Maudling, who however refused to commit himself then.[65]

Time was now running out: the Stonehouse Bill was coming up for second reading on Friday, 17 January and the Cabinet had yet to decide whether to grasp the nettle of abolition. The Sunday papers helped to focus their minds on the issue, and in such confident terms that the writers must have been briefed; for example, "Heath will announce end of retail price fixing this week" (*Sunday Times*), and "Heath will act to curb price-fixing" (*Observer*).[66] Predictably, Tuesday's Cabinet was lively, even heated. Those opposing abolition, at least for the time being, included Selwyn Lloyd, Lord Blakenham (John Hare, who was also party chairman), Quintin Hogg, and R.A. Butler. Mr. Heath was supported by Mr. Maudling ("If a little nonchalantly"),[67] Frederick Erroll, who had made the gallant attempt earlier, Keith Joseph, and Edward Boyle. After a three-hour meeting, half of which is believed to have been devoted to RPM, the issue was not resolved and had to be taken up again the following morning. Then, evidently, the reformers carried the day, since Mr. Heath told the House that afternoon that, as part of a broad modernizing policy, legislation would be introduced that session to end RPM, which "should be presumed to be against the public interest unless in any particular case it is proved to the contrary to the satisfaction of a judicial tribunal."[68] If that represented a "fall-back" policy from the almost total prohibition that he and the Department had sought,[69] it was nevertheless, considering the earlier failures, a famous victory. As a *Times* first leader (believed to have been written by the editor himself, Sir William

Haley) remarked: "Mr. Heath, within three months of arriving at the Board of Trade, has managed to push through the Cabinet proposals to abolish" RPM.[70]

That victory, of course, was so far confined to the Cabinet room, and even Cabinet members were still sufficiently ill at ease to meet again on Friday (when the Stonehouse Bill was negatived without a division) to discuss, for two and a half hours, the reactions to Mr. Heath's announcement. They decided, evidently, to persevere, but would they prevail? It was by no means certain. As that *Times* leader writer had also remarked: "Some people may be hurt. That is inevitable. It is part of the process of increasing competition and efficiency." Those "people," however, were determined not to be hurt if they could help it, and individually many of them could help it, being shopkeepers "who are often the mainstay of [Conservative] ward and constituency organization" at a time when a general election could not be more than within nine or ten months away. As TAs they were already organized nationally through the Resale Price Maintenance Co-ordinating Committee, formed by Leonard Pagliero in 1960 when the Board of Trade (under Mr. Maudling) launched its internal inquiry into RPM. Based on Wimpole Street, and advised by Gilbert McAllister, a former M.P., it had already made itself known to M.P.s, and would soon demonstrate that it enjoyed sufficient "status to be given access on occasion to Mr. Heath at the Board of Trade."[71]

It was Mr. Pagliero who greeted Mr. Heath's announcement with: "This is an absolutely dreadful statement. We challenge Mr. Heath's reasoning completely."[72] But he was hardly taken by surprise since he had booked a room at the St. Stephen's Tavern, just across from the House of Commons, for that very evening. There he put on "a private dinner party . . . for M.P.s and lobbyists," reported David Leitch.[73] The M.P.s numbered about a dozen, including the Conservative baronet, Sir Richard Glyn, who would say in the House two days later that without RPM "small shopkeepers would go to the wall."[74] "Little Man, What Now?" (as the *Sunday Telegraph* asked editorially that weekend) was to be a persistent theme throughout the campaign.

Not even an outline of that campaign as a whole can be provided here in the space available. Contenting ourselves with a sketch of the principal moves made by the pressure groups and of the salient features of the political situation in which they made them, we should first note that de facto, the first shots were fired not by the Co-ordinating Committee but by individual TAs taking aim at the Stonehouse Bill, whose basic idea, however, was perpetuated in the proposed Government Bill. On the very afternoon of Mr. Heath's announcement, the London District Council of the Federation of Retail Newsagents sent M.P.s such as Sir John Vaughan-Morgan Bt. (chairman of the Conservative backbench Trade and Industry Committee) a telegram urging "the strongest possible objection" not only to the Stonehouse bill but to "any alteration" in the existing RPM system (see Appendix B). The PATA (600 pharmaceutical manufacturers and wholesalers, plus 10,000 or more retail chemists), hand in glove with the

National Pharmaceutical Union (retail chemists as employers), sent the membership a useful campaign kit: explanatory and exhortatory letter, arguments for the retention of RPM, and a model letter to M.P.s (Appendix B). Some recipients, however, used the kit in a rather unimaginative way. On the Friday Sir John Vaughan-Morgan would remark: "When I find myself opening three letters in my morning mail which by a strange coincidence say in the last paragraph, 'This will have serious political repercussions at the next general election', my reaction is positively hostile."[75] That wording reflected a little too faithfully the penultimate paragraph of the model letter, and the exhortation (printed in black type) in the last paragraph but two of the covering letter. Perhaps the leadership should have taken the precaution of doing what Sir John thought they had done. Referring to those chemists' letters he wrote: "Although they were individually written, they were almost certainly inspired by a circular letter from the Secretary of the Trade Association which, I would hazard a guess, said something like: 'Write to your Member of Parliament in your own words, on the following lines. . . .' Of course, what then happens is that they all write virtually the same letter and, in this case, they even repeated all the same phrases."[76] He went on to acknowledge that he had later received other letters from chemists "who did not repeat their arguments in the same, monotonous form"; and that although "we are, of course, being subjected to quite a pressure campaign . . . I would not want you to think that it was all of it as stereotyped and unreasonable as the examples I have quoted above." Still, although "it is, naturally, perfectly fair that Members should be lobbied . . . it is part of our profession," lobbying annoys "when so much of it is inept and calculated, in some cases, positively to provoke hostility to the cause advocated."[77]

That risk seems to have been discounted by Mr. Stevenson, "a high powered Midlander who has the National Chamber of Trade with 450,000 retailers at his disposal as a pressure group." Before the week of the announcement was out, he had "circularized his vast membership and advised them to protest to their M.P.s at once," saying: "When the letters start streaming in I think Ted Heath will get quite a shock."[78] But it might not have worked to the NCT's advantage. Much would have turned on such variables as the quality of the write-in and the marginality of the recipients' seats.

In any event, the target was now the Secretary (and Government) rather than a private member. So it was, too, with the Co-ordinating Committee, which met in London on 17 January with some thirty TAs represented, and again at the Connaught Rooms the following Friday, when the turnout was even better: Forty TAs, represented by a hundred senior officials. This would be later described (by Maurice Corina) as "a strictly private war conference. . . . The press, which could have widely publicized their cause, was kept on the doorstep."[79] The mystery, however, had more to do with the strategy to be adopted than with the stand to be taken. After a long meeting it was unanimously agreed (and reported) that "the system of resale price maintenance, which has operated for 60 years in the public interest, should be permitted to continue."[80] They appointed what they themselves would call (on letterheads) a steering committee, drawn from five TAs that had been in the van of fixed-price free enterprise for a couple of generations: the Stationers' Association (Leonard Pagliero); PATA (H.E. Chapman); Motor Trade Association (MTA, K.C. Johnson-Davies); NCT (that high-powered Midlander, J.W. Stevenson); and the Electrical Wholesalers Federation (P.B. Etheridge). They also set up a Defence Fund, for which the PATA, for example, was quick to pass round the hat (28 January).[81]

What the Co-ordinating Committee did not announce was its strategy, merely letting it be known that the views of its constituent members would be conveyed to Mr. Heath by every means. But, insofar as these were not surreptitious, they soon identified themselves in use and included the following types of action designed to engage the governing elite both face to face and indirectly:

Mass meetings or demonstrations (e.g., St. Pancras Town Hall on 20 February, attended by some 600 delegates of various organizations who unanimously approved a resolution to retain RPM, copy to be taken to Mr. Heath at the House);

Interviews with M.P.s in constituencies (e.g., Retail news agents) and petitions (e.g., one from 500 local retail and wholesale tobacconists awaited John Cordle, the local M.P., at Conservative Party H.Q. in Bournemouth on 7 February);

Mass letter writing to M.P.s

Letter-writing had already been practised on a considerable scale, especially by the private chemists,[82] to stop the Stonehouse Bill. By 23 January, too, some Conservative backbenchers had already received "up to 40 letters of strong protest from shopkeepers in their constituencies."[83] Now the steady flow was to be turned into a flood. Direct evidence on the local response is lacking, but on 1 February a leading Conservative backbencher, Angus Maude, spoke of backbenchers having received "30 to 40 letters from retailers." On 10 February it was reported: "A Conservative backbencher in a rural area says he has had more than 40 letters, all bitterly hostile to Government policy. At the other end [of the scale] some backbenchers have had as few as 10 or a dozen letters. . . ."[84] By then Mr. Heath himself had received about 600 letters, mostly expressing opposition.[85]

One way or another, especially knowing how furious RPM supporters undoubtedly were, we may conclude that they put pen to paper in substantial numbers.

Letters written to M.P.s by TAs nationally, it is known, did pour in. The most innovative submission was made by the PATA, which circularized the evidence it had given to the internal Board of Trade inquiry (1960-61). That, like the report itself, had never been published. The PATA also made the criticism, which prima facie always carries some weight, that the decision to abolish RPM was not preceded, "as might have been expected," either by a White Paper or by "consultations with representatives of the thousands of traders affected."[86]

All this, on the face of it, seems tantamount to a shot-gun approach; in practice, the groups were more discriminating. As *The Times* political correspondent would report on 10 February:

In the past five or six weeks the pressure has been concentrated, with several signs of organization and coordination, upon Conservative backbenchers. It has been put on at both national and constituency level. Some backbenchers testify that veiled threats have come through the mail from shopkeepers in their constituencies: votes will be withheld at the general election, Mr. Heath will throw workers out of a job and they will be told who is responsible.[87]

That, evidently, was the sort of veil one sees through rather easily, and doubtless the Conservative backbenchers did not care for what they saw. To what extent were they affected? It may be true that most of the letters from TAs nationally "made little or no impact." But the "part of the mail that comes handwritten or unevenly typed bearing" the constituency postmarked may have been "really disturbing."[88] Even locally mailed letters recognized as having a common central source may unnerve a Member, depending on his/her experience, size of majority, closeness to the election, and so on. As Angus Maude put it: "Some M.P.s think the end of the world has come if they get 30 to 40 letters from retailers as part of an organized campaign. . . ."[89] Mr. Maude was that rare bird, a Conservative backbencher who spoke out publicly in favour of abolition, and obviously meant his colleagues to discount pressure of that coordinated kind. But it is indirect evidence that some of them had been moved by at least that part of the campaign.

A broader impact may be deduced from the extraordinary role of Conservative backbenchers in the House. They criticized the Secretary of State for Industry to his face, with few coming to his defence, at meetings not only of the 1922 Committeee (all Conservative backbenchers) but in its specialized offshoot, the Trade and Industry Committee, with which Mr. Heath himself had to deal at least eight times, or seven, counting from his mid-January statement.[90] For the first of the seven, about one hundred backbenchers crowded in (any backbencher may attend the specialist meetings); for the third, on the day after the publication of the Bill, two hundred. Mr. Heath's reception then (Walter Terry of the *Mail* reported) "was first frigid, then openly critical."[91] One of the critics commented, referring to Mr. Heath's earlier role as negotiator for Britain's entry into the EEC: "No wonder we could not get into the Common Market—there is no room in Europe for two de Gaulles."[92] Several of the critics had already put their money where their mouth was: "within an hour or two of the publication" of the Bill a group of Conservative backbenchers "rushed to the Table a motion to stop the Bill dead in its tracks on the formula that it be read 'this day six months' " (i.e., rejected).[93]

Two weeks later they and many others threw caution to the wind, voting against or abstaining on Second Reading, despite the entreaties of the Chief Whip, Martin Redmayne, and a meeting the night before with the former Chief Whip, Mr. Heath himself. The Government was not put at risk because Labour, although in favour of abolition in principle, was known to be playing the Parliamentary game of abstention on Second Reading, hence the voting of 287-20. But another twelve openly abstained. Of those who missed the division (including, strangely enough, the P.M. himself, who chose to keep a speaking engagement at Coventry), 20 or so were conveniently absent, making a total of over 50 rebels, all against a three-line whip. *The Times* in fact made the total a precise 56, and compared it to earlier rebellions: 27 abstentions on the Profumo affair (1963); 15 on the Suez issue (1956); and 17, with no votes against the Government, over the resignation of Sir Anthony Eden as Foreign Secretary in 1938.[94] That rather exaggerates the uniqueness of the vote: In 1961, attempting to restore capital punishment, 69 Conservatives tried to amend their own Government's Criminal Justice Bill. Above all, after 1938 came May 1940, when 60 Conservatives abstained on a vote of confidence for the Chamberlain Government, and 33 even voted with the Opposition. But the RPM revolt was one of the greatest of its kind since 1940 and may well have constituted, as a rebel claimed, "the most remarkable example in Conservative Party history of a revolt spreading in spite of the most terrific pressure from many quarters. Normally a revolt is whittled down until it loses its impetus by the time of the division."[95] No doubt he, Sir Frank Markham, partly had in mind appeals to toe the line of the type "Remember, you'll be voting not against Heath but against Alec," the P.M.[96]

All this suggests that the external pressure, too, was terrific and having substantial effect. Something approaching a half of those who voted against the Bill (including the tellers) were electorally vulnerable in holding marginal seats (some 5000 or less); about a third were holding on with majorities of under 2500, as were at least a quarter of the identifiable abstainers. Even those with cast-iron majorities, such as Mr. Cordle at Bournemouth (East), may have been influenced by the very intensity of the petitioners (see list above). At least one of those who voted against probably needed little persuasion: Sir Hugh Linstead, joint secretary of the Pharmaceutical Society. This is a professional body with a Royal Charter, whose lobbying has been mainly done by the PATA and National Pharmaceutical Union and by such ad hoc creations as the Chemists' Friends, the Chemists' Federation, and so forth, but not to the exclusion of its own efforts (see appendix B). As the other joint secretary, F.W. Adams wrote to M.P.s on this occasion: "The 29,000 members of the Pharmaceutical Society throughout the country feel strongly.... And it is probable that you have had or will receive representations from pharmacists in your constituency."[97] Among nonvoters who may really have been quiet abstainers were Sir Richard Glyn and Iain Macleod.

So Conservative backbenchers could be influenced but could Mr. Heath? Led by Sir Richard Glyn, a deputation of eight from the Co-ordinating Committee had waited upon him. Led by Sir Hugh Linstead, a joint team (Pharmaceutical Society, the Company Chemists' Association—representing Boots, Timothy Whites, and so forth—and the National Pharmaceutical Union) had waited upon him. Some groups (e.g., the MTA but also others from outside the ring, such as the Nottingham-based National Union of Small Shopkeepers) descended on David Price in the hope of influencing his boss at the BOT, Mr. Heath (whom they also corralled when he was visiting Nottingham). Other groups singled out another lieutenant at the BOT, Edward du Cann. Yet the Secretary had given no ground. Earlier he had been pictured by some Conservative backbencher from the shires as "threshing his horns among the bullocks to be first through the gate."[98] Now he had passed through the first gate, and if he had been bumped on the way, he was still out in front.

Within forty-eight hours of the Second Reading, however, he was negotiating with the rebels through the good offices of the Trade and Industry Committee. Whether that was of his own free will (the actual invitation naturally came from him), or whether he had taken a hint from the P.M. and initially entered the discussions "with bad grace and reluctance," especially when he found that he would be meeting two leading rebels, Roy Wise and Sir Hugh Linstead, and one (probable) abstainer, Sir Richard Glyn, is (at present) uncertain.[99] In any event, Mr. Heath chose to work through the Trade and Industry Committee chaired by Sir John Vaughan-Morgan (himself a former Minister of State at the BOT), who brought in the Vice Chairman and Secretary, two backbench supporters of the bill, and the three rebels to serve as a kind of armistice commission. With this body the Government, meaning first of all Peter Walker, the Secretary's PPS, and Anthony Kershaw, PPS to Selwyn Lloyd (Leader of the House) and, for the last four meetings, the Secretary himself, negotiated from Monday, 16 March to late on the Thursday night, 19 March. On that final hectic day Mr. Heath and the ad hoc negotiating group reached agreement on a rough draft of the fundamental (onus of proof) amendment in the late afternoon, but had to resume their healing work after dinner and into the night. That work was done in relays. Produced by BOT officials, drafts were taken to the Lord Chancellor's room, where Lord Dilhorne himself, Sir John Hobson, the Attorney-General, and Mr. Heath sat in judgment of them over Scotch and sandwiches. Once agreed, the drafts were taken by Anthony Kershaw to the ad hoc committee for their endorsement. In that way the ad hoc committee produced the basic amendments just in time to get them on the

Commons Order paper on Friday, which was just in time for the Committee stage due to start on Monday.

The pressure to compromise had been acute. At the beginning of the week, the Government Chief Whip knew that 71 of his flock had signed amendments to the Bill. That night Selwyn Lloyd, who "despite the principle of joint Cabinet responsibility . . . has not bothered to hide his opposition to the Cabinet decision on RPM,"[100] spoke out publicly for the rebels, having taken "exceptional measures" to find out what they would like him to say.[101] Without consulting Mr. Heath, and taking "great care" to alert the press (who might have neglected the AGM of the Fulham Conservative Association in the King's Hall), Mr. Lloyd said: "My own view is that not all RPM is good and not all RPM is bad."[102] That Mr. Heath and his men were furious when the news reached them is altogether plausible since the remark touched the central issue throughout— the onus of proof. Should there be a presumption against RPM, such that the onus would be on a TA to prove that *its* RPM scheme was *not* against the public interest? Or should it be the other way round, some central body's having to prove that a particular RPM *was* against the public interest? Apart from his original statement, the Secretary had repeated on second reading that "the burden of proof goes really to the root of the general conclusions . . . that resale price maintenance itself is incompatible with a competitive economy and, save in exceptional circumstances, should be brought to an end." This the rebels had never accepted, and this a Cabinet colleague of Mr. Heath's now obliquely, but publicly, questioned. One of the rebels exulted: "Selwyn Lloyd gave us our case on onus of proof last night."[103]

On Wednesday the pressure to compromise increased. At the annual 1922 Committee lunch for the P.M. at the Savoy, Sir Alec, before flying off to Nigeria, made an appeal for party unity. Whether that was addressed more to Mr. Heath (at fifth place to his left on the top table), Mr. Lloyd (fourth place to his right), or to the rebels out in front is uncertain. But it is known that, in a basement room in the House of Commons, within an hour after the ad hoc negotiations had been resumed that very afternoon at 2.30 (what stamina!), a settlement of sorts was reached on the central issue of onus of proof. Thursday (as already described) was given over to drafting, apart from a triumphal procession to the 1922 Committee at 6 p.m. Around midnight the Secretary, Law Officers, and ad hoc committee were enjoying a celebration drink.

What was being celebrated was a settlement, but what had been settled, on the central issue, was almost immediately in dispute. According to a leading critic, Roy Wise: "One really important new factor is that by introducing the Board of Trade as a party to the proceedings, we have brought House of Commons control back." This would mean, as he did not need to say, that the Commons could "continually bring pressure to bear on the actions of the Registrar" of the Restrictive Practices Court through the President of the BOT.[104] The Government at once denied that interpretation, and at the opening of the Committee stage on Monday, Mr. Heath said plainly that "the registrar and the court were entirely independent. They were in no way dependent on the Board of Trade, Ministers or the Government."

So what did the backbenchers and the RPM Co-ordinating Committee and the individual TAs have to show for a great deal of effort? Certainly they had won some concessions, as over the use of the loss leader in shops. But what of the really big issue—that is, the onus of proof? Manufacturers and retailers wishing to keep up their RPM agreements would have to register them. No registration: no (valid) RPM agreement. If an agreement were registered, it could be kept going for the time being—that was indeed a gain for the critics because the condemnation would no longer be automatic. As Ministers acknowledged, that at least changed the emphasis of the Bill. Moreover, the BOT would now have permissive powers, as under the 1956 Act, to direct the Registrar on the order of categories of goods to be called up for examination. That was what Mr. Wise had had in mind. But he did not say that once summoned, a petitioner would still have to prove that his RPM agreement was in the public interest. As a Conservative backbencher, Graham Page, complained on Monday: "The onus of proof . . . , should not be by the supplier, or the manufacturer or the retailer, but it should be placed on a Government department," which was greeted with Opposition cheers. Besides, until called up, any RPM agreement "which was now perfectly legal" would be left in "suspended invalidity." That night Edward Greenfield wrote, "the Tory rebels . . . gave up the ghost. They accepted the Government's complete victory on onus of proof . . . and barely pretended that the compromise amendment provided a substantial concession."[105]

Why, then, did they not continue to fight? Party loyalty, perhaps, especially in view of the P.M.'s appeal at the Savoy lunch. Possibly some mental and even physical exhaustion: They had done all that could have been expected of them, but it had not been quite enough. Also, of course, they were squeezed. As Edward Greenfield had put it the previous Friday when the main amendments were being tabled at the eleventh hour: "The beauty of Mr. Heath's timing, from the Government's point of view, is that there is hardly enough time for the concessions to be found inadequate before the Committee stage starts on Monday."[106]

That, however, prompts the question: Why hadn't the inadequacies been discovered by the ad hoc committee and the Law Officers? The bitter answer James Margach heard was that ". . . the Cabinet were fooled, the 1922 Committee was fooled, Sir John Vaughan-Morgan's steering committee on their Red Cross mission of mercy were fooled, and the rebels were fooled—all deceived into believing that an honourable truce had been negotiated."[107] And who did the fooling? Mr. Margach did not answer directly, but did record in the next paragraph that "Mr. Heath is inevitably cast as the villain of the peace by the rebels." "Fooled" may be much too harsh, but the attitudes and behaviour of the rebels were consistent with the belief. The recriminations behind the scenes constituted "an ugly manifestation of spite, venom and nervous exhaustion." On the Tuesday, they, with others, almost defeated the Government, 204-203, on the amendment to exempt drugs, medicines, and appliances from the provisions of the Bill. On that occasion, 31 of them voted with the Opposition and as many as 50 may have abstained. The rebels included a vice chairman of the 1922 Committee, Sir Charles Mott-Radclyffe, Sir John Barlow, and others commonly called "Establishment figures." Challenged to draw in his horns, Mr. Heath answered, echoing Sir Winston, "One is enough." He got his Bill, much amended in detail, that July. Within twelve months he was elected Leader of the Party. But by then the Party was no longer in office, having been pipped at the post in October.

The Peaks

Above the local chambers of commerce and of trade, the TAs and the hybrids stand the "high rises," commonly called "peaks." Beginning to be politically important from about 1860, these in the mid-1970s included, in the world of business alone, the Association of British Chambers of Commerce (ABCC); National Chamber of Trade (NCT), Retail Consortium, Multiple Shops Federation, covering the supermarkets too, the Retail Alliance, the Retail Distributors Association, recruiting the big department stores, and the Co-operative Union, the 250 or so retail coops, claiming over 11 million members, and possibly the Retail Food Confederation (the independent fresh food shops, whose owners formed the view that the Consortium in practice really spoke for the supermarkets and the department stores); the British Federation of Commodity Associations (companies and TAs); the British Importers Confederation; and the Confederation of British Industry (CBI). The political role of the peaks in the 1970s might well be worth a book to itself, but here we have to confine ourselves to a few observations about a few of them, and then only from the point of view of modes of representation to government—that is, their interaction with the political system.

Of the three that will receive some attention here, two—the NCT and the ABCC—have already been touched upon briefly. Each is more than it seems: the 88 Chambers of Commerce within the realm of the ABCC have over 750 TAs in harness; the NCT with its 835 chambers of trade (1972) harbours 34 National Allied Societies (i.e., TAs such as the Master Bakers; Fish Friers; Laundrette Owners; Retail News Agents and Motor Agents). Electing six members to the Board of Management, the National Allied Societies Committee "is an integral part of the Chamber"; it advises the Board "on the formulation of policy," which it then helps to disseminate "through the specific trade associations right down to the individual shopkeeper."[108]

In a sense the CBI, too, is more than it seems. Every one of its putative ancestors—General Chamber of Manufacturers in the 1780s, Employers' Parliamentary Council in the 1890s, Federation of British Industries (FBI), 1916-1965—was far more limited.[109] Created by amalgamation in 1965 from the FBI and two other peaks, both rivals over a certain range,[110] the CBI is unique, both structurally and functionally, in Britain. It has about 11,000 companies in membership, including 75 percent of the top 200 and 50 percent of the top 1,000 (in *The Times* Listings), the main gap being in banking and insurance. It is catholic enough to take in the nationalized industries and embraces almost all the leading TAs and EOs. The absentees include the organizations of the wholesale and retail trades and the Chamber of Shipping, a TA.[111] But the corresponding EO, the Shipping Federation, is in, as is the Shipbuilders and Repairers National Association (a hybrid). At this level finance capitalism is partly represented through several EOs (Federation of London Clearing Banks, Federation of Scottish Bank Employers, the Trustee Savings Bank Employers Council, the Finance Houses Association), and several TAs (British Insurance Association Corporation of Insurance Brokers, Corporation of Lloyds). On balance, no doubt, the city chooses to go its own way: As anyone who has worked within the Square Mile knows or senses, it is a world apart, has its own networks and its own connections with government. On the other hand, the CBI does have the Country Landowners Association and the farmers: the NFU of England and Wales; of Scotland; and of Ulster (all hybrids). Functionally, as implied above, the CBI unites under its banner what has often been kept separate, as it was in this country up to 1965: trade association work and industrial relations/collective bargaining.

How can one begin to sketch this scene, even for the limited purpose in hand? If the interaction of the peaks (NCT/ABCC/CBI) with government could ever be reduced to one word, it would be "dialogue," a term (and concept) much favoured in CBI circles but of general application: a "continuous and constructive dialogue with Ministers and their civil servants" (Michael Clapham, President, 1973); "The CBI's character, and perhaps its main raison d'être, is geared to a dialogue with Government (John Davies, Director-General, 1967).[112] Government, of course, was not always geared to such a dialogue. In 1904 the P.M.G., Lord Stanley, twice refused to receive a deputation from the NCT to discuss cash-on-delivery postal facilities, saying not that the organization was too new to be recognized (formed 1896), but that the discussion would serve no useful purpose. A campaign culminating in a protest meeting at Bolton in October apparently attracted considerable support: Within three days the P.M.G. sent a telegram offering to receive a deputation. A team of five, broadly based but led by the NCT's President, waited on the P.M.G. and got what it wanted, which, at the time, was to stop the introduction of COD facilities. (A year later the P.M.G., in the context of postal workers, would be complaining of "the amount of pressure" to which contemporary M.P.s were subjected.)[113]

Today, the interchange so contrived then seems so automatic as to be almost a natural phenomenon. The NCT makes its pre-Budget submissions to the Chancellor, touching in some detail (1972) upon income and corporation tax regulations, capital gains, and estate duty. But much of the initiative comes from government: "Consultative documents on Value Added Tax have run to many hundreds of pages and every line has been carefully studied."[114] After all that labour of Sisyphus (rather than Aphrodite), the NCT had to consider how to make its representations. Where complete unanimity prevailed with the other interests, as refracted especially through the VAT Working Party of the Retail Consortium, then NCT representations were first made through the Consortium, the targets being both the Board of HM Customs and Excise, with whom discussions followed, and Members of Parliament. Where the NCT differed from the others, it went its own way to the appropriate Minister or Department.

Evidently the dialogue does not exclude some cultivation of M.P.s. In the early seventies the chairman of the Parliamentary committee, Mr. Charles Dodd, was giving up so much time to the work that he was "becoming a well-known figure in Westminster,"[115] which in the United States at least would earn him the title of lobbyist. In 1972, Lord Jacques, the senior Coop peer, introduced into the Upper House the Landlord and Tenant (Business Compensation) Bill, the first Bill ever drafted and sponsored by the Chamber, which took "especial pride" in it even though it was not enacted. The NCT also knows where to turn: In 1972 members of the Parliamentary committee twice met the Trade Committee of the 1922 Committee to talk wholly or partly about VAT (i.e., the backbenchers of the Government of the day).

Nor does the dialogue exclude some open campaigning, as evidenced already in tracing the RPM dispute. Another example, clearly minor in comparison, was the NCT's 1968 campaign against the GPO's decision to raise the cost of first-class mail to 5d. Advising its 450,000 members to stick to the 4d post, the NCT naturally failed to keep back the inflationary tide even then. The campaign is mainly memorable for its splendid jingle: "Make a ghost of the 5d post." It also played a part in 1970 in the campaign against a further increase in SET. The burden was borne by the Retail Consortium (formed 1968), while an ad hoc group with an address in Clifford Street, W.1, worked for the more fundamental goal implied in its title, the Committee for the Repeal of Selective Employment Tax. When the Government changed hands, the Consortium itself led a deputation to the new Chancellor, Iain Macleod, to press for an end to SET. About a year earlier the Retail Alliance had campaigned to relieve specialist retailers from SET entirely. MPS were circularized ("thousands" of letters were supposed to descend on them); the Alliance chairman, Barry Austin Read, led a deputation of eleven to No.10 to deliver a statement of their case, press photographers being conveniently on hand to record the occasion.[116]

Association of British Chambers of Commerce

Older than the NCT by a generation or two (1860), the ABCC had been admitted earlier within the pale of the constitution (or political system).

Especially after 1898-1910, which saw the accession of the mighty barons previously unwilling to join (Manchester, Liverpool, Glasgow), the ABCC grew in stature, enabling the Liberal Prime Minister, Mr. Asquith to say in March 1914 (*i.e.*, before the forcing-time for government-group relations of August 1914-1918) that they "recognized in your organization the most authoritative and trustworthy exponent of the commercial interests of the United Kingdom."[117] The implied dialogue continued. Much of it was technical. The Board of H.M. Customs and Excise put to the ABCC proposals about the procedure to be followed if the standard rate of VAT were to be changed and also about possible changes in structure (April 1974). After time for reflection, there was a meeting. The ABCC team did not object, but asked for the "longest possible notice," and took the opportunity to come out strongly against "a system of multiple rates, stressing the administrative difficulties and costs which would be involved." Technical representations on fiscal matters for the spring budget 1975 were submitted to the Chancellor (December 1974) and then discussed at a meeting with officials of the Inland Revenue. A working party set up by the Lord Chancellor and Lord Advocate consulted the ABCC (May 1974) about a proposed British-American convention to work out reciprocal arrangements for the enforcement of judgments in civil matters.[118]

Some of the interchanges are naturally more political. Thus in 1974 the Association in correspondence urged on the Chancellor the view that a Capital Transfer Tax and a Wealth Tax, especially at a time of weakened business confidence, "threatened the survival of family businesses." In the context of the third London airport controversy, especially the eventual choice of Maplin Sands, the Association's National Plan for Airports (October 1973), which called for a full reexamination of the policy of concentrating air transport activity on large airports in the south-east, represented a political initiative. Press coverage "was the largest ever accorded a single activity of Chambers of Commerce"; the Department of the Environment produced an analysis to coincide with the publication of the Plan, and even the P.M. made a response.[119] When, in 1974, the Maplin decision was reversed, the Association perceived a marked resemblance between the rationale offered and its own argument the previous year for the regional development of effective airports.

Now and again the dialogue is disrupted and a public argument ensues. This may be illustrated, since it seems characteristic and kills two birds with one stone (brings in the CBI), from some aspects of the struggle against the Labour Government's transport policy in the late sixties. It started with the White Paper on Transport (Cmnd 3057) in July 1966. Diagnosing that the key to solving Britain's transport problems lay in planning to reconcile its many-sided needs (national and regional; economic and social), the Government proceeded to draw out the policy implications. Asked to comment, the Association argued that to distinguish between the uneconomic and the commercially viable railway services, and then to decide which of the former should be subsidized on social or strategic grounds, was generally sound. On the other hand, "the argument of social necessity should be used with care [since] the best initial test of what the community needed was what it was prepared to pay for."[120] The goal of better coordination of road and rail transport was sound, but a national freight policy for that purpose ought not to result "in a more rigid licensing policy than the present one."

These and other representations were made through the Transport Users' Joint Committee (TUJC), which had been thought up because (as the CBI remarked) it was doubtful whether "the transport users case was being advanced with full authority," perhaps a reflection of the fact that "the users' interests were fragmented among various organizations."[121] As a result the CBI, ABCC, British Shippers' Council, and three other bodies banded together as the TUJC, the chairmanship going to the ABCC (D.H. Joyce).[122] Thus the unified approach that marked Government policy at once tended to unify the interests (over a certain range). In accordance with the unwritten code governing group-government relations, the Minister was advised of the creation of the TUJC. Assurances were given that it would be officially accepted as an appropriate channel for consultation on problems of common interest to its members.

How did the TUJC go about its task? Before the Bill was published, numerous submissions were made to the Ministry of Transport. Members met the Minister of Transport (Mrs. Castle) accompanied by her officials. By such methods, "some desirable changes in the proposed legislation were obtained," but there were "no major concessions."[123]

Whereas the ABCC, mainly concerned to defend "the interests of the user" of transport, worked essentially through the TUJC, the CBI is of course a coalition of interests, including providers of transport. Thus it was perturbed about such other Ministerial proposals as the one to limit drivers' hours in the name of safety. Its concern, for costs naturally, was expressed through another aggregating body, the Traders' Co-ordinating Committee on Transport, a constituent of the TUJC. That body put up a paper to the Minister on the cost implications of her proposal.

Throughout much of 1967, Government proposals and White Papers on transport fell like leaves in Vallombrosa, so the CBI, as a coalition, kept aggregating through several joint bodies, with (from September) a committee of its own as, ideally, the ultimate arbiter. This was the ad hoc Transport Policy Steering Group, made up of senior industrialists to advise on broad policy ("broad" is what it would have to have been!).

In other words, the character of the CBI is such that it had to keep up its independent representations to government; it could not be contained within any organization such as the TUJC. In July the President and Director-General saw the Minister. Since that "appeared to have little effect," they were later instructed by the CBI Council to seek a meeting with the Prime Minister. He agreed and saw them in January 1968, when the CBI-ers "urged him, on cost grounds, to defer the proposed reduction in drivers' hours for at least two years."[124] The leader of the team, the President, also strongly attacked (e.g., the proposal to levy a charge on abnormal loads carried by road).

A Bill intended to combine these and many other elements in a creative synthesis had been published the previous month. The TUJC made a clause-by-clause analysis of it, then circularized all M.P.s to impress on them "the strength of opinion against many aspects of the Bill." Some Government backbenchers and even some Liberals were approached, but the principal channel consisted in the Conservative members of the Standing Committee handling the Bill. The combined efforts of the TUJC and CBI (and other TAs) in interaction with Parliamentarians produced by 23 January some 2,000 amendments for the opening of the Committee stage in the Commons. About 1,400 came from the Conservatives alone.[125] The total was astonishing even for a Bill of 169 clauses and 18 schedules. But then the transport interests had always been fertile when fundamentally challenged. Professor Samuel Finer pointed out long ago that within one month of the publication of the Transport Bill of 1946-47 (127 clauses, 13 schedules), the (Conservative) Opposition had a thousand amendments to propose. "Where had they all come from? Geographically speaking from the office of the Conservative Party's Parliamentary Secretariat. . . . In practice, this Secretariat acted as an intermediary between the transport committee of the Parliamentary Party . . . and the various interests which came to Queen Street to suggest their amendments."[126] In the resumption of that war in 1967-68, the Conservative members of the Standing Committee, armed with the 1,400 amendments, put up a great fight under the leadership of Peter Walker, who recruited Michael Spicer (formerly of the intraparty group, PEST) as an aide, and enjoyed the backing of no fewer than six economists and eight lawyers (as volunteers for the cause). In the proceedings themselves he had David Webster and Bernard Weatherill, as general staff officers, and three field commanders for specialized sections of the Bill.[127] What one of them, Gordon Campbell, said later surely applied, *mutatis mutandis*, to them all: "I and my colleagues on the committee have been continually meeting, or corresponding with, trade associations and other bodies representing every kind of industry that uses transport."[128] Such ongoing interactions produced in the end most of the final total of 2,500 amendments credited to the Opposition as a whole.

The users did not leave all the fighting to the TUJC. In March, for example, the Multiple Shops Federation circularized all M.P.s with the assessment that the Bill would increase the average distribution cost to large scale retailers by between 6.5 percent and 8.5 percent. That was also the theme of the whole-page advertisements taken by about a dozen TAs, including all the NFUs, the Food Manufacturers' Association, Wholesale Traders and Multiple Grocers:

Dear Mrs. Britain,
    We believe your food bill will go up by an unnecessary £16,000,000 . . . thanks to this ill-considered Transport Bill.

And, after the argument: "What can you do? Please help persuade the Minister to get his priorities right and reconsider this Bill. Discuss it with your housewives organizations and your local M.P."[129]

Nor, of course, was all the fighting left to the users. To some extent the providers expressed themselves through the CBI, but the Road Haulage Association (RHA) also circularized M.P.s, many of whom were said to have tabled amendments as a result. The RHA chairman, Philip Turner, linked the hauliers to Peter Walker.

Nor, as we have seen from the "Mrs. Britain" advertisements, was the battle fought only on the Parliamentary front. The PR specialists, *Aims of Industry*, launched some of their thunderbolts. The RHA turned again to PR, hiring a specialist (Richard Murphy), organizing discussions of the details of the Bill, and staging demonstrations.[130] In one of these in April, put on with the Motor Agents' Association, the Passenger Vehicle Operators' Association (mainly comprising the smaller operators) as well as the Greater London Young Conservatives, some 1,500 people and 60 gaily decorated vehicles, preceded by a stage coach drawn by a pair of greys, converged upon No.10 Downing Street from a roadhead in Hyde Park. Led by a bell-ringing town crier, traditionally dressed, a deputation then delivered two petitions, one scroll "three quarters of a mile long" bearing 100,000 signatures; the other 500,000.[131] This provided an opportunity for a picture, which had Mr. Walker in a prominent position outside No. 10, possibly in anticipation of greater glory to come.

But where was he getting to inside the House? The Walker team proved to be, in the judgment of the *Observer*, "a highly effective parliamentary opposition."[132] By the time the Committee stage ended in mid-May after a record 45 sittings, 92 of the Conservative amendments had been "accepted either in their entirety or in principle," providing grounds for Mr. Walker's claim to "substantial improvements," although it must be admitted that he and his team could not hold a candle to the Government. For the Government not only withdrew 24 of the original clauses; it even authored 200 amendments to its own Bill, described as the largest batch from that source in parliamentary history,[133] which one can well believe.

It was not quite all over. In the Lords, 258 amendments were put down, including "many which were insubstantial or to which the Government agreed."[134] One, moved by Lord Merivale (a former honorary secretary of the ABCC) but drafted by the TUJC, provided the occasion for a defeat of the Government. After discussion with the CBI, Opposition Peers threw out "many of the Bill's most contentious clauses," which may have amounted to as many as 60, touching 20 main points.[135] However, as the CBI also noted, most of those were restored by the Commons. For its part the ABCC noted that the Bill had received the royal assent (in late October) "with comparatively few substantial changes."[136] Certainly there had been some of these. For example: the Minister had conceded that the reduction of drivers' hours to a maximum of nine hours actual driving per day should now take place in two stages. The proposed charge on abnormal loads was dropped, at considerable (anticipated) loss to the

Revenue. There were some other modest gains. But there was not a great deal to show, considering, in the judgment of a close observer: "No other Bill in the history of this Labour Government [had] run into such formidable resistance."[137] The pressure groups had entered the fray over two years earlier.

Confederation of British Industry

In a birth reminiscent of Athena's surprising emergence from the head of Zeus, the CBI appeared fully grown in 1965 from the bodies of the Federation of British Industries (FBI), the National Association of British Manufacturers (NABM), and the British Employers' Confederation (BEC). Its principal objects were defined in the Supplemental (Royal) Charter that came under the Great Seal on 30 July. The one most relevant to public policy making is:

To provide for British industry the means of formulating, making known and influencing general policy in regard to industrial, economic, fiscal, commercial, labour, social, legal and technical questions, and to act as a national point of reference for those seeking industry's views.

Obviously, no clear line separates industrial from labour, or even from economic, policy, and some of the other categories are no more autonomous. The comprehensiveness of the list, in fact, reflects rather a lawyer's concern for the fullest conceivable coverage in the statement of objects. Evidently the CBI is entitled to speak on virtually every issue of public policy, and it has never been backward in claiming its birthright.

How is it organized to produce public policy? Fundamentally, as a series of committees interacting with the Director-General and some other members of the full-time staff. Committees, working parties, panels, and the like amounted to between 50 and 60 in 1971 (depending upon the mode of calculation), but it is of course the standing committees that matter. In the mid-seventies their number hovered around thirty. For internal policy making, the General Purposes Committee (GPC) and the partly overlapping Finance Committee are officially described as central, though the GPC, chaired by the President, advises on "the tactical handling of issues facing the CBI, relations with other organizations . . . " and so has an external orientation as well. However, for "representing and advancing its members' interests" (i.e., thinking about public affairs), the CBI has committees on Economic Policy, Employment Policy, for NEDC Liaison, State Intervention in Private Industry, Labour and Social Affairs, and the like. The members, who (in the late sixties) totalled "some hundreds of top-flight executives and specialists from all parts of the country . . . ,"[138] serve at the invitation of the Director-General, except for the chairmen, who are chosen by the President. He and the Vice President are elected by the membership at the annual general meeting.

Out of the committees, policy, somehow, emerges: A realistic account of the process is, as usual, most difficult to come by. But from knowledge of other bodies with the same combination of laymen and full-time staff, such as the British Legion, one would expect to be able to trace the fluctuating influence of the President (half-time or more during his two years of office); on some issues, the Vice President; senior Committee Chairmen; the Director-General, and one or more of his three deputies. In other words, the CBI is almost certainly run by a very small, partly self-perpetuating, elite. There is nothing wicked or "sinister" about that—the term Mr. Callaghan once used to characterize an element within the CBI, the Industrial Policy Group, founded in 1967 by Sir Paul Chambers and other "tycoons" as a ginger group. On the contrary, that, according to a well-known sociological law, is how substantial organizations always tend to work.

In any event, policy emerges. What happens then? It passes as a recommendation to the CBI Council. The cant word for that body in CBI circles, rivalling even "dialogue" in another context, is "Parliament." That good Welshman, John Davies, when Director-General, even called it "the Parliament of industry," a greater accolade than "Parliament of the CBI."[139] Certainly the Council is a peculiar institution. It provides (at present) no direct representation for the companies that form the basis of the whole structure and supply (1972) 80 percent of the income. Of the regular membership, it is the TAs/EOs that come off best, with 170 of the 400 or so places. The nationalized industries are entitled to 15 places. Since over a third of the 170 are full-time officials of the TAs/EOs, the ethos of the Council seems likely to be not only private enterpris*ing* but trade associationa*l*. Actual attendance at the monthly meetings may strengthen that (presumptive) tendency. Average attendance is officially put at 150-200, and even that may be an exaggeration. In any case an analysis of the attendance figures might show that the most regular and zealous are the professionals, the TA/EO officials.

In any case, the membership component in the strict sense is buttressed by a territorial component. The CBI has twelve regions, matching the Government's pattern. The regions are run by a full-time staff of some 75 and by Regional Councils, which select 50 to speak for the Regions on the CBI Council, and another 50 at large. Since they would naturally be drawn from CBI member companies, often chairmen or directors, the arrangement de facto modifies the structural peculiarity mentioned above. So does the use of the CBI's Council's own power of cooption of 75-100 executives, who also tend to come from the same broad source. In 1972 these cooptions (proposed by the GPC) totalled 80.

So we can identify about 365 (170 + 15 + 100 + 80) of the 400 or so. As one would expect from normal administrative practice, the gap is filled ex-officio by the chairmen of the standing committees, the President (who chairs the GPC), Vice Presidents, and past presidents (of whom there were four in March 1975). Between them they carry the good news from the policy-making committees to the Council. In other words, their policy recommendations are presented to Council for its approval. According to John Davies, Council "is no rubber-stamping organization," and the term—and disavowal—has been echoed by others.[140] Mr. Davies's evidence is that "occasionally papers presented are amended or referred back for further consideration." He was in a position to know. But of course a governing body of even an actual 150-200 persons turning up once a month cannot really be expected to govern such an organization as the CBI, nor does it. Council has to be carried, just as Parliament has to be carried, but it is not at the centre of policy making. Perhaps the analogy of the Council as a Parliament is more subtle than it at first appears to be.

However produced, such CBI policies are converted into inputs to government. No sketch of these is possible here (it takes, one has the best reason for knowing, at least 20,000 words, so fertile has the CBI proved to be since 1965). Instead two broad classes of policy inputs may be identified, one short term and defensive, and the other long term and constructive. The first represents a response to Government action, especially its mistaken policies, including (in Mr. Davies's view) the complete upheaval of the fiscal system represented by the capital gains tax, the corporation tax and the selective employment tax . . . the decision to go ahead with the nationalizing of steel; and the attempt to make the prices and incomes policy work by compulsion. Later examples would probably include the Transport Bill, 1967-68, the Industrial Relations Bill, 1969, the Trade Union and Labour Relations Bill, 1974, and the Industry Bill, 1975 (about which the CBI saw the Secretary once and the P.M. twice in a single month). Most of this was obviously in response to the interventionist policies pursued by Labour Governments, but the Fair Trading Bill, 1973 affords an example from the other (or Conservative) side. This Bill replaced previous legislation on mergers and monopolies; modified the law of restrictive trade practices; and produced new rules for the protection of consumers. The CBI sought some significant changes, such as block exemptions from monopoly references, and for that and other purposes approached (through an ad hoc study group) M.P.s serving on the Standing Committee handling the Bill and some members of the Lords, in addition to frequent exchanges with officials of the DTI. It failed to secure block exemptions but did gain some concessions on the subject of patent agreements. In 1972 the CBI opposed certain features of the Industry Bill, and, throughout the various stages, tried to get it amended.

Among "long-term projects for influencing Government policy," Mr. Davies mentioned the "two-year study we have commissioned from Mr. W.B. Reddaway, the Cambridge economist, into the relationship between private overseas investment and direct exports and its effect on the balance of payments," and the CBI's own study of the industrial and economic implications of entering the EEC. But under this heading we might well place CBI policy initiatives (as distinct from responses). The initiative on prices in July 1971 constitutes a striking example. By 6 August, the official closing date for replies, Sir John Partridge, the President, had persuaded 150 or so of the 200 biggest companies to agree to a voluntary limitation on prices increases for twelve months, provided that the Government would reflate the economy to an appropriate degree, that the nationalized industries would accept the same limitation, and (implicitly) that employers in both private and public sectors held out "as firmly as possible [against] excessive pay settlements. . . ."[141] The 150 ranged from the car manufacturers, American as well as British, Rolls-Royce, Dunlop, Goodyear, Renold and BP to British American Tobacco, Allied Breweries, Watney Mann, and Cadbury Schweppes. Later 90 percent success was claimed (i.e., 180 major companies).

The moratorium, meaning either no increases or not more than 5 percent across the board if absolutely unavoidable, was put into effect. When the twelve months were up, the CBI judged the policy a success insofar as the *rate* of price increases had fallen "substantially" in the intervening period.[142] By now the Government was no longer keeping the unions at arm's length: In March after the miners' strike, the P.M., for the first time since 1970, invited the TUC to meet him. Sixteen of them went along on 9 March, followed by a CBI delegation a week later. The object was tripartite talks, but these were delayed for several reasons, including the need to prepare the ground. With this the group of four was charged: the new CBI Director-General, W.O. Campbell Adamson; Victor Feather, for the TUC; Sir Frank Figgures, Director-General of NEDO; and the distinguished civil servant, Sir William Armstrong. The first of the celebrated series of ten tripartite meetings then opened at No. 10 on 18 July.

In that context, the CBI moratorium, due to end on 31 July simply had to be extended. On 19 July the Council decided on that "for a further and final period of three months," pointing to a "resumption of constructive discussions between the TUC and the CBI" and the opening of the tripartite talks "in the last few days" as factors in its decision.[143] That meant 31 October. But on 2 November at Chequers the tripartite talks collapsed. Four days later the P.M. announced a standstill on prices, pay, and dividends, and the enforcing legislation received the royal assent on the last day of the month.

As to modes of approach, "contact with Government usually takes three forms," Mr. Davies wrote as Director-General: "rather formal meetings with Ministers by the CBI President and other leading figures [including the Director-General]; the informal and far more frequent discussions with civil servants carried out more at staff level on a day to day basis; [and] more indirectly and again a top level," through NEDDY. This is still the broad pattern, but the level at which the dialogue takes place tends to be higher now than in 1967. Thus the 1972 talks were technically held under NEDDY auspices, and the rather formal meetings with Ministers may well be with the Prime Minister himself.

For the most part, the tone of these and related exchanges is urbane and reasonable, but the exceptions are remembered. After the Labour Government abandoned its (short) Industrial Relations Bill in 1969, Mr. Davies, still

Director-General, speculated about the fate of other proposals in the White Paper, *In Place of Strife*, adding "The rest of the White Paper seems fit only for the lavatory." Prime Minister Wilson answered him in the House, saying that he wished the CBI's comments had risen "a little above the level of a suburban rugby club dinner."[144] Mr. Campbell Adamson's apparent intervention during the first of the 1974 Elections (mentioned in Chapter 7) rather put a damper on things for a while, but the civilities were maintained in public.

When the limits of argument have been reached, the CBI turns to Parliament, both Lords and Commons, and probably more often than it allows, fearing to be saddled with the dread name "political," which among bodies of the kind always mean "party political." That is what Sir John Partridge means when he tells the Northern Regional Council that the CBI "has no politics."[145] But the CBI is political in the pressure-group sense. It knows exactly what to do and it does it, reaching out especially to Government backbenchers, members of the Standing Committee handling *the* Bill, and so on (on steel renationalization 1966, sponsoring a new clause and several amendments at the Committee stage and others at the Report stage; the Transport Bill, 1968; the Industry Bill, 1972; the Fair Trading Bill, 1973, and so forth).

For these and similar efforts the CBI has not failed to secure excellent press and TV coverage. For a decade or so, however, it seldom indulged in out-and-out public campaigning, tending to leave that to the interests more directly threatened or concerned. In the spring and summer of 1974, however, it did mount "a special campaign to fight the [Labour] Government's proposals for more state intervention in industry."[146] To help with the campaign, the Charles Barker City Public Relations consultancy was retained for three months. *Industry and Government*, a discussion paper prepared by an ad hoc group under the chairmanship of Lord Watkinson (Cadbury Schweppes and other companies, and a prominent CBI figure), led the way. Reduced from forty-six pages to twelve, it was circulated to M.P.s and Peers as well as CBI members. Campaigns were also mounted against the Employment Protection Bill and the proposal for a Wealth Tax.

These short-term campaigns presaged a more long-term effort at improving PR, including not only traditional ploys but indirect attempts to improve the performance of the CBI's own members and staff. These included TV training courses and commissioning a book from Bertram Mycock, former BBC Industrial Correspondent, *Don't be afraid of the Box*.

Part III:
Groups and the
Political System

Methods: Stooping to Conquer

Introduction

What are we—citizens as well as scholars—to make of all this activity? Is it good for the country? Is it in the public interest? If only we knew how to identify the public interest![1] Men and women of goodwill might argue, for example, that an incomes policy is in the public interest. That seems reasonable. It might even be said, as Peter Jay once interpreted fellow *Times*-man, Bernard Levin as saying, that "any non-traitorous fool could see that a statutory incomes policy is indispensable to national survival."[2] But in the mid-sixties Samuel Brittan reminded us that "until very recently it was a radical idea completely unacceptable to established opinion." Suddenly the pendulum swung and "the need for an incomes policy" became "*the* economic fad of the hour."[3] Pockets of resistance remained. Reviewing that very book (on the Treasury), William Rees-Mogg called incomes policy "still at best a doubtful and hypothetical objective. . . ." So, if the unions thwarted incomes policy, would they or would they not be subverting the public interest? Taking another tack, we could readily agree that the public interest is more than the sum of what pressure groups want—and yet be quite unable to speak its name when called upon in specific situations, the only ones in which we ever find ourselves.

Nevertheless it is possible and might prove useful to conceive of the public interest in another way, thinking of the cumulative consequences of group activity for the political system as a whole. In the tradition of Adam Ferguson,[4] the Italian sociologist Luigi Sturzo has distinguished between *finis operantis* (for us here, the goals pursued by the groups) and *finis operis* (the objective consequences of the pursuit as judged by some observer). Are some of the methods that groups employ deleterious, tending to cheapen and accordingly weaken the democratic attributes of the British political system? Some scholars think so. Professor J.E.S. Hayward has even characterized group-government relations as "whitemail"—that is, institutionalized blackmail—though without confining his strictures to the groups alone.[5] Whitemail and democracy go ill together. Even without whitemail, however, the cumulative effect of group activity might well be stagnation within one or more ranges of public policy. Others, again, fear a tendency towards a British version of the Corporate State.[6] To these unintended but conceivable consequences (among others), we now turn.

On Methods

In attempting to judge methods, one is not judging the arguments advanced but rather the modes of approach, although it may well be that some modes affect the quality of the debate. Are any of the methods employed deplorable or even objectionable? There are perhaps four main areas of concern: surreptitious approaches; the use of PR; the political strike; and the boycott.

Up to a point, Ronald Butt's complaint about the ALRA (and the divorce reformers) was a complaint about surreptitious methods: a minority pressure group going hard at it, with the help, never acknowledged, of the Government, notably Roy Jenkins at the Home Office and the Commons business managers at the time, Richard Crossman and John Silkin. Undoubtedly it happened: on a number of the moral issues, the (Labour) Government was really legislating but concealing its role.[7] That was reprehensible; in a democratic system, the public ought to know *who* is responsible for *what*—there should be no licence for doing good by stealth. But by that test the ALRA was scarcely at fault since it had been advocating that reform for a generation (the Divorce Law Reform Union, for two generations). The concealment was the Government's. Clearly the party managers (on both sides) are timid about the so-called moral issues,[8] as if abortion and divorce and homosexual practices have greater moral significance than food adulteration, false advertising, or dangerous working conditions. At most the ALRA might be charged with being an accessory before the fact. Some of us would promptly acquit on the grounds that the ALRA was simply fitting in as best it could with the rules of the Parliamentary game, which were not of its making.

Some groups have been guilty as charged, however. The moves to take the National Exhibition Centre to Birmingham were surreptitious.[9] The trap was sprung by a handful of the governing and nongoverning elite, with no public discussion of the Centre's location in Birmingham despite a distinct public interest and indeed money from public funds. Nor, as *The Times* commented editorially, was there even "a feasibility study into the alternatives. . . ."[10] More significant and more heinous still was the establishment of commercial TV. One need not weep for the BBC as such (no doubt they had been asking for it in many ways) in order to deplore the secrecy of the moves to provide a rival medium financed by advertising. For so fundamental a change, the Conservatives, as Lord Hailsham declaimed with passion, had sought no mandate at the general election only recently held. Certainly there was no semblance of a public debate until the whole thing had been fixed up within a section of the governing elite. Probably at a very early stage, in some quiet room in the West End (psychologically) far from the madding crowd, the franchises were parcelled out among those who cooperated, who had the right connections or pull. These franchises were the equivalent of freeholds, given away *free, gratis and for nothing* by the nation, or rather, taken away, since the nation had no idea what was really at stake.[11] Nor were the principles of allocation ever publicly discussed, no doubt because they could not stand the light of day. The franchises were of course tantamount, in the famous phrase, to permits or licenses for the franchisers to print their own money.

Once the original wheeler-dealers were ready, they went public. Some public exchanges followed—one could hardly call it a debate—between the Popular Television Association (PTA) and the National Television Council (NTC). No doubt the NTC was as much a front—for the BBC—as the PTA was for the commercial interests. But no evidence has been produced to suggest that it stooped so low to conquer—the fake letters to the press masquerading as spontaneous public opinion; pieces of propaganda planted as news stories; and the like. Twenty years later Edward Heath would refer to the "unacceptable face of capitalism." The putting across of commercial TV surely represents the unacceptable face of pressure-group politics.

There the particular use of PR compounded the felony, but of course the practice may be questionable or objectionable even when resorted to in comparative isolation. In these pages, the issue is encountered over and over again, but may be narrowed down to four contexts: the use of PR fronts; propaganda by companies and TAs to ward off nationalization; the "almost disturbingly professional" campaign at Cublington (Wing) to ward off a Third London Airport; and the development or overdevelopment of the aircraft industry on public money.

The London Foundation for Marriage Education, set up in the early sixties, through the good offices of the Westbourne Press Bureau, as a trust dedicated to the value of mechanical contraceptives, including those made of rubber, exemplifies the first area of concern. In 1964-65 another PR firm helped to launch the Genetic Study Unit. This scientific-sounding organization campaigned against the use of oral contraceptives. Despite denials, both these turned out to be emanations of London Rubber Industries, Britain's largest manufacturers of rubber contraceptives, evidently perturbed by the growing popularity of the contraceptive pill. Granted a free market in ideas, we have to concede a free market in types of contraceptives (*chacun à son gout*), but of course our choice should be made on the best evidence.

Similarly, the railway interests ought to appear under their own colours and not attempt to pass themselves off under titles seeming to indicate a broader allegiance: Road and Rail Association, National Council on Inland Transport, and Transport 2000. Journalist Ian Waller at first believed the Road and Rail Association to be "a collection of individuals who had been inspired to public action by a spontaneous desire to see different transport policies." It turned out in the end to be a pressure group for the railways: "the creation of that fertile PR man, Mr. Claude Simmons [sic], whose client in this case was the British Transport Commission."[12] (Mr. Simmonds crossed our path as someone whose services were obtained for the Cublington phase of the third London airport struggle.) In the 1970s the National Council seemed bent on stopping further rail closures, and Transport 2000 clearly tilted towards one form of transport, the railways. That was natural: it had the backing of the Railway Industry Association (the TA), and of the three unions, especially the National Union of Railwaymen, which provided money, organization, and service. The issue, of course, is subterfuge. The British Transport Commission's defence when confronted by Mr. Waller was that they were "forced" into it "by the immense volume of hostile propaganda from road haulage interests." But that surely could have been countered openly, volume for volume. One has to take a stand with the *Guardian* leader writer, in a related context: "A hidden persuader is objectionable. An open and declared persuader contributes to the democratic process."[13]

It follows that the sugar companies, including Tate and Lyle, and their TA, the British Sugar Refiners Association; the steel companies and the BISF; the RHA and associated interests, and so forth have the right to run PR campaigns in the hope of warding off nationalization. Particular points arise however. There is excellent reason to believe that in its campaign on behalf of the sugar interests, *Aims of Industry* (of which Tate and Lyle was a founder) hoped, *inter alia*, to persuade Washington to bring financial pressure to bear on the Labour Government to drop its nationalization proposal. This is consistent with the known attempt by *Aims* to go external in another sense, getting the Jamaican trade union leader, W.A. Bustamente to elaborate upon some critical remarks he had made about the nationalization policy and then publishing his reply as a statement in over a hundred newspapers. That may have been on the margin of acceptability in methods. But an attempt to activate Washington would surely have been illegitimate, and even un-British except on the assumption that Attlee and Co. were devils-on-horseback. We may need reminding that some businessmen thought just that; for example, J. Gibson Jarvie, chairman of the United Dominions Trust, saying in 1948 that if the socialists, "those reckless and incompetent megalomaniacs," continued in power "there may come a time when the only possible course is to rebel if the country is to be saved."[14]

Whether the cost of PR campaigns of this kind ought to be tax deductible (as a trade expense) is questionable. But it is not (or has not been) an open question since the Law Lords found in favour of Tate and Lyle and against the Revenue. If, as was alleged in one of the anti-steel nationalization campaigns, the PR effort included a public opinion survey that contained loaded questions and was yet passed off as genuinely scientific, that was, of course, illegitimate. The total amount spent by the steel interests was perturbing if one believes that the tendency in civilized countries is and ought to be a reduction in the power of money to influence public affairs.

The almost disturbingly professional campaign, was of course launched by WARA, straining to ward off a third London airport; specifically it was Burson-Marsteller's, under the chairmanship of Claude Simmonds. He is indeed a professional, if a somewhat controversial one among fellow professionals, at least those who run the Institute of Public Relations. No doubt the author of the phrase, John Clare, was right: The WARA campaign was not mounted by the Buckinghamshire peasantry. That in itself is perhaps not a fatal disqualification: As anyone knows who has lived or moved in Bucks, the peasants have rather more practice at mounting horses, and so forth, than ideas. The issue perhaps was less the spontaneity as such than the professionalism, and that, once again, turned on wealth. As David Crouch, a Conservative M.P. (but not for Bucks or the Home Counties) would demand later: To whom does the Government listen—high pressure public relations groups, engineering contractors, or the Roskill Commission, which had been five to one against the choice of Foulness?[15]

The charge against the aircraft industry is not simply that its "vociferous aircraft lobby" (as the Defence Correspondent of *The Times*[16] called it) received very great subventions of public money for an expansion that the nation did not need or at least could not sustain, much of which in the end had to be written off in the accounts. The charge is also that PR made that overexpansion acceptable. According to Richard Crossman in 1963: "A brilliantly successful promotion and advertising campaign has for years boosted an instinctive national pride in British aircraft, and made the public reluctant to question whether the industry has justified the sums invested in it."[17] He did not show us the colour of his money (evidence), but as in the case of TSR-2 in Chapter 5, we did observe the possibly excessive reliance of some companies, notably BAC, on PR techniques to influence Government.

The issue of political strikes mainly arose during the attempts by both Labour and Conservative Governments to reform the law of industrial relations. The call was heard first during the SOGAT-led agitation against Labour's *In Place of Strife* in the spring of 1969. But even the short Bill fell (or was pushed), and in the following year, when the parties changed places, the Conservatives picked up the torch, or, since they did it with such obvious zest, the cudgels. Against their proposals a series of stoppages was unleashed; in early December, timed to precede the Second Reading of the Bill, the shop stewards organized one of the greatest walk-outs since the General Strike. Earlier, in 1965, a de facto political walk-out occurred at Preston, where BAC workers were anticipating the cancellation of TSR-2. But that, far from displeasing management, was one of many examples of labour-capital collaboration on an issue of public policy for the aircraft industry.

Used independently or in collaboration, the political strike cannot be condoned except *in extremis*—that is, against an occupying or Quisling government or a native government busily uprooting basic civil and political liberties. The TUC would not have gone all the way with the *Sunday Times*: "No Bill in recent years has been more thoroughly publicized. . . . In unprecedented detail the Tories told the electorate what they would do, and they are doing it. When the Bill is passed, its history should fit it to become the schoolroom exemplar of the democratic process . . . the strike being organized on December 8th against the Industrial Relations Bill is a shameless attempt by one section of society to upset by force the unambiguous verdict of the majority." But the TUC—the General Council—disapproved of the action and tried to head it off, unavailingly as we know since the stewards had the bit between their teeth.

The political strike might be regarded as the limiting case of the boycott, defined as abstaining from using, buying from, selling to or otherwise dealing with a person or institution in order to exert influence. In fact we might usefully conceive of a continuum of boycotting, with the political strike at the one pole. Somewhere close to that end would go the NFU boycott of slaughterhouses and livestock markets in 1970. The Glamorgan branch was early in the field, arranging to withhold supplies from its five livestock markets "as a means of increasing pressure for a fair deal while the farm price review talks continue in Whitehall." According to the chairman of the shop stewards (the farmers' action committee), the boycott was not intended to withhold meat from consumers but "to see if we can stand together if and when the crunch comes." According to an NFU calculation, however, the boycott was expected to cut off the supply of about 2,000 head of stock, mostly cattle and pigs, so, if the chairman was correct, the men of Glamorgan would presumably be making do with mutton. Pickets were posted to make the boycott effective, but (the NFU piously announced) "persuasion rather than force will be the order of the day."[18] In May, after the annual price review had been settled (at £85 million), the NFU boycotted about thirty-one livestock markets in England and Wales. By then the mood was nastier. The president of the Federation of Meat Traders had denounced this "sabotage" as "both scandalous and irresponsible." A Manchester butcher received anonymous telephone threats that his lorry would be smashed if it came to pick up stock. At Gloucester the pickets noted the names of those who had brought in stock, and threatened them with "special attention."[19] It all had a depressingly familiar ring, except that those editorial writers usually quick to ask, *shall the unions or Parliament be sovereign?* seem to have missed this excellent opportunity. Editorially, *The Times* called it "a gentlemanly boycott," and offered not one word of criticism.[20]

With the May 1974 threat of 100,000 nurses to withdraw from the National Health Service unless salaries were increased, we seem to be on more familiar ground. A delegation of forty-four from the Royal College of Nursing put that to Mrs. Castle (Secretary of State for the Social Services) as 2,000 nurses milled around the hospital streets of London, banners flying ("Better Pay for Nurses Please"). Despite reassurances from the president of the Royal College that they did not think the action "would interfere" with their service to patients—they would simply be changing employers—the prospect was perturbing because the Royal College had "never threatened anything like this before."[21] The worst did not happen, but such a boycott of the NHS would have had something of the nature of a political strike if in a restricted sense. What of the notice given the Lord Chancellor by the Law Society that solicitors would not be able to go on doing legal aid work unless fees were increased? It threatened a kind of boycott and of a public service, in which, however, solicitors were not obliged to take part.

Along the continuum many degrees of boycott might be distinguished, but in our period it seems useful to separate out three main types. One is the refusal to carry out part of an agreed service. Thus in June 1970 some 18,000 of the nation's 24,000 family doctors were refusing to sign medical certificates in protest against the Government's refusal to refer their pay award to the Prices and Incomes Board. In Surrey soon afterwards members of the NUT, committed to the comprehensive schools policy, came to the brink of threatening to boycott selection procedures for the county's grammar schools. Already in 1969 the NAS had been pursuing a policy of noncooperation (the polite name for a boycott) as "a pinprick" to "encourage Labour backbenchers to press [the Minister] for an inquiry into the working of the Burnham system."[22]

Such actions might be read as partial political strikes. More grave is the boycott of a total institution. The outstanding case in the period surveyed was obviously the trade union boycott of the National Industrial Relations Court (NIRC). It is perhaps the classic case of this century because it not only emasculated a major Act of Parliament but also arrested a whole legislative trend, Labour as well as Conservative in inspiration. But it was not unique. After World War I the NFU boycotted the Councils of Agriculture, and so assured the failure of that early move towards a primitive sort of planning. After World War II, business and the TAs in particular, fearing to be undermined, boycotted a less primitive sort of planning, the Development Councils (DC); for example, the Master Silversmiths against a DC for jewellery and silverware, EOs against a DC for the clothing industry, and so on. The steel men went further or were more blunt about it. The Federation told the Minister (so he reported) that they would not submit to him names of leaders in the industry to serve on the new nationalized corporation and that they would make every effort to dissuade any important man he might approach from serving on it. "Deprived of such people" (the warning continued), he "would be unable successfully to plan the steel industry."[23] Certainly only one steelmaster could be found to serve on the Board, and he was from a minor company. As it happened, nationalization died the death because the Conservatives returned to office in October 1951 and returned the industry to private ownership.

Meanwhile, the BMA, too, had held up the implementation of their Act, the National Health Service Act of 1946. *Should* we participate in the new scheme was the question. The rank-and-file answered "No" through a referendum and a special Representative Meeting, whereupon the BMA Council instituted a boycott of what had to be done to make the Act work. As everyone with a long memory knows, the BMA won hands down. An American specialist, James

Christoph, has recorded: "It appeared that the Minister and his advisers had conceded almost every point raised by the BMA. . . ."[24] Quite so; the silver-tongued boy from Tredegar (Nye Bevan, of course, not the off-comer Michael Foot) had been, if not out-talked, out-manoeuvred.

There is a way of trying to undermine some new public institution other than by the direct boycott: It is to decline to continue cooperating in an important public policy, which might be regarded as the polar extreme of the boycott continuum where this merges into group sanctions in general. In 1970 the CBI was voluntarily operating an early warning arrangement under which member companies were expected to give Government Departments 28 days' notice of price increases. Infuriated by a "disastrous Bill" to create a Commission for Industry and Manpower (CIM) with great powers of intervention in industry, and the Labour Government's (Mrs. Castle's) rejection of "their strong verbal representations," the CBI Council, at a meeting attended by over 150 members, put a stop to early warnings. Companies would still tell the departments but no longer allow "time to elapse before they raise their prices," the Director-General said. This was characterized in the press as "a direct retaliation against the Government's controversial" CIM proposal.[25] In consequence, as *The Times* commented editorially, since a "wage explosion [had already occurred,] the current chapter of prices and incomes policy is closed." The CBI set about with the greatest care to brief the Opposition but was saved by Labour's loss of the election that June.

To Sum Up

Of the four area of concern, there is nothing to be said in mitigation of surreptitious approaches or, in normal times, of the political strike. Accordingly, those forms of boycott that approximate to the political strike must also be regarded as reprehensible, unless we except the Royal College of Nursing type of case in which the Government is the direct employer or the ultimate provider of the funds from which the claims would have to be satisfied. Otherwise the right to boycott a public institution, less startling if called a right to refrain from participation, probably has to be conceded. That, however, is not the view taken by some sober judges of the scene. Thus the *Sunday Times* condemned the unions for their failure to use NIRC, detecting "a minimal duty to be present when cases affecting their members' interests are being heard," and urging them to do more than the minimum: "take the legal initiative themselves."[26] Readers will decide for themselves, but it should be stressed that anyone who concedes the right, if not necessarily the wisdom or prudence of it, will have to concede that as well to such others as the steelmasters in their refusal to recognize or serve on the new nationalized corporation. With the other sort of boycott (if such it was), the CBI's withdrawal from the early warning system, there can surely be no doubt at all. As P.M., Harold Wilson amused himself in the House by likening their action to "a strike,"[27] but to drop a policy voluntarily assumed was hardly that. Such a voluntary commitment is not for all time, not even for an age.

That part of PR which is surreptitious stands condemned with other underhanded moves. The professionalization of PR is a source of anxiety, whether turned to the advantage of Cublington or the aircraft industry. Those paid to present an institution in a favourable light, may cleave too closely to the rule (expressed by Charles Churchill in *Night* two hundred years ago):

Keep up appearances; there lies the test;
The world will give thee credit for the rest.

Those paid to promote a policy or party line may give less weight to the merits of the issue than to its outcome. But PR as practised by pressure groups generally surely has to be accepted, for what determines the methods used by groups? In his generally excellent monograph on the teachers' unions, R.D. Coates distinguished between two types of explanation: the environmental (followed by "Almond, Beer, Rose, Castles, Wootton, Macridis and Clark") and the organizational (followed by "Allen, Routh, Strauss, Kleingartner, Lockwood, Blackburn and Prandy").[28] In fact the fifth "environmentalist" believes that methods are determined by both organizational (or group) attributes and environmental ones (the structure of government; previous government policy; the political culture or set of dominant values, beliefs, and emotions). But the relative strength of these factors in the blend will vary. The point for this discussion is that the attributes of a whole class of groups, here called the propagational, require these to rely heavily upon PR. They are so specialized that to name the group is to name the issue. They lack regular connections with government; they may be up against the grain of the dominant political culture; and so on. So PR *is* the method specific to them. Even a group such as the Equal Pay Campaign Committee, here classified as given on the basis of sex, may be compelled to follow the PR route. Even the unions, enjoying orderly relations with government, may find that these are disrupted, whereupon they too return, as it were, to a state of nature. PR might be defined as the method specific (not though not confined) to such a state of nature. Its use could be stopped only by interfering arbitrarily with an important class of groups or by limiting a resource held in reserve by other classes of groups. However (as one has argued with notable lack of success since 1968),[29] the public interest surely does require the compulsory registration of professional PR practitioners, as indeed of all lobbyists, and the fullest disclosure. And a state that took its democracy seriously would ensure that its citizens received (in the Leavisite phrase) that "training for critical awareness," which is the ultimate defence against specious claims and meretricious display.

10 Pluralist Stagnation

Even if group methods were never unacceptable, the cumulative effect of group actions might prove to be. One such consequence has been identified as pluralist(ic) stagnation. Is this a component of the British problem? Only a truly comprehensive study could provide an authoritative answer, but even this inquiry throws some light on the question. It suggests, in the first place, that stagnation does not prevail in every corner of the realm where the groups are active. Those who raised the issue never asserted that it did: They merely pointed to a crucial area of public policy. But subsequent discussion *has* tended to remain within the territory that they marked out. This study serves to remind us that in other sectors of social space groups take initiatives, and in so doing provide movement, not stagnation, thus tending to make the political system flexible.

Sector 4

This, it would seem, is preeminently true of sector 4, where the propagational groups reside. One may dislike or deplore what the groups accomplish in the field of moral issues, such as abortion law reform. Denying that it was reform, one may even call it retrogression. To proponents, of course, it represented an advance, for which the ground had been prepared by a very small number of determined women, starting in the mid-thirties. Either way the reform, or change, obviously did not constitute stagnation. So, too, with divorce, homosexual relations in private, capital punishment (analysis of which had to be jettisoned from these pages in order to save space) and, to some extent, racial discrimination. Such bodies as Shelter and the Child Poverty Action Group have been gadflies, making the public authorities uncomfortable and stimulating them to act in unaccustomed ways. Not much stagnation on that ground, except perhaps in the eyes of the more ardent spirits, disappointed at the slow or inadequate responses *of* the authorities. So, too, with the Friends of the Earth (FoE), drafting a new Bill (1975) to modify the rules for importing endangered species, thus advancing the cause of wildlife protection, and the Conservation Society, impatiently repeating "the main conservation thesis," that (as Dr. John Davoll put it) "in a finite world material growth must cease."[1] No doubt defensive ploys can be observed. From late 1974 to early 1975, the Conservation Society itself took part "in a major thrust against the Roads Programme," which turned into "one of the most expensive" campaigns in its history. In this the FoE was out in front, having already fired a shot by way of Mick Hamer's analysis of the road lobby, *Wheels Within Wheels*.[2] Others took a hand, and of course there were other issues in which the stance was defensive, possibly tending (some might think) towards pluralist stagnation. On balance, however, the sector seems productive of many initiatives by groups, which seem busily engaged in getting Leviathan to act, not in blocking its path.

Sector 3

Some of the expressive groups in Sector 3 bend themselves to the same task. The CPRE's prodding of the Ministry to make local authorities provide permanent camping sites for gypsies is an example, as is the role of the Civic Trust in bringing about the Civic Amenities Act of 1967. However, since expressive groups also, and mainly, give their minds to things other than political pressure, they seem likely to save most of their ammunition for the times when they are outraged or otherwise stimulated by government. If so, there will be in this sector relatively more of that defensive behaviour, which tends (it is feared) to induce pluralist stagnation. Even so distinctions need to be drawn. The Commons Society strives to amend the Countryside Bill of 1967. Carrying the fight to Standing Committee A, it secures its amendment and gains some other ground. But in 1970 the continued pressure of the National Trust made the Cumberland County Council drop its plan for a southern bypass round Keswick that would have crossed its covenanted land and increased traffic to Borrowdale. Towards the end of that year the Civic Trust, CPRE, RIBA and the Pedestrians' Association were among "the giant killers" (as the *Sunday Times* called them) who stopped the *juggernaut*—the development of the heavy lorry—in its tracks. In those instances a kind of stagnation ensued, whereas most of the Countryside Bill survived to be enacted in 1968.

Sector 1

When we turn to occupational, or producer, groups—the original cause for concern—we find that some of those in Sector 1, far from confining themselves simply to defence of their own turf, are in fact the sources of initiatives (*I'm Backing Britain*; equal pay for women; commercial TV, and commercial radio). It is true, on their other hand, that unions and other workers do try to mobilize political influence in defence of their jobs, arguing variations on the theme that their situation is special. SOGAT, the Lightermen, and the Stevedores and Dockers put themselves at the head of the column in the demonstrations against industrial relations reform, 1969-1971. Midland car workers and many others later "fell in." Pearl Assurance, the House of Fraser, and the bankers Hill Samuel, with other companies and firms, exerted themselves to stop the introduction of SET. Stewarts and Lloyds and other steel companies fought hard, disbursing much treasure, against renationalization, as earlier against nationalization. In other instances unions and companies collaborate, not always openly, in the hope of beating off some government proposal or holding it to a course of action (e.g., the development of the TSR-2).

So here, too, as in Sector 3, groups take initiatives but the danger of pluralist stagnation appears considerable, and may even be greater not only because Sector 1 will be larger (many more units available to exert pressure) but also because, as they perceive it, there will be far more at stake: jobs; new taxes; contracts/franchises; the balance of power itself in industry, certain to be affected, though in different ways, by both industrial-relations reform (the 1969 and 1971 Bills) and by nationalization. These and related issues make up ground that groups are bound to regard as vital and so to be defended at all costs.

Sector 2

As conceived in this book, Sector 2 harbours some amenity and environmental groups—those so localized or otherwise limited that they seem to be more like *of* groups than *for* groups; in other words, less like cause or promotional groups (the usual classification) and more like any other rooted interest: unions/TUC; trade associations/CBI; chambers of commerce/ABCC, and so forth. Such amenity bodies are anti- by design, having been precipitated by some government proposal; for example, in 1974, SKAR (Surrey and Kent Against the Rail-Link) determined to prevent trains racing through the Marden Valley at 100 m.p.h. *en route* for the Channel Tunnel (a project that has since slipped back to being a dream). Bristol's Campaign Against the Outer Circuit Road and the Midland Motorway Action Group, questioning the need for the Bromsgrove section of the M42, are (1972-73) cut from the same cloth as SKAR. At Dover in 1976 the Save Our Seafront (S.O.S.) Action Committee ran up distress signals to warn against the proposed new Hoverport, Western Docks, though it also offered counterproposals.[3] But the classic cases, of course, came from the Government's vain attempt to build a third London airport, an idea that did not become a project even in a decade because it was slowly suffocated by the respectable militants of Stansted and Cublington (Wing).

The central ground in Sector 2, however, is taken up by the producer peaks. At least as far as the public record goes, most of their (political) time is spent in reacting to Government policy, thus creating a potential for pluralist stagnation, as the originators of the concept clearly saw. But we hardly straddle this ground before we discover that the concept has more nuances than has been generally realized. It might simply be taken to mean the delay imposed on government by the need to carry the groups rather than an out-and-out vetoing or de facto smothering of an official proposal. The run-up to the Race Relations Act of 1968 is a case in point. It all started in August 1966 and cannot be said to have ended until October 1968. These long-drawn-out exchanges were necessary to win the consent of the CBI and especially the TUC to the employment clauses. If these were badly needed in August 1966 (as they probably were), they must have been very urgent by late November 1968, when the Act came into force, and by early 1969, when the General Council was putting the seal of its approval on a note prepared by the Race Relations Board to guide industry on the application of the controversial racial balance clause.

In that instance the Government got what they wanted, more or less; it just took them a long time to get it. That, and the energy expended by Ministers and others, represents opportunity costs, marking the opportunities missed in other policy areas, or inadequately grasped, because they were heavily or at least tiresomely engaged in this one. The defeat of the 1969 Industrial Relations Bill reveals the other and more familiar face of pluralist stagnation. Not only the First Secretary but also the Prime Minister put their authority behind the Bill in the name of the public interest: in the end they were obliged to abandon it for the sake of party unity and the survival of the Government.

The contrast between the two Bills is not confined to outcomes: The length of the run-up also varied, being less than a year in the second case. No doubt a more sophisticated assessment would soften the contrast by assessing the frequency, intensity, wear-and-tear, and political significance of the exchanges in the spring of 1969. Enough of the contrast survives, however, to suggest that two pure types of pluralist stagnation ought to be distinguished: stagnation of process (slowing down the government machine but not deflecting it from its path), and stagnation of result, which is what most commentators have focussed upon. Pound for pound, stagnation of result must be the more serious impediment to effective government, but its (ostensible) absence from a scene cannot be taken as an impeccable sign that all is well. Almost like Gulliver in the toils of the Lilliputians, Leviathan may be seriously hampered by the many groups clustered around it.

Where long-drawn-out exchanges culminate in the stultification of major government policy, there stands a third, hybrid form of pluralist stagnation, grave in itself and surely tending to erode political authority. It is exemplified at its worst in these pages by the third London airport case, which dragged on for something like a decade, entailed the spending of substantial sums of public (i.e., taxpayers') money, much of which was wasted, and ended in anticlimax at Maplin Sands. Many would also cite the national experience of wages or incomes policy. Thus the TUC's unwillingness to accede to wage restraint in 1956 has been held up in so many words (by the American political scientist, Gerald Dorfman) as a specific example of "pluralistic" stagnation.[4] The exchanges took the best part of a year because the Government's strategy was "to secure wage restraint through price restraint,"[5] which meant that the BEC and FBI had to be "jollied along" first. Some promises of price stability were extracted (and even implemented), but the TUC remained unbidden.

In August 1957 the Government tried another tack, conjuring up a Council of three (inevitably dubbed "the three wise men") to keep prices, productivity, and incomes under continuous scrutiny. But as a well-placed observer destined to become a highly placed participant would later remark: "In the light of trade union opposition," the Council was unable to survive.[6]

Its final report was issued in July 1961, when a "pay pause" (= wage freeze) was imposed by the Government wherever its writ ran, the occasion being the latest instalment of the emergent economic crisis. The stop was removed in March 1962, when the Council was superseded by NEDDY as the country drifted into economic planning. But the price of union participation in NEDDY may have been that very ending of the pay pause.[7] And the TUC would not permit NEDDY to be used as an anvil for hammering out their support for a permanent incomes policy, as economic planning presumably requires, and as Government and Chancellor (Selwyn Lloyd) had quietly hoped.[8] To fill the gap, a National Incomes Commission (NIC) was created at the urging of an impatient Prime Minister (Mr. Macmillan), but a "furious" TUC left it to its own devices—and would not answer queries, even about managerial inefficiency, prompting the NIC to "regret once more that we have been denied the assistance of the trade unions in the examination of vital questions."[9]

Returning eagerly to power in 1964, Labour produced its National Plan with great fanfare. Going for growth was the strategy; to that end the TUC (and business) promised to take part in reviewing the general movement of prices and (all forms of) money incomes and to cooperate with what turned out to be the National Board of Prices and Incomes (NBPI), the successor to NIC that was to be run by Aubrey Jones, the former Conservative Minister but "up from Merthyr" and possessor of a First in economics from LSE. He sat ex-officio on NEDDY, which was in due course charged with the broad review, thus in principle joining what the TUC had earlier left the Conservatives little alternative but to put asunder: incomes policy and planning. On this extended NEDDY, the TUC did its duty. In the voluntary phase of incomes policy from April 1965, it may even have gone beyond the call of duty, setting up (in September) an Incomes Committee to make "observations, if any" upon claims made by individual unions for better wages or working conditions.[10] While the Committee was deliberating, the union would be expected to hold off. In July 1966 the economic crisis recurred, and a lean year followed—half-freeze, half-restraint. In the policy of freeze, the General Council reluctantly acquiesced, but it naturally gave up its vetting, to which it returned, however, as the slow thaw set in.

Voluntaryism, buttressed by the Government's power to delay, returned in August 1967 only to be again replaced by compulsion after the devaluation of sterling in November. Technically that phase (from March 1968) lasted until the end of 1969, but in his 1969 Budget speech Roy Jenkins, apparently hoping to counteract the horrid medicine that was the Industrial Relations Bill, announced that the statutory powers would not be renewed. Before the due date, without reference to the NBPI, the Government itself proceeded to approve several pay settlements above the official level. From the beginning of 1970, voluntaryism was again in the saddle, backed by some delaying powers.

Successful in the June election, the Conservatives rode hell for leather into industrial relations reform of the kind that Labour had been unable to carry the previous year, but away from incomes policy. By April Fool's Day, 1971, the NBPI was no more. Yet early in 1972, following the miners' strike, the Government was sounding out NEDDY as a forum for discussing incomes policy, and in July it embarked on direct talks with the TUC and CBI. The wheel had come full circle. As Aubrey Jones would write: "After two years in office," the Conservative Government" had returned willy-nilly to the point at which Labour had begun its exercise of power in 1964."[11] The sense of *déja vu* was increased in November, when, the talks having broken down, the Government went compulsory, imposing an incomes freeze, and even more the following April when (for stage two) it created a Pay Board (and a Price Commission) to keep increases within a total of £1 a week plus 4 percent of the wages bill excluding overtime payments.

With the Pay Board the TUC would have nothing to do: Indeed, prompted from behind, it unleashed a thunderbolt in the form of the first officially supported political strike since 1926. Undeterred, the Government struggled on to November, converting stage two into stage three, only to be itself brought down two months later by the National Union of Mineworkers (NUM). Out to repeat the success of its 1972 strike, the NUM banned overtime in prosecution of a wages claim that would breach the statutory limits. Precisely because the limits were now statutory, as they had not been during the 1972 challenge, the Government picked up the gauntlet, putting industry on a three-day working week and attempting to undercut the strike that came in February by an appeal to the electorate. The Labour Party's contribution to the election debate was to claim that an incomes policy would have to be assumed by "the trade unions voluntarily (which is the only way it can be done for any period in a free society)" and that the only way to get the unions to cooperate would be for "the Government to create a much fairer distribution of the national wealth . . . ," hence the need for a "social contract."[12]

Judged by the test of votes, Labour narrowly lost the (overall) debate but won in the only way that matters—seats. Deemed a special case, the miners were granted a settlement beyond the stage three limits. In July the new Government got rid of the Pay Board, *déja vu* again except that they were much quicker with the knife than the Conservatives had been in dispatching the NBPI after the 1970 election. Bilateral trading followed. In October the Government appealed to the country, declaring that "at the heart of this manifesto and our programme to save the nation lies the Social Contract between the Labour Government and the trade unions. . . ."[13] Gaining some ground, the Government plodded on bearing the burden of a policy of swaps. As the mid-seventies merged into the late seventies, that burden was still being carried. Thus, in May 1976, the Government was proposing to swap income tax reductions for an agreement to hold average increases in wages and salaries to 4.5 percent in the twelve months from 31 July, as against against 11.5 percent from July 1975.[14]

Does all this constitute pluralist stagnation? In the particular case (say, 1956-1962), Stephen Blank has challenged both his fellow American political scientist, Gerald Dorfman and, ultimately, his own Harvard mentor, Samuel Beer. As to the mid-fifties especially, he—author of the history of the Federation of British Industries—denies that "government policy was effectively blocked by private groups." Rather the government, in effect, abdicated, being "unwilling to accept responsibility for dealing with the on-going problem of the upward pressure of prices and incomes in the new conditions of the postwar economy. . . . The Government failed, not at making a policy or at making a policy stick, but at persuading other groups to make that policy."[15]

What Dr. Blank really wants to do is to place the blame for Britain's inadequate postwar economic performance on governments, not groups. In the particular case (he argues), the Government should have been pursuing "a broader strategy of economic management," of which incomes policy would naturally have formed part. We could accept that and yet discern pluralist stagnation in the failure of the Government to persuade the groups to do what it wanted. For pluralist stagnation (of result) is about the thwarting of government, not about its own inadequacies or sins of omission, or even, in the first instance, about the usefulness of what is being proposed—that is, a judgment about stagnation on incomes policy is analytically distinct from a judgment about the virtues of that policy.

In the particular case, the (Conservative) Government was surely thwarted. Broadening the discussion, we must also agree that in 1972 the miners (if not the TUC as such) rode roughshod over the policy, and that their second challenge in 1974 precipitated the fall of a Conservative Government, after which distraction they again emerged victorious. Have Labour Governments fared better? In the first half of their 1964-1970 regime, yes; in the latter part, hardly. Here, admittedly, complications intrude upon the assessment. The Left within the Parliamentary Party represented a constraint. From 1964 some thirty to thirty-five of them met in the Commons, often in Committee Room Five, under the chairmanship of Ian Mikardo. Among other things, they opposed incomes policy (under the present economic system at least), and on that score other M.P.s rallied round, thus mustering a solid forty to fifty. In May 1968, for example, forty-four signed a reasoned amendment (sponsored by Mr. Mikardo and others) to the Prices and Incomes Bill. But there another complication lies in wait for us, since fifteen of the total were from the Trade Union Group. This group, too, is credited by a close observer, John Mackintosh, M.P., with having helped the " 'soft-line' members of the Cabinet to carry a very mild form of wages legislation in 1967. . . ."[16] Insofar as these actors were significant on this issue, pluralist stagnation is the less attributable to extra-Parliamentary groups (which invariably constitute the referent of the concept).

Whether the Social Contract of 1974 should be deemed a debit or credit in these terms remained uncertain in 1977. The thin red line (on restraint in wage increases) still held, but the TUC looked forward to a return to free collective bargaining, and in any case critics claimed that the price of its cooperation had been far too high. Allowing, for the time being, that these items cancel out, we should then have to work back to Labour's experience in the immediate postwar period. Stafford Cripps's 1948 policy of wage restraint was swallowed by the TUC but repudiated in 1950, and already rejected de facto in 1949, especially after the September Congress, when many a TUC leader went off, changed hats and reemerged as leaders of the "Confed" (Confederation of Shipbuilding and Engineering Unions), which promptly put in for a quid a week rise (at a time when the pound was still a pound). The first devaluation of the pound sterling, to which the undermining of Crippsian restraint is often ascribed, came afterwards—hard on its heels, certainly, but afterwards. Then, in 1951, Hugh Gaitskill, Cripps's successor as Chancellor, tacked bravely towards a prices and incomes policy, only to be headed off by the TUC.

Taking the period as whole, then, we should have to acknowledge a prima facie case for pluralist stagnation on incomes policy, with the TUC's bearing the main responsibility. That impression would probably be reinforced if the concept were extended to include "the rule of anticipated reactions" often credited to the German-American scholar, Carl Friedrich. From at least 1944, when the famous Coalition White Paper was published committing governments to maintain a high and stable level of employment, the need for a wages *and* prices policy was known. The 1945 Labour Government's failure to move until 1948 may well be accounted for by fear of the TUC's reactions. Subsequent governments tending to move in the same direction may also have been put off for the same reason.

***

And the CBI? Detesting a statutory (prices and) incomes policy, it generally offered no serious resistance. An exception occurred in November 1966 after the Government made an Order-in-Council freezing laundry and dry-cleaning prices. On the face of it this was hardly a death-or-glory issue, but the CBI claimed a "clear breach of the previous understanding" about the way in which the new statutory powers would be used, which meant that neither the industry nor the CBI itself had been consulted, also that the Government had reneged on a promise not "to introduce a wholesale freeze right across an industry. . . ." Incensed, a specially-convened CBI Council seemed ready for an open breach, but were mollified by the Prime Minister, Harold Wilson, who explained that to the Government "consultation meant giving to the CBI in confidence a clear indication of the circumstances in which [they] thought it necessary to exercise their powers, discussing these with the CBI and giving proper consideration to its views."[17] In 1970, too (as recorded in the last chapter) the CBI, in retaliation for a further proposed measure of State intervention, served notice of withdrawal from the early-warning arrangement, but by then the prices and incomes policy was dead if not in fact lying down.

In July 1971, on the other hand, the CBI even took a remarkable initiative, going after the 200 largest firms to sign up for a twelve-month price freeze ending 31 July 1972, or, if quite unavoidable, not more than a 5 percent increase. Within three weeks, 150 or so had come aboard, which president Sir John Partridge called "highly satisfactory." The total later rose by some 20 percent. No doubt the policy, which was extended to the end of October 1972, suited the CBI's book, but the point is that it did not constitute pluralist stagnation.[18] Similarly, the CBI is believed to have been responsible for quietly suggesting the addition of the flat £1 a week to the percentage formula for permissible increases during stage two, 1973.

No attempt can be made here to reexamine in terms of pluralist stagnation the many other issues impinging on the CBI since its formation in 1965. All one can do is assert that government-CBI relations show no sign of having suffered from stagnation (of result). Act after Act has been denounced or deplored, but somewhat modified in some instances, and put up with in the end. Aneurin Bevan's "commanding heights" of the economy have even been occupied, over the quivering but not dead body of the organization. If the change still does not seem revolutionary, it is partly because Labour apparently still finds the air on those commanding heights rather rarefied, making it dizzy ("with success," in Stalin's old phrase) and uncertain what to do next. This does not necessarily mean that the CBI lacks power, since power, denied in one sphere, may be attributed to another—that is, there may be more to power than policy or decision making. But of CBI-induced stagnation (of result), one perceives almost no evidence.

To Sum Up

Such analysts as Samuel Beer did well to alert us to the danger of pluralist stagnation as one of those "unintended consequences of purposive social action," the modern rendering of things that are the result of human action but not human design. But the gravity of it seems to vary from one sector to another, according to the mix of initiation and defence. Sector 4 with its propagational groups is almost entirely given over to innovation, endowing the political system with much-needed flexibility. Sector 2 containing the TUC does stand out as a potentially dangerous zone, but there our judgment ultimately depends upon our judgment of the policies that were tried but thwarted. These are by no means unchallengeable. Was the Industrial Relations Bill of 1969 essential for the country or, as some TUC leaders still thought in 1973, mainly designed to catch middle-class votes?[19] Incomes policy, as Sir Richard Clarke would say, was not embarked upon "with enthusiasm or for any-other reason but the lack of any credible alternative...."[20] This brings us back to Stephen Blank's point that successive governments bear a heavy responsibility for Britain's inadequate postwar economic performance. His strictures could be extended to include the other meanderings of public policy: nationalization, denationalization, renationalization; investment allowances—then grants—then back to allowances; SET introduced with a great flourish (and no consultation about its practicability), then tossed aside with purchase tax to make way for VAT, and so on, not forgetting the making and remaking of the government machine itself.

Beyond Dr. Blank stands the shade of Dean Acheson, reminding us that Britain in the postwar era had lost an Empire but not yet found a new role. Meanwhile a defence-and-foreign policy was pursued that the country in its reduced circumstances could not afford, imposing as it did an unprecedented burden—in peacetime—on the balance-of-payments account.

These and other considerations suggest that the identification of pluralist stagnation is one thing; the assessment of what it costs the country, quite another. Nor is it enough to focus on what has here been called stagnation of result. Governments normally use the group networks. These include the advisory committees (a rare list of which is printed as appendix A), and the various consultative channels, informal as well as formal. They vary in importance but they all take precious time and energy that the governing elite can ill afford and may well tend to induce stagnation of the other kind, of process. But then, as Chapter 1 attempted to convey, pressure groups are embedded in the structure of society: They are not alien forces. Only an authoritarian, possibly only a totalitarian, government could pass them by. Accordingly, stagnation of process in some sectors may be part of the cost of running a democratic political system. If, after further research, the cost still seemed high, the nation might consider ways of streamlining the existing arrangements. But in that, some would surely detect the odour, and scarcely the odour of sanctity, of the Corporate State.

11

Group, Class, and the Corporate State

Like some distant drum-beat, the Corporate State or the New Corporatism as applied to contemporary Britain began to seep into one's consciousness in the mid-seventies. But the apprehensions date at least from April 1968, when Walter Padley, M.P., a leader of the Shopworkers and member of the Labour Party's NEC, spoke out in front of both P.M. and Chancellor (Roy Jenkins) at a meeting of the Trade Union Group of the PLP, vigorously denouncing statutory wage controls "as a step towards a corporate state."[1]

Exactly what Mr. Padley meant by "a corporate state" is not clear. It is clear that other politicians could take exactly the same referent and give it quite a different name. Only a week or two earlier, "Mr. Heath and the overwhelming majority of the Shadow Cabinet" had given a "firm lead that statutory incomes policy means that a socialist economy is being fastened permanently upon the British people and must be opposed."[2] Four and a half years later Prime Minister Heath and his Cabinet "went statutory" and so, according to his own equation, took the nation a little further towards a Socialist State, which Mr. Padley, however, would have conceived of as a Corporate State.

What, then, *is* a Corporate State? This is not easily answered because, as Nigel Harris has reminded us " 'corporatism' itself was no single unified doctrine."[3] Even so, in the context of this discussion, which turns upon the possible unintended consequences of a certain class of contemporary group-government interactions, the central thread can be identified and teased out for inspection. Corporatism represents what Auguste Murat a generation ago called a "third solution," in between classical capitalism and some species of socialism, to "the social question," specifically aiming to transcend the "preposterous and inhuman class struggle."[4] Isn't *socialism* meant to do that? Yes, but corporatism attempts it while basically retaining private ownership of the means of production, distribution, and exchange. As François Perroux put it in 1938, corporatism (in the large sense) is that regime which, within a capitalist system, arranges, for the purpose of correcting the shortcomings and abuses such a system entails, the collaboration of capital and labour.[5]

That of course is doctrine, part of what another French author called "Corporatisme doctrinal" as distinct from "Corporatisme législatif." But if we check doctrine against enactment as the first *stato corporativo* gradually took shape in Italy in the late 1920s, we do find confirmation (e.g., in the Labour Charter of April 1927) that its base was still to be private ownership. The state would intervene in economic production only to make good deficiencies in priv̇ate enterprise, or to further state policy. Nor need such intervention be undertaken by direct management; the state might rely upon controls or exhortation.[6]

Responding more to the Depression than to doctrine, the state began intervening in that sense in the early thirties, making the IRI (*Istituto per la Recostruzione Industriale*) its principal instrument for salvaging certain firms in shipping, shipbuilding, and engineering and for canalizing investment funds. What was meant to have been a rescue operation survived, and so the Corporate State almost stumbled upon its well-known hybrid form—a public corporation, wholly state-owned but enjoying substantial independence, and itself controlling many ordinary, or normally constituted, companies that would have to face the arbitrament of the market. Thus, under what came to be called "the IRI formula," a government's broad economic calculations would be conveyed to the micro level, where companies would enjoy the bracing breezes but also the bounteous rewards of private enterprise.

It was at this working level that the most novel arrangements for reconciling capital and labour could be discerned. Accepted by both sides in 1925 (after dispensing with the services of the free trade unions), this collaboration was put on a statutory basis the following year in the celebrated Law on the Legal Regulation of Collective Labour Relations, commonly known as the Rocco Law after the Minister of Justice, Alfredo Rocco. Employers and employees were to line up in associations that would negotiate a collective labour contract, disputes about which would be settled by specially-created sections of the Courts of Appeal acting as Labour Courts. Lockouts and strikes were forbidden. Just over a year later the Labour Charter, to which Alfredo Rocco put the final touches, sketched the outline of the corporate state. Its basic building block, the corporation was deemed to "constitute the unitary organization of the forces of production. . . ." Since the corporations were to be composed of associations of employers and employees enjoying legal equality and sole bargaining rights, the several provisions amounted to an ambitious attempt to clamp down on the class war at its point of origin. Social insurance, whose burden was to be equally shared, was also provided as "another manifestation of the principle of collaboration."

In accordance with these ideas, corporations were created to cover seven fields, making for thirteen national associations or syndicates (one being "single"), the whole structure capped by a Ministry, then by a National Council, of Corporations.[7] By now, 1934, twenty-two corporations were authorized, one for each field (though the original thirteen "sections" were cut to nine). These twenty-two would lead up to three "production cycles" (agriculture and trades; industry/commerce; public services), and then to the National Council.

Evidently the third solution was gradually emerging. But who or what was making it happen? From the start the corporations had been manned by the "right sort of chap," politically "sound." Later the Party was directly represented in the twenty-two corporations. That indicated fusion of one sort, but a fusion of the State and the Party was also under way. Political opponents of the regime were driven out, jailed, killed, or cowed, leaving the field to a *partito unico*. This single party ceased to be private and became an organ of government, creating a *Stato-Partito* (as Sergio Panunzio christened it). The interpenetration of the economic, governmental and party orders was then intensified by allowing eight out of ten of the nominees for the list of candidates to the reconstituted Chamber of Deputies to be put up by the sections within the corporations. One touch was still needed for the sake of symmetry: a place for the corporations as such in the sun of the Chamber of Deputies, which, in the manner of Parliaments from the beginning, had been territorially based. Immolating itself to that cause, the existing Chamber gave up the ghost in 1938 to make way the following year for a Chamber of Fasces and Corporations. On paper at least, the three orders had fused, and the corporate state was indistinguishable from the party state.

Although too rapidly sketched, this real-life model ought to enable us to judge whether, and if so to what extent, the warnings of a Walter Padley in the late sixties—and of a Jo Grimond and others in the mid-seventies—were well grounded. Certainly in 1974 the Labour Party fought and (just) won two general elections on manifestos undertaking to create a National Enterprise Board (NEB) "to administer publicly-owned shareholdings," and the NEB was quickly seen by "many eyes" to be "closely reminiscent of Italy's state holding company, IRI."[8] By then the IRI had become in effect a great conglomerate, including Aeritalia (aerospace), Alitalia (aviation), and Alfa Romeo (if not Fiat) in addition to its original acquisitions (e.g., in banking, shipbuilding and shipping) among its 150 or so companies. By that test the NEB, legislated in 1975 but relying on persuasion, had in the later seventies some way to go, with holdings in eight companies, in four of which it was the sole or a principal shareholder, several acquired because they had failed that other test—of the market.

In 1974 Labour also promised "a system of Planning Agreements between the Government and key companies to ensure that the plans of those companies are in harmony with national needs and objectives and that Government financial assistance is deployed where it will be most effectively used." Inspired by Italian and especially French planning experience in the previous decade, the proposed system was also bound up with the IRI concept: "Wherever we give direct aid to a company out of public funds we shall reserve the right to take a proportionate share of the ownership of the company."[9] That sentence embodied the carrot and the stick that might be needed to get companies to cooperate. They showed no hurry to do so, however, after the new scheme was enacted in 1975. By the following summer six companies were talking about signing, and three nationalized industries were talking about talking.

No doubt it is true that under the sponsorship system (recall Chapter 8) a high proportion of the major companies were already in close touch with Government Departments. Even so, if all these policies did portend a New Corporatism, the nation was not exactly rushing headlong into it. And where was the evidence for that class collaboration which seems to constitute the inner core of the concept? Like sponsorship proper, the planning agreements would in practice almost certainly not include (rather than say "exclude") the unions. The CBI doubtless spoke for its members in characterizing the proposals as "neither necessary nor desirable," adding that "the compulsory disclosure of information would be damaging to industrial relations."[10] Thus (extrapolating) the workers would get to know of unpalatable or even harsh but unavoidable decisions too far in advance (so to speak). In short, a planning agreement would probably be perceived by management as a Pandora's box, which they would resist opening.

Conversely, the Social Contract, presented for the second of the 1974 elections as lying "at the heart of this manifesto and our programme to save the nation," was to subsist "between the Labour Government and the trade unions. It is not concerned solely or even primarily with wages. It covers the whole range of national policies." In exchange for some such (social) policies, the unions would freely acknowledge that "they have other loyalties—to the members of other unions too, to pensioners, to the lower-paid, to invalids, to the community as a whole."[11] This meant voluntary wage restraint, hence the Communist Party's characterization of it as a "social con trick." But on whom? The TUC did not revive the formal wage-vetting arrangements it had used in the sixties to monitor pay claims in good time. In early November it was calculated that its own advice to government on wages "took up only six column inches" in one of its broadsheets: Its successful representations to government occupied two pages, and it was asking for more (in terms of the proposed Employment Protection Bill, pensions, and nationalization).[12] In any event, the CBI had not been consulted about the Social Contract, to which it declared itself "in no way committed."[13] Their leaders complained "that the Government was making no attempt to reach a balanced view on critical industrial questions"—rather it was a situation in which the unions got what they asked for, even one in which "the Government seemed to be at the beck and call of the TUC."[14]

Before November was out, however, the Government was showing signs of preparing to overcome the limitations of their approach. The Chancellor, Denis Healey floated the idea of a separate social contract, to which the CBI president (Ralph Bateman) responded. Ministers, he argued, would either have to "impose statutory wage controls which few people want, or they must begin to balance the scales again and return us to the healthy situation whereby both sides of industry can negotiate pay and conditions from a more equal base of power and responsibility."[15] But May 1975 found the CBI Council still asking the Government to formulate an effective pay policy "in conjunction with both sides of industry."[16] It was not until July that the Government was compelled by soaring inflation not only to think again, but tripartitely, as disclosed in the White Paper *The Attack on Inflation* and in the House. There the Chancellor, opening the Second Reading of the Remuneration, Charges and Grants Bill, which gave the Government powers for its counterinflation policy, announced that, after the year of restraint—the £6—was up, he envisaged "returning to the TUC and the CBI to work out new rules that would continue into 1977."[17] Soon journalists were taking such an arrangement for granted; thus, in January 1976, the Labour Editor of *The Times* would write that "the time is fast approaching when the TUC, the CBI and the Cabinet will have to decide what is to take the place of the £6 policy when it expires in a little under six months' time."[18]

Corporatist ideas have found institutional expression in several forms, starting (in our period) with the National Economic Development Council (NEDC) and its tributaries. Conceived in 1961 against a background of the most recent balance-of-payments crisis and at work (or at meeting) in March 1962, NEDC (T.C. Fraser recalls) was designed "specially to reach agreement between the three parties, government, management and trade unions, on how to break the vicious circle which our post-war economic experience has been following, that is the regular cycle of go and stop...." Nor was it designed to be yet another advisory body. The Conservative Chancellor, Selwyn Lloyd, said (according to Mr. Fraser) that he "wanted something more purposeful than that. He wanted both sides of industry to share with the government the task of relating plans to the resources likely to be available, and would not arrogate to ministers the right to settle the agenda."[19] As First Secretary of State at the DEA, Michael Stewart spoke (September 1966) in the same vein for the incoming Labour Government: "We emphatically want NEDDY to be a body at which the CBI and the TUC can be there at the formative stages of policy."[20]

By then NEDDY had been diminished by the loss of its economic director and a large section of the economic division of the National Economic Development Office (NEDO) to the DEA for the macroeconomic calculations that had gone into the ill-starred National Plan. If diminished, NEDDY was not denuded. Its Industrial Division kept going "as the external agency for conducting the dialogue between government and the major part of private industry...." That took the specific form, even before Labour returned to office in 1964, of Economic Development Committees (EDCs, or "Little Neddies"), of which about a score had been created by the time Mr. Stewart spoke.[21] The intention (their organizer, Mr. Fraser, has said in language that unconsciously echoed some corporatist writers) was to bring together "the 'three estates' of industry, i.e., the government departments concerned, the management organizations and the trade unions, [starting] with the initial objective of ensuring that these parties should have from the first a real sense of responsibility for the establishment of the committee and thus for the success of its work." Virtually all the EDCs were formed by that process, although the several nominees were not meant to be delegates. Chairmen were appointed after consultation with the three estates, as were the (up to three) independent members.[22]

How far these new structures proved in practice to be genuinely tripartite, tending to mitigate "the preposterous and inhuman class struggle," is of course quite another question. T.C. Fraser, who ended up as acting head of NEDO and had been a trade-association executive, saw the NEDC as fulfilling that function, though expressing it as "partnership." As general secretary of the TUC, Len Murray has seen the NEDC exercise as a stimulus to thinking the almost unthinkable, which may be evidence for the same tendency.[23] Before the NEDC monthly meetings, a CBI Liaison Committee meets under the chairmanship of the President to go through the NEDC agenda and "to formulate where possible a united view of 'management members'."[24] But far from ruling out a moderating role for NEDC, that practice might be a precondition of it.

On the other hand, the NEDC has not become what one industrial leader, Sir Peter Runge, expected of it. Director of Tate & Lyle and prominent in its "Mr. Cube" campaign, and President of the FBI from 1963 to 1965, he once declared: "There is only one body which looks at the economy in the broad and which tests policies by the criteria of the efficiency of the nation as a whole. I refer to the NEDC. . . . Its image is that of a planning body. . . . but its grazing rights cover a much more extensive field."[25] That was corporatist in tone if not in actual words, but the implied growth did not take place.

The general reasons for arrested growth cannot be discussed here, but a specific one has to be touched upon because it bears so closely on the corporatist theme. As Trevor Smith, a keen observer of British political economics, has put it: "There was an element of legerdemain in NEDC tripartism," which, a Minister had told him, was "not so much a confidence trick as a trick of confidence."[26] On that view, the NEDC was simply a vehicle for the mobilization of group consent to planning, never intended to serve participation—that is, in our terms, never intended to be corporatist at all. So, too, with the EDCs, about which Mr. Smith is even more forthright: tripartism there was "something of a sham" because it did not confer equal participation, as between industrialists and trade unionists, on the Committees, in the distribution of chairmanships, or in NEDO's service. That, for our theme, may not be decisive, however, because corporatism does not appear to require precise numerical equality in the representation of capital and labour, only their collaboration.

In any event, the incoming Conservative Government of 1970, after a thorough review, retained all but five of the (by then) twenty-one EDCs as well as the parent body. The new administration proved to be strongly interventionist, as in the 1972 Industry Act which, over the opposition of the CBI, gave the Secretary of State for Industry power to take equity holdings in private industry (echoes again of the Italian IRI). More specifically, in August 1972, the

Secretary of State for Employment unveiled the possibility of handing over many of his Department's responsibilities to a body later identified as a Manpower Services Commission (MSC), an idea already favoured by the TUC. By New Year's Day 1974, the MSC was in existence: In April it took over the Training Services Agency from the Department; in October, the Employment Services Agency. "A major innovation," Dan McGarvey (General Council) told the TUC Congress because in addition to advising on manpower questions it was "an executive body."[27]

Did this development contribute, unintentionally, to "creeping corporatism"? In the House, the Secretary (Maurice Macmillan) had emphasized the MSC's tripartite structure. On inspection, tripartite turned out to mean TUC, CBI, and local authority/educational interests groups (three of each), with an independent chairman (Sir Denis Barnes). If this was not exactly the triad of the *stato corporativo*, it was in the tradition, since the chairman would be chosen with an eye to the public interest, of which the state is expected to be the guardian. Moreover, against the wishes of the TUC, the staff of both Commission and Agencies became civil servants. On the Commission itself, the TUC and CBI, with the others certainly, would have a job to do, even though the functions would actually be discharged by the Agencies. Real work as distinct from debate is often conducive to fruitful collaboration.

This form of self-regulation had been recommended in the Robens Report on Safety and Health at Work, which appeared in July 1972, just before the idea for a manpower services commission had been aired. Here it would be a Health and Safety Commission and Executive, responsible to Ministers for administering a new comprehensive and integrated system of law covering the health and safety of virtually all people at work. This Commission, too, would be tripartite in the same broad sense, which both CBI and TUC vigorously opposed, arguing at a meeting with a junior Minister in February 1973, that "to command the support of industry," only industry should be represented.[28] The consultative document (July 1973) retained the pattern, however, and the Bill, introduced in January 1974, followed the document. A change of Government followed, but in March the incoming Labour Administration reintroduced the Bill. Now the TUC in particular rehearsed its criticisms, especially about the composition of the new authority. Some changes to the Bill were accepted and "incorporated either before it was introduced or at the Committee stage."[29] But in the Act (31 July) the composition remained tripartite in the broad sense of the term, and so the Commission came to have both a local-authority component and independents. Again, the functions would actually be discharged by an executive (January 1975), the old Factory Inspectorate writ large and unified. However, on the Commission itself, Capital would again be sitting down with Labour under the aegis of the State, not merely to talk but to do a specific job.

On its face, the Conciliation and Arbitration Service (CAS), which began work in September 1974 even before it had been legislated, appeared to be another apt example of the general trend. For its immediate source was to be found in direct capital-labour negotiations in 1972, following the miners' and railwaymen's strikes. In July, under the CBI roof, the two sides unanimously agreed to set up a conciliation and arbitration service, to deal, initially, with disputes of major importance in which a stoppage of work has occurred or is apprehended.[30] Started in September, this service was run by a joint TUC/CBI Committee, which had its first test in January 1973.

Just over a year later, for the first of the 1974 elections, the Labour Party offered such a CAS to the electorate, though as a nongovernmental body. Having won (more or less), the Labour Government sent out its consultative document in May, adhering to the increasingly common-ground plan of a Council of ten: three each from the TUC, CBI, and outside, who proved to be academics. J.E. Mortimer, for long a full-time official of the Draughtsmen's union, was placed in the chair by Prime Minister Wilson. To some extent, then, the development represented a detachment from the State, although the staff doing the actual work were to remain civil servants after transfer from the Department. Despite persistent TUC objections, they remained so when the Advisory, Conciliation and Arbitration Service (ACAS) was legislated in 1975. In any case, the Council embodied some measure of class collaboration (i.e., apparently sustained the corporatist trend).

So it goes on—but whither? The net result of the government-group interactions outlined above is not easy to characterize, but this at least is clear: It is not the corporatism of *lo stato corporativo*. When sociologists R.E. Pahl and J.T. Winkler were writing just before the October 1974 election, they were confident that corporatism in that sense was coming. "Corporatism is fascism with a human face.... What the parties are putting forward now is an acceptable face of fascism; indeed a masked version of it, because so far the more repugnant *political and social* aspects of the regime are absent or only present in diluted form."[31] Whether they were simply referring to the coercion (including castor oil for putting opponents out of commission) is not clear. In any event, something fundamental *was* absent, a necessary condition of corporatism: the *Stato-Partito* (or fusion of party and state), or, as a minimum, the *partito unico* (or single party). No *partito unico*, no *stato corporativo*. The authors came within hailing distance of recognizing that connection in noting, among the signs of creeping corporatism, "the advocacy of a temporary suspension of party politics in favour of national or coalition government." But that is a far cry from a one-party *system*, of which there was no sign when they wrote or in the late seventies.

What of corporatism in some looser sense? In all discussions of the kind, a fundamental weakness is observable: a tendency to mistake structure for function, to assume identity of purpose and achievement from identity or close similarity of institutional form. It is only too easy to see in the National Enterprise Board a reincarnation of the IRI, in something like the same circumstances. But who can say how they will be used and so what paths they will be made to follow? From the point of view of State tutelage or even guidance, the IRI proved to be a wayward child. So, notoriously, did ENI (Ente Nazionale Idrocarburi), the great energy corporation started in 1953: Under Enrico Mattei, it became a state within a state, one that seems to have remained intact despite his death. If EGAM (operational from 1971 in metals, textile machinery, and so forth) appears to have been less "feudal," that may be because it found itself struggling financially to survive. In any event, compare the NEB. Its (former) head, Lord Ryder, though no Enrico Mattei, was credited with dreams of quasi-autonomous power. From the very drafting of the 1974 White Paper, however, the "NEB has been clearly seen as an instrument of government policy, even though, as civil servants are quick to point out, Ryder's own remarks do not always convey that impression." In three important NEB initiatives up to early 1976, Lord Ryder was "merely . . . asked to help implement" government policy decisions. There is (a close observer judged) "no question that Ryder is under Whitehall control."[32] We have similar structures, then, but different control relationships and so the possibility of quite varied uses and political meaning, as between countries at any given time or within one country over time (hence the significance of freedom of association in general and for parties in particular).

That holds good for the system of sponsorship even in form, and de facto for the Little Neddies and planning agreements, which, even with the best intentions, seem fated to tilt towards capital, like the Italian corporations in the later years. Earlier, when the influence of Edmondo Rossoni was still strong, they had been tilted the other way. The Social Contract affords the most striking reminder of the need to study how an institutional arrangement, as well as a formal structure, is actually made to work. Not only is it, despite some official lip-service to CBI participation, a bilateral arrangement in fact, but it has been used (many analysts have judged), not to sustain a Corporate State, but to prepare the way for a Socialist one. "A social contract of sorts there undoubtedly is, but it is increasingly more about socialism than about wage restraint," wrote the labour correspondent of *The Times*, Paul Routledge, in 1974. He went on to list the debits and credits (as recorded above), which on balance doubtless tended towards socialism in at least some mechanical sense of the term.

Still resorted to in the mid-seventies, the Social Contract continued to be interpreted in that light, by Sir Keith Joseph, for example, and by that other intellectual Conservative, Ian Gilmour, who perceived the development as "a sort of state sponsored syndicalism. . . ."[33] In 1976 the Liberal M.P., David Steel was writing in the same vein, immediately about the Budget, ultimately about the Social Contract. How would Labour like it, he wondered:

. . . if a Tory Chancellor, presenting his Budget, said: "I have in mind two rates of company tax and I'll let the Commons know which one to vote for once the

CBI has told me, by the end of June please, what levels of prices increase they are willing to try to get their members to accept for next year."[34]

Like formal structures, then, institutional arrangements can be made to work in quite different ways. This means that we cannot with complete confidence strike a balance—as to net tendencies—within the framework of the debate as so far conducted. We need to delve, as others have not, into informal corporatism. This would have to be inquired into on another occasion, but it has already been illustrated in these pages, if not pursued; for example, the collaboration of capital and labour on certain issues, not only at the top but at lower levels, as recorded in Chapter 5 (TSR-2) and in Chapter 8. The RPM case is not without its irony. Who was it that, in 1964, made common cause, in effect, with the manufacturers and shopkeepers against the Government and, on the face of it, the public interest? The Union of Shop, Distributive and Allied Workers. And who was their spokesman in the House? None other than Walter Padley.[35] Four years later he would be detecting, on other grounds, the dangerous drift towards a Corporate State.

The movement of persons in and out of government and group service, possibly with stopping-points *en route* in the hybrid institutions, would also repay study in order to test the hypothesis that it makes for a kind of cultural corporatism. The movement itself has been observed but little documented.[36] It goes back at least half a century, and includes: from Foreign Office to the first Director-Secretary of the FBI; Ministry of Transport (Permanent Secretary, no less) to be Director-General of the National Union of Manufacturers; then—now post-World War II—a lesser light, but still senior, to the same position from the Board of Trade (BOT), which also supplied a Secretary for the British Scrap Metal Federation; an Under-Secretary at Housing and Local Government to be chief executive of a landlord's organization; an Assistant Secretary there to take charge of the Country Landowners' Association; from Foreign Office, former ambassador, to the managing directorship of the British Electrical and Allied Manufacturers' Association; another former ambassador to be chairman, overseas policy committee, of the Association of British Chambers of Commerce; head of division, Department of Employment and Productivity to Director-Generalship of the National Farmers' Union; Under-Secretary at the Department of Prices and Consumer Protection, ex-Ministry of Food and Department of Trade and Industry, to the Director-Generalship of the Food Manufacturers' Federation, Director-General of Fair Trading to be Director-General of the CBI, and from Ministry of Social Security to Child Poverty Action Group.

All that is in addition, in the narrower sense, to *pantouflage* that delightful French term ("*la pantoufle*" means "slipper") denoting the equally delightful switch from Whitehall to the board room and hence (switching languages) *la dolce vita*, the sweet life. For example, Assistant Secretary to the Board of Inland Revenue, later Commissioner, to be Finance Director, Boots Pure Drug

Company; Permanent Secretary to the Ministry of Aviation to be chairman of British Aluminium, the Canadian British Aluminium Company, Aluminium Foils, and managing director of Tube Investments; from the Treasury to the board of Midland Bank; Ministry of Transport (chief scientific officer) to take charge of group planning and development at Vickers, appointed by a new managing director who had met him when serving on the British Steel Corporation.

Movement into the government arena if not exactly the government has of course been common since the 1960s, quite apart from the irregulars brought in by Harold Wilson. As illustration, economic director of the Iron and Steel Board to direct NEDO; from Wool Textile Federation (before that Lloyds Bank) to be industrial director of NEDO; president of the Birmingham Chamber of Commerce (active in the National Exhibition Centre case) to be industrial adviser at the Department of Economic Affairs (DEA), whose chief such adviser came in from British Aluminium, moved on to be managing director of NEDO, and exited, in the fullness of time, to John Laird and Son, the construction company, whose deputy chairman had been on NEDO in the early days (the managing director of a subsidiary had also served on a Little Neddy); chairman of Nabisco to be another DEA adviser, joined in that role by the managing director of the Peter Jones store. These industrial advisers were to be coordinated by a steelman, who later moved over to the CBI when its Director-General went off in search of a Parliamentary seat, and, finding one, was transported within weeks—a miracle—into the Cabinet Room as Minister of Technology. Other industrial advisers, inherited by that Ministry after the DEA folded, came from such firms as Metal Box, Imperial Tobacco, British Sidac, and Reckitt and Colman. Rio Tinto-Zinc, Hambros Bank, and Marks and Spencers were among companies supplying men on attachment to the Civil Service Department (under a Conservative regime). Nor was the City of London (Wall Street) neglected; for example, a managing director of Lazards (the merchant bankers) exchanged places for two years with an Assistant Secretary at the Treasury, and a city solicitor was recruited as managing director of the Industrial Reorganization Corporation.

All this surely represents no more than the tip of the iceberg. Exactly what it portends no one, at present, can say. In 1965, Peter Nettl thought (to paraphrase crudely) that business was being "nobbled" by government, but he was long on hypothesis, short on evidence.[37] Since 1965, the exchanges have multiplied, with relatively more forays into government from the outside, making it more likely that the outsiders will leave their mark on that species of primary group that increased interaction may be expected to produce. In other words, the interaction may be expected to produce some common values and beliefs, some common definition of the situation, which, if unobstructed, would be likely to foster corporatist modes of thought at least and, with other variables, a Corporate State.

Does the tendency, then, go unobstructed? The question can hardly be pursued in the few remaining pages, but the answer must be a firm "No." Some objections have already been mentioned: alternate parties in office (alternate = coming after one of the *other* kind, as in alternate generation, first by budding, then by sexual reproduction). The *Stato-Partito* is not even a dot on the horizon; nor is the *partito unico*, even. Quite apart from that, those who predict corporatism seem always to forget the limitations of their analysis—that they have been cutting a swathe through the complex reality. Abstraction there must be of course, leaving a residue, but "out of sight" should not mean "out of mind" when it comes to prediction. Of the residuum, only one component can be singled out here as peculiarly relevant to the New Corporatism: the class conflict that persists despite all tripartite arrangements and other modes of collaboration, informal as well as formal. If, as Andrew Shonfield pointed out long ago, one cannot simply call the present system capitalist,[38] it retains a substantial capitalist sector and, accordingly, a substantial source of class antagonism that, in certain circumstances, tends to be articulated in the political arena. That is hardly news, which such Liberals as Giolitti in Italy and John Stuart Mill in Britain conveyed as effectively, up to a point, as Marx and Engels. But, in discussing the prospects of corporatism, many seem to need reminding that "the standing feud between Capital and Labour," as Mill characterized it, flourishes still, and with it a standing stimulus to class politics.

Even in these pages the class lines can be discerned, in part, by identifying one or more of the principal antagonists. The unions in one form or another have often been singled out. Discussing the Trade Union Group of the PLP in 1970, David Wood of *The Times* wrote: "They are trade unionists first and socialists (if at all) second, and the industrial class war continues to have a menacing reality for them that it has for nobody else."[39] Thinking of the unions in the usual sense, and the risk (December 1973) of confrontation with the Heath Government, Peregrine Worsthorne (*Sunday Telegraph*) pronounced: "The current crisis has a very substantial element of class war about it...."[40] But, remembering what those issues were about (industrial relations reform; prices and incomes), one would do better to examine the substance of pressure-group politics for evidence of class conflict. A preliminary analysis of sectors 1 and 2 (mainly Chapters 5, 7, and 8 but even, to some extent, 6) suggests that a high proportion of the representations actually made by groups could be subsumed under three headings: social control, especially for mastery or advantage within the industrial setting; public expenditure; and taxation.[41] These could be properly represented as class issues.

The possibility of reconciling, up to a point, class analysis with group analysis has been remarked upon even by scholars apparently writing within the Marxist tradition, who might have been expected to disapprove. The Pole, W. Wesolowski, for example, has stressed that there is no essential contradiction between the model of an antagonistic society derived from Marxism or from the theory of group interests. His fellow countryman, Stanislaw Ehrlich has gone even further, arguing that, far from being in contradiction with the Marxist theory of social classes, the analysis of group interests forms its indispensable complement.[42]

With that line of thought one is inclined to agree. In this book, certainly, there is evidence for the view that in certain sectors at certain points in time, group politics is virtually a continuation of class politics by other means. But that would hardly hold for other sectors (3 and 4 in this book), where different bases of cleavage stand revealed, making group the more appropriate concept.[43]

Evidently one's final judgment of these conceptualizations depends at any given time upon the relative importance of the sectors. Everyone readily agrees that sectors 1 and 2, occupied by the given groups, are of profound importance. It is there that observers have reported seeing the Corporate State developing. For all the reported signs, however, the system, retaining a substantial capitalist foundation, retains the standing feud as well and so a tendency to class politics, which may be supplemented, deflected, and even civilized by group politics but not eliminated. Not at its source, at least. There does remain a conceivable political solution, which is to eliminate class antagonism by eliminating politics—basic rights, rival parties for public office, and the like. That was the way the *stato corporativo* actually went, of course, but it will not be the British way or—in deference to Ernest Barker, the English way—for as far ahead as we need to look.

Appendixes

Appendix A
Advisory Bodies in British Government as of 1973

Department	Name of Body	Date of Appointment	Expected Date of Report
Ministry of Agriculture Fisheries and Food	Committee of Inquiry into the Veterinary profession	March 1971	In up to 2 years' time
	Advisory Committee on Pesticides and other Toxic Chemicals	March 1954 (Reconstituted July 1964)	Ad Hoc
	Food Standards Committee	1947 (Reconstituted 1960)	Ad Hoc
	Food Additives and Contaminants Committee	December 1964 (Formerly a sub-committee of the Food Standards Committee)	Ad Hoc
	Farm Animal Welfare Advisory Committee	July 1967	Ad Hoc
Civil Service Department	Task Force on the interchange of scientific talent	September 1972	Progress report by end of 1972 and thereafter as appropriate
	Computor Agency Council	December 1972	As required
Ministry of Defence	Defence Lands Committee	January 1971	End of February 1973
	Committee of Enquiry into Service Catering	December 1972	April 1973
	Committee of Inquiry into the Medical, Dental and Nursing Services in the Armed Forces	April 1971	March 1973

Department	Name of Body	Date of Appointment	Expected Date of Report
Department of Education and Science	Advisory Committee for Handicapped Children	Set up pre-1960 Reconstituted August 1969	–
	Library Advisory Council (England)	1965	–
	Library Advisory Council (Wales)	1965	–
	Standing Commission on Museums and Galleries	1930	–
	National Advisory Council on Education in Industry and Commerce	1948	–
	Advisory Board for the Research Councils	September 1972	From time to time
	Advisory Committee on Agricultural Education	January 1971	–
	Committee on Reading	April 1972	End of 1973
Department of Employment	Commission on Industrial Relations	Constituted as a Statutory body in November 1971 under the Industrial Relations Act 1971	Annual and Ad Hoc
Department of the Environment	Ancient Monuments Board for England	1914	Annual
	Royal Commission on Environmental Pollution	February 1970	No set frequency
	Sub-Committee of the Royal Commission on Environmental Pollution	November 1971	

Department	Name of Body	Date of Appointment	Expected Date of Report
Department of the Environment (Cont)	Royal Fine Art Commission	May 1924	As necessary
	Central Housing Advisory Committee	1935	Reports not made by Committee (reports from time to time by Sub-committees)
	Central Advisory Water Committee	Under S2 of the Water Act 1945	No regular reports made
	Clean Air Council	1957	–
	Noise Advisory Council	April 1970	No set frequency
	National Consultative Council of the Building and Civil Engineering Industries	1943	–
	Technical Committee to examine large steel box girder Bridges (appointed jointly by Secretary of State for the Environment and Secretaries of State for Scotland and Wales)	December 1970	(Interim report received, June 1971); Early 1973
	Historic Buildings Council for England	October 1953	Annual
	Freight Integration Council	February 1969	From time to time
	Construction and Housing Research Advisory Council	November 1971	–
	Planning and Transport Research Advisory Council	November 1971	–

Department	Name of Body	Date of Appointment	Expected Date of Report
Department of the Environment (Cont.)	Local Government Boundary Commission for England	November 1972 (existed as a body designate since Nov. 1971)	Report to Secretaries of State for the Environment and Home Affairs from time to time
	Advisory Committee on Pop Festivals	August 1972	March 1973
	Advisory Committee on Aggregates	August 1972	Interim Report—Mid-1973
Department of Health and Social Security	National Insurance Advisory Committee	October 1947	From time to time
	Industrial Injuries Advisory Committee	November 1947	From time to time
	Central Health Services Council (and seven associated Standing Advisory Committees—Medical, Dental, Pharmaceutical, Ophthalmic, Nursing, Maternity and Midwifery, Mental Health)	July 1948	From time to time
	Joint Committee on Vaccination and Immunization	October 1962	From time to time
	Joint Working Party on the organization of Medical Work in Hospitals	April 1966 (Reconstituted 1972)	1974
	Committee on Medical Aspects of Chemicals in Food and the Environment	September 1972	No set frequency
	Medicines Commission	November 1969	Annual
	Advisory Committee on the application of Computing Science to Medicine and the National Health Service	June 1969	From time to time

Department	Name of Body	Date of Appointment	Expected Date of Report
Department of Health and Social Security (Cont)	Committee on One Parent Families	November 1969	Mid-1973
	Committee on Safety of Medicines	June 1970	Annual
	Attendance Allowance Board	October 1970	Ad Hoc
	Council for Post-Graduate Medical Education in England and Wales	December 1970	From time to time
	Committee on Hospital Complaints Procedure	March 1971	Spring 1973
	National Health Service Staff Advisory Committee	April 1972	None
	Committee on the working of the Abortion Act	May 1971	1973
	Standing Scientific Liaison Committee on Smoking and Health	June 1971	From time to time
	Working Party on Collaboration between Local Authorities and New Health Authorities in England and Wales	August 1971	A series of recommendations until winding-up probably in early 1974
	Central Council for Education and Training in Social Work	October 1971	No set frequency
	Food Hygiene Advisory Council	May 1955	No set frequency
	Committee on Medical Aspects of Food Policy (Nutrition)	Originally set up 1941 Reconstituted July 1965	No set frequency

Department	Name of Body	Date of Appointment	Expected Date of Report
Department of Health and Social Security (Cont)	Joint DHSS/BMA Working Party on Medical Certification	July 1970	Spring 1973
	Working Party on the Dental Services	March 1972	Early 1974 with interim reports if necessary
	Central Manpower Committee (Medical and Dental)	March 1972	From time to time
Department of Health and Social Security and Home Office	Committee on Mentally Abnormal Offenders	September 1972	1974
Home Office	Advisory Council on the misuse of Drugs	January 1972	As necessary
	Advisory Council on the Penal System	September 1966	As necessary
	Advisory Council for Probation and After-Care	October 1962	Does not make formal reports
	Boundary Commission for England	1944	General reviews every 10-15 years (next report between 1979 and 1984); interim reviews as necessary
	Boundary Commission for Wales	1944	General reviews every 10-15 years (next report between 1979 and 1984); interim reviews as necessary
	Royal Commission on the Constitution	April 1969	Mid-1973
	Criminal Law Revision Committee	February 1959	As necessary

Department	Name of Body	Date of Appointment	Expected Date of Report
Home Office (Cont)	Electoral Advisory Conference	Pre-1939	As necessary
	Conference on Local Government Electoral Law	1968	As necessary
	Home Office Scientific Advisory Council	November 1965	As necessary
Inland Revenue	Tax Reform Committee	December 1969	No fixed times
	Working Party on Mining Capital Allowances	April 1971	Early 1973
Lord Chancellor's Department	Law Commission	June 1965	Reports on special subjects about 8 times a year, and submits an annual report
	Council on Tribunals (also Scottish Committee which reports annually)	1958	Annual
Northern Ireland Office	Northern Ireland Commission	May 1972	Does not make reports
Ministry of Posts and Telecommunications	Television Advisory Committee	October 1945	As necessary
	Frequency Advisory Committee	April 1958	–
Scottish Office	Committee on Adult Education in Scotland	May 1970	1973
	Committee on Scottish Licensing Laws	April 1971	Early 1973
	Scottish Advisory Council on Social Work	July 1970	As necessary
	Scottish Health Services Council (and Associated Committees)	May 1948	(a) Annual (b) As necessary on specific subjects

Department	Name of Body	Date of Appointment	Expected Date of Report
Scottish Office (Cont)	Ancient Monuments Board for Scotland	October 1969	Annual
	Scottish Council on Crime	February 1972	As necessary but advice can be conveyed without formal report
	Royal Fine Art Commission for Scotland	August 1927	As necessary
	Boundary Commission for Scotland	1949	General reviews every 10-15 years (next report between 1979 and 1984); interim reviews as necessary
	Scottish Housing Advisory Committee	1935	Subcommittees on specific subjects; reports from time to time
	Scottish Water Advisory Committee	Under S1 of the Water (Scotland) Act 1946	No regular reports made
	Scottish National Health Service Staff Commission	August 1972	As necessary
	Clean Air Council for Scotland	1957	—
	Historical Buildings Council for Scotland	November 1953	Annual
	Advisory Committee on Electoral Areas	May 1972	As necessary in 1972 and 1973
Scottish Office and Lord Advocate's Department	Scottish Law Commission	1965	From time to time
	Committee on Criminal procedure in Scotland	January 1970	Late 1973 for main report (interim report already issued)

Department	Name of Body	Date of Appointment	Expected Date of Report
Department of Trade and Industry	Monopolies Commission	January 1949	Reports on all references; over 1966-1970 an average of 6 reports each year
	Industrial Development Advisory Board	October 1972	Annual (within 6 months of end of financial year) as part of Annual Report to Parliament under Industry Act 1972)
	Committee on Property Bonds and Equity-linked Life Assurance	February 1971	End 1973
	Metrication Board	May 1969	Annual
	Departmental Committee on Trade Mark Law and Practice	February 1972	End of 1973
H.M. Treasury	Committee to Review National Savings	March 1971	Spring 1973
	Review Board for Government Contracts	August 1969	General review expected towards end of 1973 then at three-year intervals
Welsh Office	Ancient Monuments Board for Wales	1914	Annual
	Historic Buildings Council for Wales	October 1953	Annual
	Welsh Council	May 1971 for a period of three years	No set frequency
	Women's National Commission	July 1969	–

Appendix B
Organizing Pressure on M.P.s: Resale Prices Bill, 1964

THE PROPRIETARY ARTICLES TRADE ASSOCIATION

THE NATIONAL PHARMACEUTICAL UNION

Urgent—For Immediate Action   January, 1964

To All Retail Pharmacists.

RESALE PRICE MAINTENANCE

On Friday, 17th January, 1964, there will be a full day's debate in the House of Commons on Resale Price Maintenance, when Mr. John Stonehouse (Labour/Co-operative Member of Parliament for Wednesbury) will be moving the second reading of a Private Member's Bill to abolish Resale Price Maintenance. The reception which this Bill receives, and the nature of any Government statement which may be made on the same occasion, will largely depend on what Members of Parliament learn from their constituents on this issue **before that date.**

ACTION IS REQUIRED NOW

from every pharmacist, by making his views known to his M.P. by letter and, if possible, by interview.

In Conservative-held seats every vote is of the utmost importance. In Labour-held seats as well, M.P.s cannot ignore the views of their constituents.

Let your M.P. know that you take an extremely serious view of this matter, that the retention of resale price maintenance is of the utmost importance to your livelihood, and that your M.P.'s attitude may well influence your decision at the General Election.

Enclosed is a statement covering important points in favour of the retention of Resale Price Maintenance. Also enclosed is a model letter which can serve as a basis for a letter on your own headed paper to your M.P., preferably in your own words. After reading the enclosures you may wish to compile a different letter using some of the arguments contained in them. If so, so much the better, but in any event

IT IS VITAL THAT YOU ACT IMMEDIATELY

Please let us know the name of the M.P. to whom you write and what reply he gives. A reply-paid envelope is enclosed for this purpose. After you have written to your M.P., why not show this letter to other retailers in the area?

ARGUMENTS FOR THE RETENTION OF R.P.M.

What we are asking is that the law as it now stands should remain the law and that, where the manufacturer so desires, the practice of individual price maintenance shall not be banned from the British trading system. In so many industries, R.P.M. has proved of benefit not only to manufacturers and distributors but also to the consumer.

The price-cutting of the big chain stores is not, as they so glibly claim, designed to help reduce the cost of living; it is for the sole purpose of taking for themselves the trade of the smaller businessman and therein creating a real danger of monopoly formation which is never in the interests of the consumer. These price-cutters stock only the fast selling brands of any particular type of product and members of the public who prefer other brands are compelled to go to the independent retailer. No retailer can exist by selling only slow-moving products and if the independent retailer is forced out of business the consumers' choice of products will be seriously restricted.

It is claimed that R.P.M. keeps prices high, but all the evidence available from Canada and America proves that products protected by R.P.M. have held the line against inflation in a remarkable manner. In Canada R.P.M. was abolished in 1951, but in 1960 amending legislation was passed restoring to the manufacturer the right to withhold supplies from traders who use their products as loss leaders because of the damaging effects of such practices.

No one can deny the intensity of competition among branded products and no manufacturer could afford to ignore competition. If a manufacturer fixes an excessive price for the product he offers he leaves the door wide open to all his competitors.

To abolish R.P.M. would strike at the fundamental right of the individual to enter into contract with another.

The report of the Monopolies Commission on the tobacco and cigarette industry and the judgment given in the case of the Net Book Agreement by the Restrictive Practices Court both stated that R.P.M. did not operate against the public interest.

Practically every government department and nationalised industry which engages in selling to the public adopts a policy of R.P.M. If, therefore, it is right for the Post Office, right for the Stationery Office, right for the Government itself to adopt this policy, why should it be wrong for the manufacturer of a branded article?

MODEL LETTER TO M.P.s

Esq., M.P.,
House of Commons,
London, S.W.1.

Dear   ,

As a retail pharmacist with a business in your Constituency, I am very anxious that the private traders' interest should be safeguarded on Friday, 17th January, when the House gives a full day's debate to the second reading of the Bill being introduced by Mr. Stonehouse to abolish resale price maintenance.

The retention of Section 25 of the Restrictive Trade Practices Act, 1956, is essential to the livelihood of retail chemists like myself who are giving a specialised service to the community. Retail pharmacies in Great Britain provide a comprehensive and essential dispensing service both for N.H.S. and private prescriptions to members of the public. Should R.P.M. be declared illegal there is no doubt that many retail chemists at present providing that dispensing service would be forced to close down and, as a result, the public would suffer.

Under R.P.M. the consumer is assured of fair value for money because the quality of advertised branded products must always be maintained and the price to the consumer is kept as low as possible by the intense competition between manufacturers of similar type products.

If R.P.M. is abolished the consumer will be subjected to many undesirable practices such as "phoney" bargains and "false" price cutting, practices which are in existence at present. It would clearly be against the public interest for any Legislation to stimulate the buying of more medicine than is needed by encouraging "cut price" and "special" offers.

This matter is of such vital importance to me that I look to you to convey to the Government my deep concern and that of thousands of other independent traders, and I trust that you will take any opportunity presented to you to speak against the proposed Bill in the House on 17th January.

I cannot stress too strongly that any action to weaken the existing system of individual price maintenance would be regarded by me, and I am sure by all other private traders, as a betrayal of our interests and could have serious repercussions at the time of the next General Election.

It is impossible to state a case in full in a letter but I would be very pleased to meet you with other of my colleagues to discuss this matter further at any time to suit our mutual convenience.

*

TELEGRAM

RT HON SIR JOHN VAUGHAN-MORGAN, BT, M.P.

THIS LONDON DISTRICT COUNCIL OF THE NATIONAL FEDERATION OF RETAIL NEWSAGENTS BOOKSELLERS AND STATIONERS URGES THE STRONGEST POSSIBLE OBJECTION TO ANY PRIVATE MEMBERS BILL TO ABOLISH RESALE PRICE MAINTENANCE OR ANY ALTERATION IN THE SYSTEM OF RESALE PRICE MAINTENANCE AS ALLOWED UNDER SECTION 25 OF THE RESTRICTIVE TRADE PRACTICES ACT 1956 =

BLEASDALE +

Sir John Vaughan-Morgan's Response

"Most people accept that retail performance maintenance is going. I prefer the Government's approach, but I am not impressed by some of the lobbying that is going on. I suppose we have to accept it as part of our profession, but I do not think that a printed circular telegram is a very forceful argument. And when I open three letters in my morning mail which all say in their final paragraph, by a strange coincidence, 'This will have political repercussions at the next election,' my reaction is positively hostile. I do wish that public relations officers and some of the secretaries of trade associations would be a little more circumspect and intelligent in their lobbying of Members of Parliament. They sometimes forget that the reaction is quite the contrary of what they seek" (Parliamentary Debates, vol. 686, 17 January, 1964, col. 666).

*

THE NATIONAL PHARMACEUTICAL UNION

13th February, 1964

To: Members of the N.P.U. and the C.D.A. in England, Wales, Scotland, and Northern Ireland.

Dear Sir or Madam,

The N.P.U. has now had advice from Counsel on the wording of a clause which could be included in the Government's Bill to abolish Resale Price Maintenance, which would exclude drugs, medicines and surgical appliances from the provisions of the Bill.

It has been agreed that Sir Hugh Linstead, M.P., should write to the President of the Board of Trade and the Minister of Health seeking their support for the inclusion of the suggested clause in the Bill.

Would you please write to your Member of Parliament *now* asking him to support the inclusion in the Bill of a clause exempting "any drug, or any substance recommended as a medicine (as defined in the Pharmacy & Medicines Act, 1941) or any medical or surgical appliance" from the provisions of the Bill.

The following extract from an article in *"The Times"* of 10th February by that paper's Political Correspondent explains why it is essential that *you* should write: —

"Letters from the trade associations pour in, and it is hardly surprising that most of them have made little or no impact on backbenchers. The really disturbing part of the mail comes handwritten or unevenly typed bearing his constituency postmark. These letters are sent by shopkeepers whom the M.P. knows as members or officials of his local association, of the local Conservative club, and perhaps even of the local council."

The Bill will be published shortly. Time is therefore very limited. Write now.

*

THE PHARMACEUTICAL SOCIETY OF GREAT BRITAIN

IMPORTANT NOTICE ABOUT PRICE CUTTING

The intention of the Government to abolish Resale Price Maintenance is a matter of great concern to pharmacy and the collective views of the Society and other bodies representing pharmaceutical interests have been made known to the Government and widely publicised.

Some retail businesses (including at least one pharmacy) have anticipated the proposed legislation and indulged in spectacular price-cutting in certain commodities despite the fact that manufacturers' conditions of resale still attach to the products concerned. The intention of these retailers is clearly to steal a march on their competitors and to obtain as much free publicity as possible, even though some of it may be unfavourable.

To cut the price of an article which is still the subject of a resale price condition is a breach of the terms on which the article is supplied, conduct which is professionaly unacceptable. Furthermore, the deliberate attraction to a pharmacy of publicity of a controversial nature is not in the best interests of the profession. It is contrary to the general principles expressed in the Statement on Matters of Professional Conduct regarding the conduct of a pharmacy.

At present some commodities sold in pharmacies are not subject to Resale Price Maintenance and prices to the public are decided by the pharmacist or firm concerned. Following Government action it may be that the list of such items will be increased. The right of each retailer in these circumstances to fix his own

214

prices is not disputed, but the Council of the Society wish to make it clear that any blatant publicity relating to price levels will be regarded as conduct liable to bring the profession into disrepute. Whatever the outcome of the proposed legislation, pharmacists are urged to act with restraint in meeting competition from sources outside pharmacy.

February 1964

Notes

Notes

Notes

Chapter 1
A Paradise of Groups

1. "Maitland as a sociologist," in Ernest Barker, *The Citizen's Choice* (Cambridge University Press, 1938; reprint of 1937 ed.), p. 175.

2. For further information on these and related bodies, consult, to begin with, Graham Wootton, *Pressure Groups in Britain, 1720-1970* (Allen Lane, Penguin Books Ltd., and Archon Books, Conn., U.S.A., 1975), documents 45, 46, 81, 38, 72-74, and 64-71; Stephen Blank, *Industry and Government in Britain: The Federation of British Industries in Politics, 1945-65* (Saxon House/Lexington Books, 1973); and Wyn Grant and David Marsh, *The Confederation of British Industry* (forthcoming).

3. *Report* of the Commission of Inquiry into Industrial and Commercial Representation (Association of British Chambers of Commerce and Confederation of British Industry, 1972), pp. 23-25. Hereafter: The Devlin Report. In addition to the chairman, Lord Devlin, the members were Anthony Howitt, Patrick Macrory, Lord Netherthorpe, Leslie Robinson, and Allen Stock.

4. Such banks clear cheques or, technically, bills of exchange for settlement.

5. See Wootton, *Pressure Groups*, docs. 55, 56, 77, and 78 for further information.

6. *Democracy in America* (Oxford University Press, World's Classics ed., 1946), p. 376.

Chapter 2
Pressure Groups

1. 13 May 1962. Quoted in Henry Fairlie, *The Life of Politics* (Methuen, 1968), p. 208.

2. *The English Constitution* (Oxford University Press, 1945, reprint).

3. Radio 3 talk. *The Listener*, 8 March 1973.

4. *The Times*, 20 June 1969.

5. In Maine's *Ancient Law* (John Murray, 1924; reprint of 1906 ed.), p. 186.

6. *The Times*, 6 November 1968.

7. Fabian Tract 404, 1971, and *Manchester Guardian Weekly*, 8 May 1971.

8. *New York Review of Books*, 11 November 1965. For Samuel Beer, see Elke Frank, ed., *Lawmakers in a Changing World* (Prentice-Hall, Inc., 1966), pp. 37-38.

217

9. Gerald A. Dorfman, *Wage Politics in Britain, 1945-67* (Iowa State University Press, 1973).

10. "Pressure Groups and Propaganda," *Annals* of the American Academy of Political and Social Science (May 1935).

11. *Parliamentary Affairs*, vol. IX, 1956; *Political Quarterly* (January-March 1958); *Organized Groups in British National Politics* (Faber, 1961). He also used "attitude group" for the second category.

12. Graham Wootton, *Official History of the British Legion* (Macdonald and Evans, 1956), p. 1.

13. J.B. Sanderson, *Political Studies* (October 1961), pp. 236-53. He referred to S.E. Finer, who had made similar distinctions to Potter's. See also the pioneering book by a British author, J.D. Stewart, *British Pressure Groups* (Clarendon Press, 1958).

14. Robert E. Dowse and John Peel, *Political Studies* (June 1965).

15. Graham Wootton, *Interest-Groups* (Hemel Hempstead, Prentice-Hall International, 1970), p. 39.

16. Ibid.

17. Allen H. Barton, "The Concept of Property-Space in Social Research," in Paul F. Lazarsfeld and Morris Rosenberg, *The Language of Social Research* (Glencoe, Ill.: Free Press, 1955).

18. Robert H. Salisbury, *Midwest Journal of Political Science* XIII (February 1969).

19. David Neeson Levinson, *British Pressure Groups: Three Case Studies*, Harvard University thesis (HU.92.57.518). The other two groups were the NFU and BMA.

20. *The Guardian*, 12 May 1967.

21. Richard Crossman, *Diaries of a Cabinet Minister* (Hamish Hamilton & Jonathan Cape, 1975), vol. 1, p. 24.

22. Wootton, *Interest-Groups*, pp. 36-37. The groups there identified as second- and third-order are here subsumed under "representative."

23. TUC Annual Reports, 1975, p. 458; 1970, pp. 503-4; 1971, p. 133; 1966, p. 161.

24. Wootton, *Pressure Groups in Britain, 1720-1970* (Allen Lane, Penguin Books Ltd., and Archon Books, Conn., U.S.A., 1975), pp. 6-7.

25. Annual Report, 1970, p. 71; Commons Society Annual Report, 1969, p. 11.

Chapter 3
Expressive Groups: The Amenities of Life

1. Graham Wootton, *Pressure Groups in Britain, 1720-1970* (Allen Lane, Penguin Books Ltd., and Archon Books, Conn., U.S.A., 1975), doc. 80(b).

2. National Trust, Report and Accounts, 1971, pp. 17 and 6.

3. S.K. Brookes and J.J. Richardson, *Parliamentary Affairs* (summer 1975), p. 320.

4. Ibid., p. 7.

5. Report and Accounts, 1972, p. 8.

6. Report and Accounts, 1970, p. 7.

7. Wootton, *Pressure Groups*, doc. 54.

8. Robert Waterhouse, *The Guardian*, 22 October 1968.

9. *The Guardian*, 16 September 1967.

10. *Oxford Times*, 21 March 1969.

11. Association of British Chambers of Commerce, 108th Annual Report, 1967-68, p. 7.

12. 110th Annual Report, 1969-70, p. 12.

13. 16 December 1970. H.C.D. 5th series, 808, c.350.

14. 21 September, 1969; 5 October 1969; 4 January 1970.

15. Tony Dawe, *Sunday Times*, 13 December 1970.

16. Tony Aldous, *Battle for the Environment* (Fontana, 1972), pp. 53-54.

17. Term attributed to Harold Jackson of *The Guardian* by F.R. Lyon, PRO to the Road Haulage Association. *The Guardian*, 25 October 1969.

18. Tony Dawe, *Sunday Times* 13 December 1970.

19. Tony Aldous, *Battle for the Environment*, p. 64.

20. *Sunday Times*, 16 June 1974.

21. Mick Hamer, *Wheels Within Wheels: A Study of the Road Lobby* (Friends of the Earth Ltd., 1974), pp. 6, 7 and 39.

22. Richard Kimber, J.J. Richardson, and S.K. Brookes, *Political Quarterly* (April-June 1974), p. 193, citing Richard Rose, *Politics in England* (Little, Brown, 1964), p. 131 (pp. 269-71 of the 1974 ed.).

23. Michael Baily, *The Times*, 14 April 1976.

24. *Sunday Times*, 13 February 1977.

25. Ibid., 3 July 1977.

26. William Plowden, *The Motor Car and Politics in Britain* (Penguin Books, 1971), p. 369.

27. "The Motor God," *The Guardian*, 15 May 1964.

28. Leaflet for Sponsored Walk, 3 May 1970.

29. *The Times*, 5 July 1968.

Chapter 4
Propagational Groups: Conservation, Human Rights, Morals

1. For the earlier years, see Robert J. Lieber, *British Politics and European Unity* (University of California Press, 1970).

2. Ross Davies, *The Times*, 7 May 1974. The physicist is John Treble.

3. *Options for Political Action*, 1973/75 (5 September 1973). At Potter's Bar is Mr. S.G. Lawrence; operations director is Edward Dawson.

4. *The Crisis of Life Styles* (Conservation Society, 1975), p. 3. Emphasis in original. Mr. Hutchinson had been chairman for four years. See also Margaret Laws Smith, *Towards the Creation of a Sustainable Economy* (Conservation Society, 1975). On the Campaign, see *Conservation News*, November, 1975, p. 11.

5. Oral evidence by Edward Dawson to Mrs. Sylvia Armour, assistant secretary to the Wolfenden Committee on Voluntary Organizations, 20 January 1976 (Society doc. 1976/54). This Committee under Lord Wolfenden was established in October 1974 to review the role and function of voluntary organizations in the last quarter of the twentieth century. Sponsors were Carnegie U.K. Trust and the Joseph Rowntree Memorial Trust.

6. Annual Report, 1975, p. 9.

7. *The History of FoE*, in *Supporters' Bulletin*, summer ed., 1976. It was at first a gleam in the eyes of Edwin Matthews (European representative of FoE Inc.,) and Barclay Inglis, who met on Clare Island, Ireland, in August 1970. Mr. Matthews floated the organization at a dinner for environmentalists at the Travellers' Club the following month. Graham Searle, who was there, became the first full-time Director. He now presides over Earth Resources Research Ltd. (ERR), which like FoE, is a company limited by guarantee, but, unlike FoE, enjoying charitable status. The current Director of FoE is Tom Burke.

8. Evidence (n.d.), p. 1.

9. Oral evidence record, 20 January 1976, sec. 6.

10. *Towards a National Energy Strategy*, 22 June 1976. See also the address by Lord Avebury (Eric Lubbock), president of the Conservation Society, at the London School of Economics, 16 November 1973, *The Energy Crisis: Growth, Stability or Collapse?* (Conservation Society, 1974).

11. See Graham Wootton, *Pressure Groups in Britain, 1720-1970* (Allen Lane, Penguin Books Ltd., and Archon Books, Conn., U.S.A., 1975), doc. 92, for the recruiting letter.

12. NCCL: Tony Smythe, in Robert Benewick and Trevor Smith (eds.), *Direct Action and Democratic Politics* (Allen and Unwin, 1972), and Robert Benewick, *The Annals*, May 1974. Amnesty International: Harry M. Scoble and Laurie S. Wiseberg, *The Annals*, May 1974.

13. Annual Report, 1971-72, pp. 3-5.

14. In William B. Gwyn and George C. Edwards III (eds.), *Perspectives on Public Policy-Making* (Tulane Studies in Political Science, vol. XV, 1975), p. 123. The general source is Frank Stacey, *The British Ombudsman* (Clarendon Press, 1971). Justice is treated as an organization *for* because, although lawyer-led, its membership in 1974 split 63 percent legal (barristers and solicitors) and 38 percent other. See Professor Gwyn, ibid., p. 100.

15. Ibid., p. 131.

16. *Let's GO With Labour for the NEW Britain* (n.d.), p. 3.

17. *The Times*, 25 June 1970.

18. The current literature is not much help specifically on the relative weight of inputs and withinputs. But for Canada, see the work briefly reviewed by Donald V. Smiley (Toronto), "The Dominance of Withinputs?: Canadian Politics," *Polity* (winter 1973), pp. 276-81.

19. *Sunday Times*, 5 April 1964.

20. Leo Ormston founded Youth Impact. In Glasgow the initiator was a Mrs. Middleton. The councillor was J.W. Pepper. *Sunday Times*, 5 April 1964, and *The Guardian*, 23 March 1964.

21. *Sunday Times*, ibid.; Sandra Salmans, *New York Times*, 15 March 1977.

22. In March 1965 Mr. Oliver was appointed Secretary-General of the Public Morality Council, the first Catholic to hold the job. It had been held by the late George Tomlinson, a Methodist. *The Guardian*, 3 March 1965. On the flaws, see *The Times*, 4 February 1964. See also *Daily Telegraph* and *The Guardian*, same date.

23. Roy Wallis, *New Society*, 13 July 1972.

24. *Observer*, 7 April 1974. The Salvation Army man is Edward Shackleton, of Swindon.

25. Ibid.

26. Sandra Salmans, *New York Times*, 15 March 1977.

27. *Observer*, 20 June 1965.

28. "Portrait of a Lobby," *The Listener*, 19 June 1969.

29. Paul Ferris, *Observer* Colour Magazine, 10 November 1968.

30. *The Times*, 13 April 1964. The speaker is Mr. W.G. Smith.

31. *Sunday Times*, 5 April 1964.

32. Peter G. Richards, *Parliament and Conscience* (Allen and Unwin, 1970), pp. 64-66.

33. *The Times*, 14 May 1954.

34. Antony Grey, secretary of HLRS, in Brian Frost (ed.), *The Tactics of Pressure* (Galliard, 1975), p. 43. Cf. Richards, *Parliament*, p. 73.

35. Grey, ibid. Mr. Robinson, a future Minister of Health, had also busied himself with abortion law reform.

36. *The Guardian*, 14 November 1961.

37. Richards, *Parliament*, pp. 74-75.

38. Grey, in *The Tactics*, p. 47.

39. Richards, *Parliament*, p. 77.

40. In the House of Commons, the Arran Bill apparently went down to defeat. Richard Crossman, *The Diaries of a Cabinet Minister* (Hamish Hamilton and Jonathan Cape, 1975), vol. 1, p. 97, n. 2.

41. Grey, in *The Tactics*, p. 49.

42. Ibid., pp. 49-50.

43. Ibid., p. 53; see also *Sunday Times*, 27 November 1966 ("Red Duster lobby blow to Abse's Bill"). The Armed Forces had already been excluded (also Scotland and Northern Ireland).

44. Ten Minute Rule: The rule is the standing order permitting brief discussion on motion for leave to introduce a Bill. The time is supposed to be a curb on loquaciousness.

45. Crossman, *The Diaries*, vol. 1, p. 161.

46. Ibid., vol. 2, p. 97.

47. Ibid., vol. 2, pp. 171-72.

48. Ibid., p. 407.

49. Ibid., p. 97, n. 1.

50. At one point the Chief was taking a very hard line about keeping opponents off the Standing Committee, which technically could have been done. See ibid., p. 172.

51. Ibid., p. 68.

52. Letter to *The Times*, 24 June 1969. By 1975 Mr. Grey was inclined to give his Society higher marks for achievement. See Frost (ed.), *The Tactics*, p. 39.

53. Basic sources for the ALRA are Keith Hindell and Madeleine Simms, *Abortion Law Reformed* (Peter Owen, 1971), and in *Political Quarterly* (July-September 1968); Richards, *Parliament*; and Bridget Pym, *Pressure Groups and the Permissive Society* (David & Charles, 1974) and in *Political Quarterly* (July-September 1972). See also John Barr, *New Society*, 9 March 1967; Jeremy Bugler, *Sunday Times*, 2 July 1967; and Norman St. John-Stevas, *The Spectator*, 26 May 1967. On this and other such issues, consult Leo Abse, *Private Member* (Macdonald, 1973).

54. Wootton, *Pressure Groups*, doc. 93.

55. Hindell and Simms, *Abortion Law Reformed*, pp. 158-59.

56. Ibid., pp. 177-79.

57. *Observer* political correspondent, 14 May 1967.

58. Bugler, *Sunday Times*.

59. Ibid.

60. Crossman, *The Diaries*, vol. 2, p. 423.

61. Ibid., p. 424.

62. Ibid., p. 411.

63. *The Times*, 24 June 1969.

64. Ibid., p. 496.

65. Ibid., p. 516.

66. *The Guardian*, 1 November 1967.

67. *The Guardian*, p. 564.

68. *Sunday Times*, 3 December 1967.

69. Crossman, *The Diaries*, vol. 2, p. 610.

70. Lena Jeger, M.P., *The Guardian*, 3 April 1968.

71. George Clark, *The Times*, 12 July 1968.

72. J.M. Cartwright Sharp, Secretary to the Law Commission, *The Times*, 23 June 1969.

73. Laurence Marks, *Observer*, 8 December 1968.

74. Norman Shrapnel, *The Guardian*, 18 December 1968.

75. The lines got crossed with the Matrimonial Property Bill introduced by Edward Bishop (Labour) after winning third place in the ballot. A former engineering draughtsman, Mr. Bishop may have been less skilled as a draftsman. The Bill in any case was severely criticized by the Law Commission. Epithets like "rough-hewn" and even "nonsensical" were bandied about. Since the provisions crucially affected the Divorce Bill and appealed to the Parliamentary Labour Party, if not to Labour Ministers, the lines took some time to be disentangled. Ian Aitkin and Francis Boyd, *The Guardian*, 21 January 1969, and 26 February 1969.

Chapter 5
Operational Groups: Labour and Capital

1. Annual Report of the Council of the Law Society, 1955-56, pp. 22, 115-22.

2. Graham Wootton, *Pressure Groups in Britain, 1720-1970* (Allen Lane, Penguin Books Ltd., and Archon Books, Conn., U.S.A., 1975), pp. 21-24, 32.

3. Nicholas Tomalin, *Sunday Times*, 3 March 1968.

4. Vincent Hanna, *Sunday Times*, 28 November 1971.

5. Christine Eade, *The Guardian*, 18 January 1969, and 22 November 1968. The woman in the chair was Mrs. Audrey Hunt.

6. *The Guardian*, 6 May 1969.

7. *The Guardian*, 14 February 1963.

8. Byron Rogers, *The Times*, 2 May 1969.

9. Clifford Webb, *The Times*, 3 and 5 November 1970.

10. Paul Routledge, *The Times*, 1 December 1970. "Possibly" is used because he was then relying on an expected turnout of 500,000.

11. *The Times*, 9 December 1970.

12. Hugh Noyes, *The Times*, 9 December 1970.

13. *The Times*, 16 December 1970.

14. TUC Annual Report, 1971, p. 97.

15. Anthony Crosland, *Sunday Times*, 4 April 1971.

16. Alan Watkins, 5 March 1971.

17. *Let's Go With Labour*, p. 9.

18. See Richard Rose, *Influencing Voters* (Faber and Faber, 1967), for the earlier jousting.

19. *The Guardian*, 29 January 1958.

20. *The Guardian*, 4 February 1964; Clause 4 of the Labour Party Constitution.

21. Of the British Iron and Steel Federation, and of *Aims of Industry*. For the latter's slogan, see Wootton, *Pressure Groups*, doc. 75.

22. Richard Crossman, *The Diaries of a Cabinet Minister* (Hamish Hamilton and Jonathan Cape, 1975), vol. 1, p. 498.

23. DEA Progress Report, July 1968.

24. *The Times*, 7 December 1971.

25. "Mammon" quoted by Myfanwy Jones, *The Guardian*, 26 July 1961.

26. H.H. Wilson, *Pressure Group* (Secker and Warburg, 1961), p. 194 and fn. This basic source should be here and there corrected and supplemented by Peter Forster, *Spectator*, 25 August 1961. On Professor Wilson's use of primary material, see Morris Davis, *Ethics* 80 (October 1969), p. 53, and Cecil Miller, *Ethics* (April 1970), p. 227.

27. Geoffrey Moorhouse, *The Guardian*, 18 March 1961.

28. Harold Jackson, *The Guardian*, 3 July 1968. Those entrepreneurs with enough political influence to get their companies in on the ground floor with a programme contract were given (said one of them, Roy Thomson, later Lord Thomson of Fleet) "a permit to print your own money" (*Guardian* editorial, 25 July 1959). Sometimes quoted as "licence." Another version, attributed to entrepreneur Harley Drayton: "a licence to mint your own threepenny bits."

29. *The Guardian*, 18 March 1961.

30. John Heilpern and Laurence Marks, *Observer*, 10 January 1971. Other members included Lady Tweedsmuir, active in the commercial TV campaign; Sir Peter Rawlinson; and Mr. Geoffrey Johnson Smith.

31. Cited in *The Guardian*, 1 June 1964.

32. *The Guardian*, 4 November 1966.

33. Ibid.

34. *Sunday Times*, 9 March 1969.

35. Robert Chesshyre, *Observer*, 21 June 1970. Cf. also Heilpern and Marks, *Observer*. Later Sir Paul Bryan, director of Granada TV.

36. Heilpern and Marks, ibid.

37. Adam Hopkins, *Sunday Times*, 9 March 1969.

38. *The Times*, 21 March 1969.

39. *The Listener*, 17 April 1969.

40. Ibid., 17 July 1969.

41. *The Times*, 28 March 1970. In January 1971, it had 700 members, each paying 7/6d.

42. *The Times*, 24 June 1970.

43. *The Times*, 30 June 1970.

44. *The Times*, 10 September 1970.

45. Ibid.

46. *The Times*, 28 December 1970.

47. *Sunday Times*, 21 February 1971. See note 28.

48. *Sunday Times*, 28 March 1971: "Radio Lobby Defeats Chataway."

49. *Observer*, 17 January 1965.

50. *The Guardian*, editorial, 2 January 1959. "Basically" is used because Bristol Aircraft was also incorporated.

51. *Observer*, 13 December 1964, and 17 January 1965. The industry naturally tried to qualify the totals quoted. But even the quality press seemed muddled. Cf. *Observer*, 13 December 1964, and 17 January 1965; the defence correspondent of *The Guardian*, Claire Hollingsworth, 15 January 1965. See also *Sun*, 3 February 1965.

52. Not only Sir George Edwards, managing director BAC, and its chairman, Lord Portal, but also the chairmen of the parent companies, Lord Nelson (English Electric), Sir Charles Dunphie (Vickers), and Sir Reginald Verdon Smith (Bristol Siddeley, makers of the engines for TSR-2 and the vertical-take-off fighter).

53. David Fairhall, *The Guardian*, 12 January 1965.

54. *Observer*, 17 January 1965.

55. *Sun*, 13 January 1965.

56. *The Guardian*, 13 January 1965.

57. *The Guardian*, 15 January 1965. Crossman, *The Diaries*, p. 128, gives 10,000, which had been "guess-timated" the day before in the *Guardian*.

58. *Sun*, 14 January 1965.

59. Harold Wilson, *The Labour Government 1964-70* (Weidenfeld and Nicolson and Michael Joseph, 1971), p. 61.

60. *Observer*, 17 January 1965.

61. Kenneth Owen, *The Times*, 15 January 1968.

62. George Brown, Michael Stewart, Denis Healey, James Callaghan, Frank Cousins, Ray Gunter, Roy Jenkins, Sir Frank Soskice, George Wigg, Herbert Bowden and Arthur Bottomley. *The Guardian*, 30 January 1965.

63. Trevor Williams, *Sun*, 30 January 1965.

64. Crossman, *The Diaries*, p. 146.

65. Norman Shrapnel, *The Guardian*, 3 February 1965.

66. David Fairhall, *The Guardian*, 14 January 1965.

67. *Sunday Times*, 7 February 1965.

68. Not 31 March, as in Wilson, *The Labour Government*, p. 90.

69. *Sun*, 2 April 1965, and Wilson, ibid., pp. 89-90; Crossman, *The Diaries*, pp. 191-92, reports about ten for (c), including himself.

70. Kenneth Owen, *The Times*, 15 January 1968.

71. *The Guardian*, 2 January 1959.

72. *Sunday Times*, 7 February 1965.

73. *New Statesman*, 22 January 1965.

74. Graham Wootton, *Interest-Groups* (Hemel Hempstead, Prentice-Hall International, 1970), pp. 49 n. 53.

75. Andrew Wilson, *Observer*, 2 May 1965.

76. Richard Scott in Washington, *The Guardian*, 19 June 1968.

Chapter 6
Representative Groups (I): Third London Airport
and Equal Pay for Women

1. Matthew Coady, *New Statesman*, 9 June 1967.

2. Ronald Wraith, *Political Quarterly* 37, no. 1 (1966).

3. Inquiry held December 1965-February 1966; Inspector, G.D. Blake and Technical assessor, J.W.S. Brancker.

4. Sir Roger Hawkey: "We won the public inquiry," *The Guardian*, 27 May 1967. John Lukies: "We won the last inquiry, . . . ," *The Guardian*, 26 February 1968.

5. Patrick Gordon Walker, *The Cabinet* (Heinemann Educational Books, 2nd rev. ed., 1972), pp. 184-85. See also Wraith, *Political Quarterly*; G.B. Lamb, *Public Inquiries as an Instrument of Government* (Allen and Unwin, 1971); and Richard Crossman, *The Diaries of a Cabinet Minister* (Hamish Hamilton and Jonathan Cape, 1975), vol. 1, p. 624, and vol. 2, p. 346.

6. Coady, *New Statesman*, and Crossman, *The Diaries*, vol. 2, p. 346.

7. Coady, ibid.

8. Crossman, *The Diaries*, vol. 2, p. 383.

9. *The Times*, 23 May 1967.

10. George Clark, *The Times*, 23 February 1968.

11. *The Times*, 29 June 1967.

12. Olive Cook, *The Stansted Affair* (Pan Books Ltd., 1967), p. 106.

13. *The Times*, 29 June 1967.

14. The P.M. believed that the issue had "not been well-handled by the Departments." Harold Wilson, *The Labour Government, 1964-70* (Weidenfeld and Nicolson and Michael Joseph, 1971), p. 392.

15. *The Times*, 1 November 1967.

16. Ibid.

17. *The Guardian*, 6 November 1967. See also Ronald Butt, *Sunday Times*, 25 February 1968.

18. Crossman, *The Diaries*, vol. 2, p. 551.

19. Ibid., p. 563.

20. *Sunday Times*, 25 February 1968.

21. "The Folly of Foulness," *Manchester Guardian Weekly*, 8 May 1971.

22. *The Guardian*, 13 February 1968.

23. Political staff, *The Times*, 23 February 1968.

24. *The Guardian*, 23 February 1968.

25. George Clark, *The Times*, 23 February 1968.

26. *The Times*, 21 May 1968.

27. *The Guardian,* 2 May 1968.

28. *Observer*, 8 March 1969.

29. Robert McKie, *Guardian*, 6 March 1969.

30. *The Times*, 4 March 1969.

31. Arthur Reed, *The Times*, 27 February 1968.

32. With Hertfordshire, well over £100,000.

33. *The Times*, 18 March 1969.

34. Arthur Reed, *The Times*, 21 May 1968.

35. David Perman, *Cublington, a Blueprint for Resistance*, (Bodley Head, 1973), p. 94. Cf. p. 93. Mrs. Carol Walsh, whose Cublington home would have been demolished, said: "I know there are many people who are pleased that Cublington might be the choice, but they are frightened to say so in the open." On her ostracism, see *Times*, 22 December 1970.

36. *The Times*, 16 June 1967.

37. Cook, *The Stansted Affair*, pp. 93-94. This is in marked contrast to the frequent reminders that the development was opposed by Stanley Newens, the Labour M.P. for Epping, thrice called "sincere." To a colleague in the Parliamentary Labour Party (Terry Boston), Mr. Newens was simply being used by "a conservative middle-class lobby," in which there was a bit of truth, Richard Crossman agreed. Crossman, *The Diaries*, vol. 2, p. 391.

38. Perman, p. 97.

39. *The Times* and *Guardian*, 10 March 1969.

40. Perman, *Cublington*, p. 106.

41. *The Times*, 17 July 1969.

42. Perman, *Cublington*, p. 94.

43. *The Times*, 7 July 1969.

44. Perman, *Cublington*, p. 107.

45. Brian Cashinella and Keith Thompson, *Permission to Land* (Arlington Books, 1971), p. 14.

46. Ibid., p. 16. See also John Clare, *The Times*, 5 April 1971, p. 1.

47. Graham Wootton, *The Politics of Influence* (Routledge and Harvard University Press, 1963), Ch. XXV.

48. *The Times*, 27 April 1971 (interview with Tony Aldous).

49. Ibid.

50. Tony Aldous, *Battle for the Environment* (Fontana, 1972), p. 249.

51. *The Times*, 19 December 1970, and 27 April 1971.

52. Perman, *Cublington*, p. 150.

53. Ibid., p. 152.

54. *The Times*, 19 December 1970.

55. George Clark, *The Times*, 21 December 1970.

56. Clark, *The Times*, 19 December 1970.

57. Ibid., and 22 December 1970. The housewife is Mrs. Carol Walsh.

58. Aylesbury correspondent of *The Times*, 21 December 1970.

59. *The Times*, 5 January 1971.

60. *The Times*, 19 and 20 December 1970. The Vice Chairman is William Manning, a farmer.

61. Brian Cashinella, *The Times*, 10 January 1971. Cf. Perman, *Cublington*, p. 140.

62. *The Times*, 22 and 23 December 1970, and 13 January 1971.

63. *Manchester Guardian Weekly*, 8 May 1971.

64. Through its Director, Peter Conder. *The Times*, 14 January 1971.

65. *The Times*, 5 January 1971.

66. *The Times*, 5 April 1971.

67. H.C. Deb., 5th series, 1970-71, vol. 816, c. 42-3.

68. *The Times*, 28 October 1971.

69. *The Times*, 27 April 1971.

70. Patrick Rivers, *Politics by Pressure* (Harrap, 1974), pp. 94-95.

71. Stanley P. Johnson, *The Politics of Environment* (Tom Stacey, 1973), p. 226.

72. In Brian Frost (ed.), *The Tactics of Pressure* (Galliard, 1975), pp. 80-81. Kimber and Richardson, two leading academic specialists on environmental issues, did not directly address this question, but cautiously concluded that "In effect the Government had taken the line of least resistance. . . ." In Richard Kimber and J.J. Richardson (eds.), *Campaigning for the Environment* (Routledge, 1974), p. 208.

73. Peter Self, *Econocrats and the Policy Process* (Macmillan Press Ltd., 1975), p. 163.

74. Ibid.

75. During the Stansted dispute, speaking for the Town and Country Planning Association and as "an important member" of the South-East Regional Economic Planning Council, he had disputed, although "not technically qualified," the official view that "an airport at Sheppey would interfere with Heathrow from an air traffic control point of view. As a planner I believe that a new airport should be sited in the Thames Estuary, either at Sheppey or Foulness." Cook, *The Stansted Affair*, p. 99. For his slashing attack on the Roskill methodology and subsequent exchanges with Professor Alan Williams, see Self, *Econocrats*, pp. 171-77.

76. In his "Rambler at large" column reviewing David Perman's book (note 35) above. *The Countryman* ("a miscellany of rural life and work"), autumn 1973, pp. 127-28.

77. Bernard Levin, *The Times*, 30 March 1971.

78. *British Record*, no. 12, 25 September 1972.

79. Nora Beloff, *Observer*, 17 June 1973.

80. *To the Point*, vol. 1, no. 9, 6 May 1972. *The Times*, 26 June 1973.

81. Earlier: "the white elephant of the century." *Manchester Guardian Weekly*, 8 May 1971.

82. Beloff, *Observer.*

83. Interview with Mr. Ian Gilmour, at Ministry of Defence, 14 June 1973.

84. *The Guardian*, 2 October 1973.

85. Tom Congdon, *The Times*, 6 June 1974.

86. John Pudney, *London's Docks* (Thames and Hudson, 1975), p. 183.

87. No. 2, January 29, 1975 (British Information Service, New York).

88. Allen Potter, *Political Studies*, 1957, pp. 49-64.

89. *Daily Herald*, 8 December 1961.

90. Quoted in the *Bulletin* of the Women's Freedom League, no. 6, 25 March 1960.

91. *Daily Herald*, 8 December 1961.

92. Ibid., p. 10.

93. Annual Report, 1966, p. 158.

94. Ibid., p. 14.

95. Ibid.

96. That is, definition, cost, method of implementation, and so forth.

97. Annual Report, 1966, pp. 416-17; spokesman: G.H. Lowthian.

98. Annual Report, 1968, pp. 178-79.

99. Annual Report, 1969, p. 174; CBI Report, 1968, p. 41.

100. *The Guardian*, 4 March 1968.

101. Annual Report, 1968, pp. 455-59; Miss J. O'Donnell, Draughtsmen's union.

102. Annual Report, 1969, p. 172.

103. Ibid.

104. *The Guardian*, 22 November 1968.

105. Christine Eade, *The Guardian*, 18 June 1969.

106. *The Guardian*, 3 April 1969.

107. Ibid., and 22 November 1968.

108. Annual Report, 1969, p. 173.

109. Annual Report, 1970, p. 209; CBI Report, 1969, p. 37.

110. Hugh Noyes, *The Times*, 10 February 1970.

111. *Times* Parliamentary Report, 10 February 1970; Barbara Castle, *Sunday Times*, 19 December 1971.

112. *Sunday Times*, 19 December 1971.

113. David Jones, *The Times*, 19 May 1970.

114. Annual Report, 1973, p. 68.

115. CBI Report, 1972, p. 9.

116. TUC Report, 1974, p. 52.

117. *Observer*, January 1972.

Chapter 7
Representative Groups (II): Trade Union Congress

1. Ivor Jennings, *Cabinet Government* (Cambridge University Press, 1947), Ch. I. On unions as pressure groups, see Timothy C. May, *Trade Unions and*

Pressure Group Politics (Saxon House/Lexington, 1975), and V.L. Allen, *Trade Unions and the Government* (Longman, 1960).

2. Annual Report, 1967, p. 267.

3. Anthony Lester and Geoffrey Bindman, *Race and Law in Great Britain* (Harvard University Press, 1972), p. 128.

4. Annual Report, 1967, p. 269.

5. CBI Annual Report, 1967, p. 35.

6. Richard Crossman, *The Diaries of a Cabinet Minister* (Hamish Hamilton and Jonathan Cape, 1976), vol. 2, p. 433.

7. CBI Annual Report, 1967, p. 35.

8. TUC Report, 1968, pp. 297-301.

9. *Sunday Times*, 10 March 1968.

10. *The Guardian*, 10 February 1968 (Eric Silver).

11. *The Guardian*, 15 April 1968 (Martin Adeney).

12. TUC Annual Report, 1968, p. 302.

13. James Margach, *Sunday Times*, 14 April 1968.

14. Ibid; Crossman, *The Diaries*, pp. 784-85.

15. *Anonymous Empire* (Pall Mall Press, 1966), pp. 74-82.

16. Lester and Bindman, *Race and Law*, pp. 116-17.

17. CBI Annual Report, 1968, p. 38.

18. Lester and Bindman, *Race and Law*, pp. 136-7.

19. Ibid., pp. 138, 140.

20. Ibid., p. 141.

21. CBI Report, 1968, p. 38.

22. Lester and Bindman, *Race and Law*, p. 141.

23. Harry Eckstein, *Pressure Group Politics* (Allen and Unwin, 1960), p. 23.

24. *The Times*, 9 July 1968.

25. Ibid., where eight is the total. But see Philip Rawstorne's list in *The Guardian*, 10 July 1968.

26. Dennis Barker, *The Guardian*, 11 July 1968.

27. *The Times*, 12 July 1968.

28. CBI Report, 1968, p. 38.

29. Annual Report, 1969, pp. 373-74.

30. Mrs. E.A. Hunt, an elected member of the Women's Advisory Committee. TUC Annual Report, 1966, p. 416.

31. Mrs. C. Page (USDAW). Annual Report, 1966, p. 415.

32. D.E. Wilson (AEU). Annual Report, 1967, p. 458.

33. Ibid., p. 540.

34. Annual Report, 1968, p. 458.

35. Peter Jenkins, *The Battle of Downing Street* (Charles Knight, 1970), p. 27.

36. Ibid., p. 37.

37. Eric Wigham, *The Times*, 13 June 1969.

38. TUC Report, 1969, p. 204.

39. Eric Wigham, *The Times*, 31 December 1968.

40. John Torode, *The Guardian*, 1 January 1969.

41. Harold Wilson, *The Labour Government 1964-70* (Weidenfeld and Nicolson and Michael Joseph, 1971), p. 592.

42. Patrick Gordon Walker, *The Cabinet* (Heinemann Educational Books, 1972), rev. ed., pp. 51-52, 133, and John Mackintosh, M.P., *The Times*, 21 June 1968.

43. Gordon Walker, ibid., pp. 52-53; Crossman, *The Diaries*, vol. 2, pp. 772-73.

44. 24 January 1969.

45. *New Statesman* editorial, 16 May 1969.

46. *The Times*, 15 May 1969.

47. Peter Jenkins, *The Guardian*, 19 June 1969.

48. James Margach, *Sunday Times*, 22 June 1969.

49. TUC Annual Report, 1969, pp. 21, 23-4. That is, change a rule to increase its own authority, enabling it to do some of the things that the Government was trying to do legislatively.

50. Annual Report, 1970, p. 239.

51. Wilson, *Labour Government*, pp. 778, 781. This body may have been a continuation of the Parliamentary Committee.

52. Annual Report, 1970, p. 576.

53. CBI Annual Report, 1970, p. 33.

54. David Wood *The Times*, 8 October 1970.

55. TUC Annual Report, 1971, p. 346.

56. Paul Routledge, *The Times*, 14 October 1970.

57. *The Times*, 16 and 29 October 1970.

58. V. Flynn (SOGAT); Annual Report, 1971, p. 431.

59. Eric Heffer, *The Class Struggle in Parliament* (Gollancz, 1973), p. 186.

60. TUC Report, 1971, p. 78.

61. Ibid., p. 96.

62. Ibid., p. 98.

63. *The Times*, 11 January 1971.

64. William Hardcastle, *The Listener*, 4 February 1971.

65. Annual Report, 1971, p. 423.

66. Ibid., pp. 354, 355.

67. W.C. Anderson (NALGO); Annual Report, 1971, p. 433.

68. Annual Report, 1973, p. 438.

69. *Sunday Times*, 23 April 1972. TUC Annual Report, 1972, p. 91.

70. Annual Report, ibid.

71. Annual Report, 1974, p. 81. The T & G paid its own fine.

72. *The Times*, 1 May 1974.

73. Heffer, *The Class Struggle*, p. 320.
74. Eric Jacobs, *Sunday Times*, 5 November 1972.
75. CBI Press Release, P.74.72.
76. *The Times*, 3 August 1972.

Chapter 8
Representative Groups (III): Business

1. T.C. Fraser, *Chambers of Commerce and Trade Associations* (Royal Society of Arts lecture, 5 April 1973). Lloyds Bank, wartime gunner, Wool Trade Delegation, industrial director of NEDC, staff director of Devlin Commission, temporary director-general NEDO.
2. National Chamber of Trade Handbook (London, n.d.), p. 20.
3. Historical sketch in National Chamber of Trade publicity brochure, (London, n.d.), p. 13.
4. P.J. Mortlock in NCT *Journal*, May 1973, p. 492.
5. Brochure, p. 14. Graham Wootton, *Pressure Groups in Britain, 1720-1970* (Allen Lane, Penguin Books, Ltd., and Archon Books, Conn., U.S.A., 1975), doc. 73.
6. The Devlin Report, p. 19 (see note 3, Chapter 1).
7. Ibid., p. 4.
8. Ibid., Appendix VII.
9. Wootton, *Pressure Groups*, doc. 74.
10. NCT *Journal*, May 1973, pp. 475, 469-70.
11. The Devlin Report, p. 11.
12. *Report* of Herbert Committee on Intermediaries, para. 121 (p. 45).
13. Clifford Webb, *The Times*, 27 July 1971.
14. ABCC, Annual Report, 1974, p. 63.
15. Arthur Osman, *The Times*, 14 February 1970.
16. Giles Smith, *The Times*, 29 January 1970.
17. Clifford Webb, *The Times*, 29 January 1970.
18. Malcolm Dean, *Manchester Guardian Weekly*, 21 February 1970.
19. Julian Mounter, *The Times*, 5 March 1970.
20. Giles Smith, *The Times*, 14 July 1970.
21. Ibid.
22. D.G.A. Smallcross (Hove); *The Times*, 9 July 1970.
23. *Serving Industry* (n.d., c.1974), p. 9.
24. V.G. Munns, Royal Commission on Trade Unions and Employers' Associations, Research Papers no. 7, 1967, p. 53.
25. *Report*, para. 6.
26. Ibid., and para. 117.
27. Ibid., para. 118.

28. Leonard Tivey and Ernest Wohlegemuth, *Political Quarterly* (January-March 1958).

29. Devlin Report, p. 123.

30. *The Times*, 23 June 1969.

31. Keith Richardson, *The Times*, 27 February 1972.

32. Maurice Corina, *The Times*, 13 November 1968.

33. Richardson, *The Times*.

34. Hugh Clayton, *The Times*, 15 May 1974.

35. *The Times*, 19 March 1970.

36. Maurice Corina, *The Times*, 19 February 1970.

37. T.C. Fraser, in *Journal of Management Studies*, May 1967, p. 163 (his 1966 lecture at LSE).

38. Quote by T.C. Fraser in his 1970 lecture at Dundee College of Technology, *Putting an Industrial Dimension into Economic Policy Making*.

39. Fraser, in *Journal of Management*, p. 155. See also note 1.

40. Fraser, Lecture.

41. *The Times*, 7 February 1968.

42. Ibid., 20 September 1967.

43. Fraser, in *Journal of Management*, pp. 163-64.

44. Fraser, Lecture.

45. Fraser, in *Journal of Management*, p. 164.

46. *The Times*, 9 May 1974.

47. Quoted in *Steel Review*, April 1964, p. 35.

48. P.H.S., *The Times*, 3 May 1967. Wootton, *Pressure Groups*, doc. 64.

49. *The Times*, 6 August 1963.

50. *Observer*, 19 January 1964.

51. *Observer*, 24 November 1963.

52. *The Guardian*, 1 January 1964.

53. For example, *The Guardian*, 7 January 1964; *New Statesman*, 10 January; *Observer*, 23 February; *Listener*, 7 May.

54. *The Guardian*, 14 August 1964.

55. British Iron and Steel Federation, *Steel: Leave Well Alone*, n.d. (c. June 1974).

56. *Observer*, 24 March 1964.

57. *Steel Review*, April 1967.

58. *New Society*, 23 January 1964.

59. *Pharmaceutical Journal*, editorial, 25 January 1964.

60. Ronald Butt, *The Power of Parliament* (Constable, 1967), pp. 255-58.

61. Ibid., p. 259.

62. Maurice Corina, *The Times*, 1 October 1968.

63. *Daily Telegraph and Morning Post*, 5 December 1963.

64. For example, *Daily Telegraph*, 23 January 1964.

65. James Margach and Ian Coulter, *Sunday Times*, 12 January 1964.

234

66. Ibid.
67. *Observer*, 19 January 1964.
68. *The Times*, 16 January 1964.
69. Butt, *The Power*, pp. 262, 270. *Observer*, 22 March 1964.
70. *The Times*, 16 January 1964.
71. *The Times*, 10 February 1964.
72. *The Times*, 27 September 1968.
73. David Leitch, *Sunday Times*, 19 January 1964.
74. *Daily Telegraph*, 18 January 1964.
75. *The Guardian*, 18 January 1964.
76. Letter to author, 22 January 1964.
77. Ibid.
78. Leitch, *Sunday Times. The Guardian*, 21 January 1964.
79. *The Times*, 27 September 1968.
80. *The Guardian*, 25 January 1964.
81. *Pharmaceutical Journal*, 1 February 1964.
82. *The Retail Chemist*, February 1964.
83. *The Times*, 24 January 1964.
84. *The Times*, 10 February 1964.
85. *Daily Telegraph*, 7 February 1964.
86. *The Guardian*, 18 February 1964.
87. *The Times*, 10 February 1964.
88. Ibid.
89. *Sunday Times*, 2 February 1964.
90. 11 December 1963; 15 January 1964; 4 February 1964; 26 February 1964, 17, 18, and 19 March 1964 (twice). These count as negotiations. There were three meetings not graced by his representatives.
91. 27 February 1964.
92. *Daily Express*, 27 February 1964.
93. *The Times*, 26 February 1964.
94. Political correspondent, *The Times*, 11 March 1968.
95. Sir Frank Markham, *The Guardian*, 11 March 1964.
96. James Margach, *Sunday Times*, 15 March 1964; Alec is Sir Alec Douglas-Home, Prime Minister for just short of a year from October 1963.
97. Political correspondent, *The Times*, 10 February 1964.
98. Ibid., 27 January 1964.
99. *The Times*, 23 March 1964, and *Sunday Times*, 29 March 1964. The reference to Sir Richard Glyn, however, derives from the author.
100. *Sunday Times*, 22 March 1964.
101. Francis Boyd, *The Guardian*, 18 March 1964.
102. *Sunday Times*, 22 March 1964.
103. Francis Boyd, *The Guardian*, 18 March 1964.
104. *The Times*, 21 March 1964.

105. *The Guardian*, 24 March 1964.

106. *The Guardian*, 20 March 1964.

107. *Sunday Times*, 29 March 1964. "Fooled" may have been too strong. But there is no doubt who should have been wearing the laurel wreath. Within a year or so Mr. Heath was leader of the Party.

108. NCT Handbook, n.d., p. 17.

109. Wootton, *Pressure Groups*, introduction, pp. 43-44, 93-96.

110. Sir Henry Benson and Sir Sam Brown, *Report on the Formation of a National Industrial Organization*, April 1964.

111. The Devlin Report, paras. 80 and 109, and CBI membership list (unpublished).

112. (Sir) Michael Clapham, CBI Press Release P.22.73, 19 March, and John Davies, *Steel Review*, January 1967.

113. Wootton, *Pressure Groups*, doc. 53.

114. NCT Report, 1972, p. 12.

115. Ibid., p. 8.

116. *The Times*, 7 July 1969.

117. A.R. Ilersic (with P.F.B. Liddle), *Parliament of Commerce* (ABCC and Newman Neame, 1960), p. 164.

118. ABCC Report, 115, 1974, pp. 7-8.

119. ABCC Report, 114, 1973.

120. ABCC Report, 107, 1966-67, p. 7.

121. CBI Report, 1966, p. 46.

122. Traders Co-ordinating Committee on Transport, Traders Road Transport Association, the National Traders Traffic Association.

123. ABCC Report, 108, 1967-68.

124. Ibid.

125. *The Times*, 24 January 1968. The CBI claimed 2400 (1968 Report, p. 66). There may have been 2,500 from the Opposition as a whole; *Guardian*, 16 May 1968.

126. *Anonymous Empire* (Pall Mall, 1958), p. 67.

127. Edward Taylor, Michael Heseltine, Gordon Campbell. See Alan Watkins, *New Statesman*, 23 February 1968.

128. *Sunday Times*, 12 May 1968.

129. *The Times*, 10 April 1968.

130. See Richard Rose, *Influencing Voters* (Faber and Faber, 1967), for the earlier PR efforts.

131. *The Times*, 8 April 1968.

132. *Observer*, 14 April 1968.

133. *The Guardian*, 16 May 1968. Also David Wood, *The Times*, 20 May 1968.

134. *The Times*, 16 October 1968.

135. Ibid., and CBI Annual Report, 1968, pp. 66-67.

136. ABCC Report, 109, 1968-69, p. 6.

137. *Observer*, political correspondent, 14 April 1968.

138. John Davies, D-G, *Steel Review*, January 1967.

139. Ibid.

140. W.P. Grant and D. Marsh, *Political Studies*, vol. XIX (December 1971).

141. CBI Report, 1971, pp. 8-9.

142. CBI Report, 1972, p. 8.

143. Press Release, P.77.72, 19 July 1972.

144. *The Guardian*, 27 June 1969.

145. CBI *Review*, December 1971, p. 7.

146. CBI Report, 1974, p. 31.

Chapter 9
Methods: Stooping to Conquer

1. Within the context of pressure groups, the discussion may be dated from E.P. Herring, *Group Representation Before Congress* (Johns Hopkins University Press, 1929) and *Public Administration and the Public Interest* (McGraw-Hill, 1936).

2. *The Times*, 10 July 1975. Two years later Mr. Jay would become British Ambassador to the United States.

3. *The Treasury under the Tories* (Penguin Books, 1964), p. 171.

4. See Chapter 2.

5. *European Journal of Political Research*, vol. 4 (1976), pp. 350-52.

6. R.E. Pahl and J.T. Winkler, "The Coming Corporatism," *New Society*, 10 October 1974. See also Wyn Grant, "Pressure Groups in Britain," discussion paper for Anglo-American Conference on Research Trends in British Politics, University of Stirling, 1976.

7. See Chapter 4.

8. Bridget A. Pym, *Political Quarterly* (July-September 1972).

9. See Chapter 8.

10. *The Times*, 14 July 1970.

11. Peter Jay, "Giving Away Public Assets," *The Times*, 6 August 1970.

12. *Encounter*, August 1962, p. 8.

13. *The Guardian*, 27 March 1969.

14. Arnold Rogow with Peter Shore, *The Labour Government and British Industry, 1945-51* (Blackwell, 1955), pp. 143, 180.

15. Mr. Crouch's eloquence must have made an impression. In 1974 he was reported to be a director of Burson-Marsteller. *The Times*, Business Diary, 3 May 1974, citing the recently-published edition of the *Hollis Press and Public Relations Annual.*

16. *The Times*, 8 January 1963.

17. *The Guardian*, 17 May 1963.

18. *The Times*, 7 February 1970.

19. *The Times*, 21 April and 12 May 1970.

20. *The Times*, 12 May 1970.

21. *The Times*, 13 May 1974.

22. *The Guardian*, 10 March 1969. Also *The Times*, 17 June 1970; *Manchester Guardian Weekly*, 20 June 1970; and *Sunday Times*, 2 August 1970.

23. Rogow and Shore, *The Labour Government*, p. 197.

24. In James B. Christoph and Bernard E. Brown, *Cases in Comparative Politics* (Little, Brown, 2nd ed., 1969), p. 63.

25. Giles Smith, *The Times*, 19 March 1970.

26. *Sunday Times* editorial, 23 April 1972.

27. *The Times*, 20 March 1970.

28. *Teachers' Unions and Interest Group Politics* (Cambridge University Press, 1972), p. 115.

29. Graham Wootton, "Controlling Lobbyists: Lessons from America," *The Times*, turnover, 3 December 1968.

Chapter 10
Pluralist Stagnation

1. Conservation Society, Annual Report, 1975, p. 3. Friends of the Earth Supplementary Bulletin, summer 1975.

2. Friends of the Earth Ltd., 1974.

3. A.J. Woolford, Temple Ewell: *Proposed New Hoverport Western Docks–Dover*, 5 February 1976.

4. Gerald Dorfman, *Wage Politics in Britain 1945-57* (Iowa State University Press, 1973), p. 97.

5. Allan Fels, *The British Prices and Incomes Board* (Cambridge University Press, 1972), p. 9.

6. Aubrey Jones, *The New Inflation* (Penguin Special, 1973), p. 50.

7. Ibid., pp. 51, 209.

8. Dorfman, *Wage Politics*, p. 101.

9. Fels, *The British Prices*, p. 21.

10. TUC Report, 1966, pp. 312-13.

11. Jones, *The New Inflation*, p. 130.

12. Manifesto, February 1974, p. 9.

13. Manifesto, October 1974, p. 5.

14. *British Record*, no. 9 (New York, 24 May 1976).

15. *The Politics of Economic Policy in Britain: The Problem of 'Pluralistic Stagnation'*, p. 18 (British Politics Group of the American Political Science Association, September 1975).

16. *Westminster Bank Review*, May 1968, p. 28.

17. CBI Annual Report, 1966, p. 13.

18. *The Times*, 11 August 1971, and CBI Press Release, 19 July 1972.

19. Len Murray, Assistant General Secretary, TUC, interviewed by author, 28 June 1973. (He became General Secretary the following September.)

20. *The Times*, 10 July 1975 (Peter Jay). Also author's interview with Sir Richard at Guiness Mahon in Greatchurch Street, London, 25 June 1973.

Chapter 11
Group, Class, and Corporate State

1. *The Times*, 3 April 1968.

2. David Wood, *The Times*, 22 March 1968.

3. *Competition and the Corporate Society* (Methuen, 1972), p. 65.

4. *Le Corporatisme* (Les Publications Techniques, Paris, 1944), p. 187.

5. Quoted from ibid., p. 35. "Capital and Labour" is author's version of *l'élément patronal et de l'élément ouvrier*.

6. Carta del lavoro (Labour Charter), VII and IX.

7. The basic documentary source is Shepard Bancroft Clough (with Salvatore Saladino), *A History of Modern Italy*: documents, readings, and commentary (Columbia University Press, 1968). But see also Giampiero Carocci, *Italian Fascism* (Penguin Books, 1975), pp. 83-88.

8. David Blake, *The Times*, 17 May 1974. Manifesto, October 1974, p. 10.

9. Manifesto, p. 10.

10. Annual Report, 1975, p. 13.

11. October Manifesto, p. 5.

12. Paul Routledge, *The Times*, 4 November 1974.

13. Annual Report, 1974, p. 9.

14. Malcolm Brown, *The Times*, 21 November 1974.

15. *The Times*, 25 November 1974.

16. Annual Report, 1975, p. 8.

17. Hugh Noyes, *The Times*, 24 July 1975.

18. Paul Routledge, *The Times*, 9 January 1976.

19. T.C. Fraser, *Putting an Industrial Dimension into Economic Policy Making*, Dundee College of Technology lecture, 1970, p. 2.

20. Ibid., p. 3.

21. Ibid., p. 7.

22. T.C. Fraser, *Journal of Management Studies*, May 1967, pp. 156-57.

23. Interview with author, 28 June 1973.

24. *The Policy Work of the CBI* (CBI, London, August 1971), p. 3.

25. Fraser, Lecture, p. 17.

26. In Jack Hayward and Michael Watson (eds.), *Planning, Politics and Public Policy* (Cambridge University Press, 1975), p. 63.

27. Annual Report, 1974, p. 350.

28. TUC Report, 1973, p. 124.

29. TUC Report, 1975, p. 75.

30. CBI Press Release, P.74.72, July 1972.

31. *New Society*, 10 October 1974.

32. Keith Richardson, *The Times*, 7 March 1976. Lord Ryder has since moved to greener pastures.

33. *The Times*, 7 October 1975.

34. *The Times*, 12 April 1976.

35. For example, *The Times*, 11 March 1964.

36. J.W. Grove, *Government and Industry in Britain* (Longmans, 1962) for a few examples. The rest are derived from the Press or from civil servants.

37. *Political Studies*, vol. XIII (1965), pp. 22-44.

38. *Modern Capitalism: The Changing Balance of Public and Private Power* (Oxford University Press, 1965).

39. David Wood, *The Times*, 23 November 1970.

40. Peregrine Worsthorne, *Sunday Telegraph*, 16 December 1973. But cf. Peter Jenkins, *The Guardian*, 26 January 1974, p. 6: "Nowhere, except in a section of the executive council of the National Union of Mineworkers, is there evidence of class war."

41. For a crude first attempt at classification, see author's *Interest Groups in Britain and the United States*, paper read at American Political Science Association annual meeting, Washington, D.C., 1972.

42. *Le Pouvoir et les groupes de pression* (Mouton, Paris, 1971; from the Polish), pp. 5, 3.

43. This clarifies, and in emphasis qualifies, one's earlier formulation that pressure politics "tends to . . . [be] the continuation of economic bargaining by other means." Graham Wootton, *The Politics of Influence* (Routledge and Harvard University Press, 1963), p. 7.

Index

National Federation of Retail News-
agents, 141, 212
National Incomes Commission, 177
National Industrial Relations Court,
116, 120-121, 169, 170
Nationalization, and pluralist stagna-
tion, 182; steel, 55-56, 137, 160,
166, 169, 175; and Social Contract,
186; sugar, 166, 188; transport, 30,
152-156. *See also* Public Relations
National Joint Action Campaign for
Women's Equal Rights, 96
National Joint Advisory Council, 102
National Parks Campaign, 26
National Pharmaceutical Union, 142,
145, 146, 209, 212
National Plan for Airports, by ABCC,
152
National Society for Clean Air, 6
National Television Council, 60, 165
National Trust, 6, 22, 26, 174
National Union of General and Munici-
pal Workers, 95
National Union of Journalists, 59
National Union of Mineworkers, 178
National Union of Railwaymen
(NUR), 19, 166
National Union of Small Shopkeepers,
146
National Union of Teachers (NUT), 9,
169
National Union of Vehicle Builders
(NUVB), 96, 111
National Viewers' and Listeners' Asso-
ciation, 39
Naturalists' Trust, 32
NCCI. *See* National Council for Com-
monwealth Immigrants
NCCL. *See* National Council for Civil
Liberties
Neal Working Party, Len, 116
Nelson, Lord, 225, fn 52
Nettl, Peter, 193
New Corporatism. *See* Corporatism
New Feudalism. *See* Feudalism, the
New
Newens, M.P., Stanley, 73, 74, 75

Newspaper Publishers Association, 126
Newspaper Society, 126
New Scientist, 35
New Statesman, 55, 114
NFU. *See* National Farmers' Union(s)
Nicholas, Harry, 114
Nichols, J.W., 132
1922 Committee (Conservative back-
benchers), 109, 139, 144, 147;
"fooled" over RPM, 148; Home
Affairs Committee of, 105; Trade
and Industry Committee, 144, 146,
151; Transport Committee
Noble, M.P., Michael, 86, 89, 129
Noise Abatement Society, 6, 33, 39,
75
North-West Essex and East Hertford-
shire Preservation Society, 16, 71-
72, 74, 75, 76
Norwood, M.P., Christopher, 53, 96
Nuthampstead Preservation Society,
77, 78

Obscene Publications Act (1959), 39
Observer, 34, 46, 56, 66, 77, 140, 155
Office of Manpower Economics, 99
Oliver, Edward, 39, 221 fn 22
Ombudsman, in Britain. *See* Parlia-
mentary Commissioner for Admin-
istration
Osborn, M.P., John, 140

Padley, M.P., Walter, 183, 192
Paedophile Information Exchange, 13
Page, M.P., Graham, 148
Pagliero, Leonard, 141, 143
Pahl, R.E., 190
Pannell, M.P., Charles, 74
pantouflage, 192
Panunzio, Sergio, 185
Parents' Group for Educational Stan-
dards, 13
Pargeter, John, 79
Parkes, Joseph, 15
Parkinson, Harry, 128
Parliamentary Commissioner for Ad-
ministration, 37-38, 41

About the Author

Graham Wootton studied at the London School of Economics and Political Science where he received the B.Sc. with first-class honours and later the Ph.D. There followed two years at the Cabinet Office as a temporary civil servant researching into aspects of strategic policy during the 1939-45 War. For the next decade and a half he taught politics and sociology at the Delegacy for Extra-Mural Studies, University of Oxford, becoming senior staff tutor at Rewley House, the University centre for continuing education. He is now professor of political science at Tufts University in Massachusetts. Professor Wootton has published five other books, on the theory of workers' participation in industry as well as on interest groups. The most germane to this volume is *Pressure Groups in Britain, 1720-1970* (1975), a collection of original documents prefaced by an essay in interpretation.